Praise for
Every Family Has a Story

International Bestseller

"I love every word she writes and long for every reader to experience her unique and generous way of being in the world."
—Cathy Rentzenbrink

"A deeply wise book that will help a lot of people." —Johann Hari

"I am a huge admirer of Julia's work." —Elizabeth Day

"Enriching and beautifully written. Anybody who has a family, or is building a family, will benefit from this book's wisdom."
—Mohsin Zaidi

"Julia Samuel writes with unfailing grace, tenderness and consummate storytelling. Everyone who reads this will learn something profound." —Dr. Rachel Clarke

"This is a wonderful, wonderful book. . . . Everybody needs to read it." —Dr. Rangan Chatterjee

"Offers vivid insights in a book for all families. . . . I was utterly drawn in." —Kathryn Mannix

"Fascinating. . . . Julia Samuel's compassionate work never fails to inform, comfort and make me think." —Pandora Sykes

"Truly wonderful—wise, compassionate, thoughtful and always inspiring." —Justine Picardie

"Full of insight into the pain and beauty at the heart of family life. There is so much to learn in this book." —Clover Stroud

"A profoundly important and compassionate book. . . . Highly recommended." —Liz Earle

"Wonderful, wise and empathetic, so useful but also so beautifully written. . . . [Samuel] is engaged in the process of working with clients, changed by them and their stories, as we are by reading about them. Every family should have one, to consult in times of trouble." —Gavanndra Hodge

"[Samuel's] writing is honest, heartfelt and wise. . . . Over and over she extracts the extraordinary from people who didn't know they had it in them." —Raffaella Barker

"Engaging, informative and very well written." —Philippa Perry

"An essential, clever and kind book that reminds us that we can never hope to understand ourselves without deeply understanding our families. A testament to the ongoing relevance of psychotherapy and to Julia Samuel's preeminent skill as an author and therapist." —Alain de Botton

"[Samuel] excels at distilling shrewd insights from her subjects. . . . [Her] candor offers an unusually intimate look at how therapists work. . . . Covering a broad array of family structures and dilemmas, this quietly dazzling consideration of what it means to be a family is sure to resonate." —*Publishers Weekly*

Every Family Has a Story

How to Grow and Move Forward Together

JULIA SAMUEL

ANCHOR CANADA

For Catherine and Rachel, with my love

Copyright © 2022 Julia Samuel

Anchor Canada paperback published 2024
Doubleday Canada hardcover published 2022

Previously published in hardcover with a different subtitle:
How We Inherit Love and Loss

Library and Archives Canada Cataloguing in Publication
Title: Every family has a story : how to grow and move
forward together / Julia Samuel.
Names: Samuel, Julia, 1959- author. https://id.oclc.org/worldcat/entity/
E39PCjx6439R9qmvY7rvwVT6qP
Identifiers: Canadiana 20220273278 | ISBN 9780385684415 (softcover)
Subjects: LCSH: Families. | LCSH: Families—Psychological aspects.
Classification: LCC HQ519 .S26 2024 | DDC 155.9/24—dc23

Cover design: Penguin Random House UK
Cover image: Adapted from *The Garden of Eden* by C. F. A. Voysey
© Victoria and Albert Museum, London.
Set in 11/13pt Bembo Book MT Pro
Typeset by Jouve (UK), Milton Keynes

Printed in the USA

Published by Anchor Canada,
a division of Penguin Random House Canada Limited,
a Penguin Random House Company

www.penguinrandomhouse.ca

10 9 8 7 6 5 4 3 2 1

Penguin
Random House
ANCHOR CANADA

Contents

Introduction

Every family has a story. A story of love and loss, joy and pain.

The story of the family I was born into was one of great privilege and multiple traumas. But we didn't tell stories. There was no narrative or understanding of what had been, what was going on, or how to deal with it. My parents were young adults during the Second World War. My father was in the Navy and my mother was a land girl, or farm worker. But that was not where their injuries lay. My mother's parents and two siblings had all died suddenly and unexpectedly by the time she was twenty-five years old. My father's father and brother had also died, without warning, when he was still a young man. Their fathers had fought in the First World War.

As with the majority of people living in that era, and as my generation of baby-boomers can attest, they abided by the need to survive and multiply. They had admirable tenacity, grit and courage. Their route to survival, the only one open to them, was to forget and move on. They lived by the adage that what you don't talk or think about won't hurt you. Putting on a good show, hiding vulnerability and, yes, a stiff upper lip were the mantras of my childhood and that of most of my generation. But even when it's out of sight—perhaps especially when it's out of sight—the fingerprint of love and loss inside us continues to gather complexity. It isn't always visible to the naked eye, but is still complicated, still textured, still painful.

What is often not recognized is that behaviours like these are the legacy of trauma. Trauma doesn't have language. Trauma has no concept of time. It sits on high alert in our bodies, ready to be ignited many decades after the original traumatic event. It doesn't allow for the processing of emotion. For me it meant many pieces of the jigsaw were missing. I remember looking at black-and-white photographs of my dead grandparents, aunts and uncles, examining them for clues because I knew practically nothing about them. The first time I saw a photograph of my maternal grandfather was this year. There were so many secrets and so much was left unsaid that I look back at my parents now and wonder: What did they know? What did they think about? Did they know what they felt? As a couple, did they ever talk about the things that mattered to them? And those secrets, did they tell each other or not? They certainly didn't voice any of it within my earshot.

This meant I was constantly observing and listening for clues. As it turned out it was the perfect brew to ferment a psychotherapist: I was always curious, listening intently, keenly interested in what was happening behind the façade, like a detective looking in the dust for footprints.

My parents have died. While I have been writing this book my love for and understanding of them have changed and grown. They live on in me, continually shaping and influencing me, as do all our key relationships. I am hugely grateful to them. I learnt from them many crucial skills, behaviours and ways of being that serve me well. I still benefit now from the immense opportunities they gave me.

I came to write this book about families because every client I have ever had has focused on their family. They want to know why they have difficulty with their relatives or describe why they love them, and everything in between. I am no different from my clients. In my therapy, I spent great tracts of time exploring my family of origin and my family now, trying to make sense of what was going on.

Families and their roles today

The phrase "nuclear family," meaning two married parents and their children, no longer fully describes the 95 million families who live in North America. Families come in many forms: single-parent families, same-sex families, adopted families, extended families, polyamorous families, blended families, families with no children and families made up of friends in which there are no blood relationships.

In the past, a family's central purpose and function was to raise children. A big shift has taken place socially in that more mothers are working and have fewer children. Since we live longer, rearing children takes only half of our adult lifespan. We therefore live as adults in our family for much longer than we did in the past, carrying with us the burden or gifts from it. Every person living in these different models of family will have their unique response to them, which will be informed by their genetics, environment and experience.

I wanted to look beneath the skin of some of these types of families to find out what went on and to ask questions: what is it that enables some families to thrive despite enormous adversity when others fragment? What predicts family breakdown? Why do our families drive us mad?

This book aims to explore those questions and deepen our understanding of them. It isn't about how to raise perfect families. They don't exist. Families operate on a spectrum of dysfunction and function depending on internal and external stressors. Instead, I tell the stories of the lived experience of eight families as they face a particular challenge, charting them through multiple generations. The level of influence of one generation on the next is often underestimated. The unresolved stressors of one generation can be passed down to intensify the daily pressures of life for the next.

Families are in constant flux, which is why they are so complicated and why they are such hard work. While the older generation is facing old age, their adult children are dealing with their own offspring leaving home, and those young people are adapting to and stepping into adulthood. Nowadays what was seen as the normative four-stage life cycle—establishment (marriage), expansion (children), contraction (children leaving home), dissolution (partner dies)—is by no means the case for everyone. Relationships often end in divorce, children choose not to leave home or return home after some years, or perhaps there are no children. We see from the stories that follow that at times families need to pull together, and at others to step back. It is this dance—the moving in and out as a family, seeking harmony while allowing for differences—that supports stability.

I am fascinated by families for good reason: families matter. Family is the single most important influence on a child's life and their outcome. They carry that reliable love into adulthood, as it strengthens their emotional, physical and spiritual well-being, which enables them to live a happy, healthy and productive life. At its best, family is the safe place where we can be our whole selves, with all of our frailties and fault-lines, and still be loved and deeply understood. Ideally, it is a place where the roots of our development are fully known, the atmosphere we grew up in acknowledged.

At the centre of our well-being is relationship. The quality of our lives depends on the quality of our relationships. As a therapist informed by the attachment theories of John Bowlby, I see that all our "relational stuff" began with our family. It is the centre of how we learn to relate to each other and how we manage emotions in every aspect of our lives—ourselves, love, friendship, work—as well as family. The basis of our beliefs and values is programmed into us through our family, whether we follow or rebel against that family system. Most importantly, we gain our sense of our own value from our family: we come innately to believe we are of worth, or not.

When they are "good enough," as Donald Winnicott, the eminent paediatrician and psychoanalyst, termed it, families form the bedrock of our lives, a foundation that keeps us steady when we face the brickbats of life. When functioning well, we can turn to our family in adversity, and for team support. When the external world feels fractured and alienating, home and family can be a refuge to heal and rebuild our strength.

We may not see our family, but they are still part of us, genetically, in our memories and our unconscious. We can never leave them, as we can a partner or a friendship.

Exceptional families are ordinary families

The families I write about are both exceptional and ordinary. My belief is that I could pick any family at any point in their life, and between us we would learn a great deal about what is hidden beneath their external selves, what informs and influences them. It could be the "ghosts from their nursery," their childhood influences, their parents and grandparents, or how their own children are forcing them to face aspects of themselves they haven't dared look at before. What we'd find would be uniquely theirs and, in some ways, familiar to us all.

Discovering these further truths about themselves gave my clients, and would give any family, clarity and confidence to navigate their life in all its turbulence.

I am intrigued that in families most of what is talked about is of no consequence, and much that matters is left unsaid. It means our imagination goes to unknown and scary places: the stories we tell ourselves are full of gaps and assumptions. Knowing that family scripts are passed down through the generations, I was particularly interested in the power and influence of those secrets and silences. I came to understand that what is rejected in us, what is exiled to a dark unspoken place, tends to ferment and may become hostile and dangerous.

My clients did not come to see me because they wanted therapy to come to terms with those wounds from the past, but due to a painful present. We discovered, though, that their present was woven with threads from their past. Among much else, I saw clearly how trauma can be passed down from one generation to the next.

I knew the theory that when a traumatic event isn't addressed and processed in one generation it continues through the generations until someone is prepared to feel the pain. I also knew the research about epigenetics: how trauma changes the chemical charge in our genes that impacts our operating system, heightening our response to external events, switching on the fight/flight/

freeze part of the brain, our amygdala. I noted that the amygdala stays on red alert decades after the event if the trauma has not been processed. For instance, if we had not addressed the trauma of the suicide in the Rossi family, one of the grandchildren might have been beset by fears, body images and sensations they could not explain; they would have believed something was wrong with them. The messages I take from this are, first, that it will serve us and our future generations to recognize that perhaps our psychological wound didn't start with us, that this is not our failure as a person. And, second, that by addressing the pain and processing it, we protect the future generations.

Each of the eight families faced tough life challenges, as we all do. It is at those peak points of change—like death, illness and separation—that families often falter. It can be a propensity to hold on to the past, fearing the future, that makes family transitions both threatening and exciting, each family member offering different, sometimes conflicting, attitudes. These families showed it takes enormous dedication and commitment to nurture family, to prioritize it over other life demands, to hold together in crisis. They demonstrated that families in transition, indeed at most times, require us to draw on our deepest reserves of love, patience, self-awareness, time, effort and, of course, money. I aimed to shine a light on the minutiae of what happens in a particular family, believing that the most personal and intimate details of ourselves can be translated most broadly to a universal perspective.

Generations

I am increasingly drawn to work with family systems because I see our lives as interconnected and interdependent, not separate. I see the process of change as a collective business. I have come to understand through this work that it is not what happens to a family but the quality of the connection and the intentional goodwill between its members that affect our capacity to manage.

The power of grandparents and parents to influence even adult children for better or worse was an important new insight to me. In these case studies we see that family is more than the individuals in it. Each member holds their own narrative, but they also combine to create the family system and way of being. They show that the family life cycle, from birth, adolescence and adulthood into old age, is the primary context of human development. It is through looking at their different stories from generation to generation, and how they influence each other, that we begin to understand ourselves.

In each chapter the family is the structure that holds the emotional system of each living generation, three and even five generations. How that emotional system is managed by everyone in the family, led by the parents and grandparents, shapes their resilience when they face big life changes or even traumatic losses.

We see that emotional systems are not logical. We may want our child/parent/grandparent not to be upset by something we see as trivial—or, at the other end, traumatic—but that doesn't work. The purpose of our emotional system is to give us messages that flow through our body about safety, danger, that allow us to experience pleasure and to have our needs met. It is important to know that the emotions can flow freely through us, whether they are painful or joyous. It is when emotions are shut down that dysfunction sets in. In families, dysfunction can be passed down from generation to generation, as the parent models it in their behaviour to their children, and the cycle continues.

A dysfunctional family comes in many hues and levels of dysfunction. It is generally one in which there are more negative interactions than positive. There is not a predictable attitude of goodwill in each family member, or reciprocal care and support for each other. They do not know how to deal with difficulty: a conflict can escalate into a stand-off that may last months, years or even generations. They tend to be rigid, with fixed views of right and wrong, and close down communication rather than open it up. Behaviourally and psychologically, they are unpredictable and a source of distress to each family member when resolution is not sought or found. It may mean family members feel both abandoned and trapped. They may experience the addictive pull of variable reward, sometimes receiving the longed-for love and attention, and then, for no reason, experiencing its withdrawal: everyone is hooked, waiting for the next hit.

Those families who are rigidly dysfunctional, at the extreme end of it, who don't move along the spectrum, are unlikely to present themselves to me. I often wonder about the seemingly intractable issue that many of those who most need support and insight are least likely to ask for it. Or, worse, unable to access it.

Family systems carry more than just our scripts and emotions. They also, implicitly and explicitly, set the patterns of behaviour and connection between each member of a family—who has what role; who holds the power—as well as the beliefs and rules around what may be communicated, what is blocked, what behaviour is sanctioned. When negative, family dynamics can contribute to the problems of a particular family member and the root of individual and collective anguish. If, for example, the father is weak, his child may be domineering. The dynamic between them is co-created and affects everyone. Rather than dealing only with the weak father, it is important to address the whole family dynamic, since the family in its entirety is the medium for change.

Sometimes an individual acts out a behaviour as an expression of a systemic difficulty. For example, where money worries are not being addressed by everyone in the family, one of the children may have control issues. Families can get stuck at points of change and crisis, using an outmoded pattern of coping, hoping the outcome will be different, then find themselves more entrenched in their difficulty. It is the family as a whole that needs understanding. And at times they need more than understanding: they require active change and help in adopting different behaviours. When I worked with these families I looked at the patterns between all of the members, and what might be causing problems, rather than just a "problem person."

Anyone looking at their own family would benefit by examining their inherited family patterns and behaviours to see what may need adapting. It is often small unexpected changes that bring improvements. For instance, the Wynne family helped their depressed son by watching the whole series of *Modern Family* together.

Love matters

Love, the underpinning predictable resource for families to manage their emotions, is key. Love in all its forms: the capacity to give it, receive it, in action, by standing back, letting go or moving towards, through rupture and repair.

At the root of fracture and heartbreak in families there is often jealousy and competition for what can be seen as the limited resource of love in all those forms. It plays out in misery and hurt, and in the consequent battles of siblings and couples or in intergenerational rivalry.

There are ongoing debates about nature and nurture. When we are born we are given a genetic blueprint: our propensity for intelligence, athleticism and character traits, and we know that their potential can be fulfilled or blunted by our environment. The random luck of what kind of family we are born into, wealth or poverty, history, psychological health and family patterns, influences the quality of the nurture. But at the heart of well-being is our core identity: "I am loved and I belong. This family is my home and safe place whatever happens to me or them."

From my own experience and what I have learnt from the families in this book, when comparing non-biologically and biologically related families, the stories we tell ourselves become who we are. When we are told truthful stories, we trust that we are loved and belong. And we thrive, whatever our genetic inheritance or connection.

Families are messy, chaotic and imperfect. Where we love and care most, we also hurt most, fight hardest and make our deepest mistakes. Yet we thrive when our family is held securely within and around us. It is worth the effort, heartache and strife. When we can trust in it, it can be the force that holds us together when our world is upended. Even across great distances, when our family is at the centre of our being it can help us find our own equilibrium despite the disorder and madness in the world.

The best thing we can do to help this is to prioritize our family, in our hearts, our minds—and with our time.

The Therapy

I am indebted to my clients who gave me permission to write about their most personal and difficult issues. I describe their narratives as stories, which is true, but it is worth remembering that I am describing their innermost personal lives. It is no "story" for them. Their generosity and courage were based on their hope that in telling the story of their family, others may gain insight into theirs, perhaps healing wounds. I believe the wisdom gleaned by clients and therapists in the secrecy of the therapy room has for too long been an untouched resource of value to everyone.

I have disguised the real identity of my clients to protect their privacy. Some are composites and, apart from one family, all the client relationships in this book took place during the pandemic of 2020/21 and over Zoom. I have only mentioned the impact of Covid-19 when it materially affected my clients. With all the challenges Covid presented, it turned out to have some unexpected upsides for the therapeutic process. From a practical perspective it meant I could see more people at an agreed time: trying to get more than one or two people into a room with me, juggling travel and schedules, is a much bigger logistical challenge. I also saw that remote therapy was less intimidating, particularly for the older generations. Sitting in the safety of their own homes, perhaps with a cup of tea in hand, looking at other family members and me on the same screen became a friendly environment within which to discuss important, often intense, issues. At the end of the session I would leave the Zoom call, but quite often the family would stay on and talk more about what we had discussed. I often thought those would have been the best conversations to be a part of and regularly asked for an update but none came. For all the downsides of not picking up on visceral body signals from my clients, intermittent connectivity, seeing up someone's nose rather than their eyes, the benefits of Zoom far out-weighed the negatives. I will always want to work with clients in my room, but for families, in my practice, this is the way forward.

Many of the families were already part of my caseload. Others I chose because of the diverse lens they bring, like the Bergers, and the Singh/Kelly family, or the particular struggle they faced, like the Craigs. Each story can be read on its own or they can be read in sequence. The connection between them was that the families had the courage to come forward for support in the difficulties they were fa-cing. They recognized they had to find new ways of dealing with them.

Conversely, when I listen to my clients who have painful and intractable problems with family members, who don't join them in therapy, their parent or sibling is fixated on being right, rather than willing to look at what else might be contributing to the issue. Hold-ing rigid positions is a hallmark of families that are stuck in negative patterns. I believe the families in this book show it is their capacity to adapt and shift their perspectives while looking for closer connection and stability that marks them as functioning. Our therapy was, and usually is, an extremely good place to begin to explore and even to practise this important skill. The ability of these families to learn to manage their emotions, as well as allow them, was a significant factor in their robust surfing of life's challenges through the generations.

It's helpful, with this in mind, to turn to Daniel Goleman's *Emotional Intelligence: Why It Can Matter More Than IQ*. His definition of emotional intelligence: "the ability to identify, assess and control one's own emotions." If we are not to be hijacked by the sustained stresses of modern family life we need to be intelligent about our emotions. We need to grow in self-awareness—acknowledging what we feel and why we feel it. If we are self-aware, we can remind ourselves when we are in a state of overwhelm that other moods and emotions exist: this isn't all we are for ever. It enables us to practise habits to rebalance, like mindfulness, or even just step out of the room for a moment, which helps us to judge better how to recover from upset, not act it out. It gives us the discipline to filter words and feelings in the service of the relationship, not as an attack on it, to engage our thinking and feeling, tune into others with empathy. Once we can steady ourselves and see others do the same, we don't need to impose ourselves but trust there is enough love within the family system.

Family therapy is often more intense than one-to-one. Every experience in the group is magnified by the number of people. For the parent, who holds responsibility (even if they don't wish to) for the place they're in, it can be particularly hard. Listening to the criticisms or pain of one's children requires forbearance. It takes courage and commitment to sit with those feelings. Painful revelations cut deep but unexpected positives may arise. Yet I believe that those families daring to embrace the force of their feelings, letting them run through them and shift their connection with each other, was in some cases transformative, and in others extremely helpful. Pain, unfortunately, is the agent of change. Avoiding it blocks change. Each of these families' new willingness to name, experience and process their obstacles will form their new family pattern.

I am not a family-systems therapist, which is a particular model of psychotherapy. My work is informed by its theories. I counselled these families with the aim of forming a strong attachment with them, which builds trust: the predictor of good outcomes in therapy. There are more matrilineal than patrilineal perspectives: there are more women in my therapy practice, which reflects the numbers of men in therapy as a whole. More men are accessing it, but in much lower numbers than women.

My contracts with my clients vary. I see couples who want maintenance a few times a year, some families monthly for similar reasons and most individuals weekly or bi-monthly. After the therapy I appreciate it when clients send me updates of their lives or Christmas cards but there is no expectation that they will. Yet their stories live on in me. They shape and influence me, as all important relationships in my life have done.

Therapy is not for ever. It always has an end. Through ongoing reviews there comes a time when we agree together a client's readiness to end. They are empowered to get on with their life without the need for psychotherapy. Hopefully they have strengthened their resilience for when obstacles and losses face them, and to take responsibility for moving forward. They have acknowledged the injury from their parents, partner or an event but are not trapped in a blaming loop. Therapy doesn't fix what went wrong: it helps us learn to adapt, grow and change despite what went wrong.

An ending with a client is a significant, integral and vital element in the process of therapy. Acknowledged as part of the initial contract, it is important that it does not come as a shock to them. Endings are planned and tend to happen gradually. Having developed such a close and meaningful relationship, I am always sad when it ends. It can be tempting to continue as friends, but this is not advisable. A key consideration when I'm thinking about a different kind of relationship with a former client is not to cause harm. Honouring the therapy and the space it holds inside us both is best protected by clear boundaries. I have occasionally developed dual roles with previous clients, usually professionally, which are not harmful, but I tend to avoid it.

I mention my supervisor multiple times throughout the text. All therapists incorporate supervision into their clinical practice to protect clients from missteps by the therapist. For the counsellor it is the place for learning: the opportunity to reflect on their thoughts, feelings and behaviours in their approach to their client. My supervisor is my much-respected, valued and needed colleague, to whom I take my ethical questions, my mistakes, my dilemmas, my fury, or my worry about my clinical practice—and at times my satisfaction or clients' good outcomes. Without my supervisor I don't think I could work effectively. Working with people always brings up questions, conflicts and our own issues, which a wise and trusted person will help to clarify.

Having groups rather than individuals to work with and write about was a psychological juggle. It meant I had to exclude many aspects of people's lives, choosing to write about the parts that affected the whole family. Everyone I worked with, the majority of whom had never had therapy before, found it illuminating and bonding. They were glad of the opportunity to look at themselves and face thorny issues while I took responsibility for conflicts and facilitated greater insight. Revealing their fears, experiencing painful emotions, was difficult, powerful and healing. I could see my clients' energy shift as new understandings emerged. A key element of psychotherapy is the opportunity to hear yourself, and each other, in a new way: the magical power of listening and being heard.

The families I worked with navigated many complex issues. They found the capacity to live with unanswered questions and learn to love again, despite huge losses. I came to see that in the process they shared the ability to straddle the uncertainty of life with a strong commitment to hope.

When practising therapy with my clients I am always writing in retrospect. When I looked at our work together, I took a third position. I accessed the intensity of our process, stepped back, and oscillated between the two views of client and therapist generating greater clarity. The idea was to consider their and my thinking. The psychologist Dan Siegel calls it "mindsight." I would also do a version of this with my clients: I would step back and offer my thoughts to them to give them fresh viewpoints. We know from behavioural science that we tend to support our past decisions even if new information suggests they are wrong. We confuse patterns of familiarity with safety. It can take an outsider's view, like mine, to shine a light on those intractable responses. The therapy room becomes a portal that allows the client to see themselves with greater depth, unpick stuck narratives, gain new perspectives of what has been going on and how they are in relation to each other.

One can never know how much time therapy will take or its outcome. I saw most of the families for just six or eight sessions. Considering how fixed family patterns and dynamics can be, I was encouraged by the speed and level of change that emerged. For someone using time as a barrier to seeking therapy I would suggest (with a smile) it takes less time than watching a TV series.

I understand how daunting it is to take time out to reflect, but the power of therapy as preventive medicine for families in the present and the generations to come can be profound.

The Wynne Family

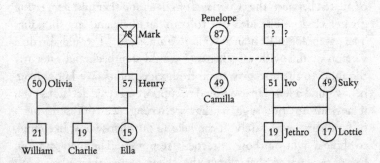

The Wynne Family

Who am I? Am I the sum of my genes or do I make myself?

Case conceptualization

Ivo Wynne was fifty-one years old, a cabinet-maker, married to Suky, aged forty-nine an American-born documentary-maker. They had two children: Jethro, nineteen, and Lottie, seventeen. Ivo came to see me because he wasn't sure of his paternity, whether he was his father Mark's son or not. He wanted to explore this perplexing question, to help him decide the best direction to take: to find out more or live with the status quo—uncertainty. Ivo had an older brother, Henry, aged fifty-seven, and a younger sister, Camilla, who was forty-nine. Mark, Ivo's father, had died five years ago, leaving his mother, Penelope, aged eighty-seven, a widow who self-medicated with alcohol, a just-about-functioning alcoholic. We met in my counselling rooms.

"I'm fifty-one and right now, against every bone in my body, I know I have to find out who my biological father is. It seems incredibly asinine, but it never seemed weird to me that my dad rarely gave me attention when I was a child. Friends at school kept saying, 'Why doesn't your dad ever come and watch you on Sports Day?' I was very sporty, winning every race, and I was captain of the cricket team. I'd say, 'Oh, he's very busy,' and, honestly, I didn't think it was wrong or weird. It was all I knew."

As I heard Ivo's words, I could see his confusion but also a deep pain in his hazel eyes, which were set in a handsome face, with swept-back brown wavy hair. Designer glasses propped on his aquiline nose gave an impression of someone with aristocratic blood. But it was the way he crossed his legs, the arc of his elegantly clad limbs when he moved, that reminded me of highly bred horses. Knowing our parents' history is a fundamental part of our identity for all of us, but if, as in Ivo's case, it also brings high status, then its loss would be another layer of complexity.

I asked Ivo to tell me more of his story. He was a craftsman, with his own company, which designed and made high-end kitchens and furniture. I found myself drawn to look at his hands with renewed interest, their capacity to create beautiful objects. I've always admired people who can make things, since everything I do is invisible. But I needed to turn my attention to his story.

Ivo was the middle brother of a family of three. His elder brother Henry had inherited the title and estate on Mark's death. Henry, aged fifty-seven, was married with three children. He ran the estate and was modernizing it to make it profitable. Camilla, his younger sister, had "always had problems." I imagined a whole world of sibling rivalry in that mix: the eldest son inherits the lot, leaving Ivo, labelled "the heir and spare," with "second-son-itis."

Camilla, aged forty-nine, was (hopefully) one of the last of a generation of upper-class women born into a systemic patriarchy, their education for the purpose of marriage, not a career. She'd had multiple relationships, but now lived alone on the family estate, working part-time for a country auctioneer. She'd had a close bond with her father. They had all been brought up with the formal arrangement of a nanny and nursery life, quite separate from their parents. Henry and Ivo had been sent away at seven, as boarders, to a preparatory school. Camilla went at eleven. All three had been at the cruel end of corporal punishment and must have shut down on their vulnerabilities and emotions to survive that harsh environment, away from home, at such a young age.

Ivo told me, "Twice I asked for my father's help. Once he gave me sleeping pills and the other time he suggested we go on holiday together in Italy to escape . . . He didn't know how to listen and be with me, but in offering the fix I knew he meant well. I remember him reaching to hold my hand once, when we went to see my mother in hospital after her attempted suicide."

I took a breath in shock: he'd spoken of a traumatic event in such a light tone. I asked him how old he'd been and he replied, "Fifteen." I acknowledged how traumatic it was while I logged it as an example of his initial response to pain: glide over it, don't go there. I left a gap for other feelings to surface.

Ivo wrapped his fingers around his thumb, turning them back and forth, with a faraway look, tears in his eyes. He didn't mention his mother's attempted suicide, which he still blocked, just a memory of his father: "I held his hand when he had dementia. That felt nice . . . he didn't know who I was . . ." He was smiling through his tears. "I felt close to him." Then he coughed, and turned his attention to the distance between them: "I don't think he knew my birthday, or my middle name—he certainly didn't know what I was interested in, who my friends were or anything about me . . . but the agony for me isn't that. It's his chilliness towards me, which felt different from Henry and Camilla." His head cast downwards, he said, with some awkwardness, "He could never look me in the eye." There was a long pause while we took in the devastation of his words.

I wanted to get beneath the surface, delve more into the mechanics of Ivo's early years. I was thinking that the roles each child adopts, reinforced by their parents, can have the greatest influence on the behaviour of a family. They are often formed in our family of origin to stabilize the family system. I wasn't clear yet as to who in the Wynne family took which role: had Ivo been "the quiet one" and Henry "the fixer"? While this might work well in their birth family, now that they were adults, joining other family systems, it may no longer fit and could even cause fracture. If it came up, I'd suggest they explore it with openness to see what might need adapting.

Three children can be brought up in the same house by the same parents and have entirely different childhoods. I've often heard a parent say, "I don't know why so-and-so is difficult when her brother is easygoing—they've had exactly the same upbringing."

Yet each child evokes their own unique response from their parents, and memories of each event are shaped by that response.

Henry was organized, ambitious and a leader, all characteristics of an eldest child. I hypothesized that being the heir would give him power and self-importance yet add a layer of expectation from his parents and envy from his younger siblings.

Middle children, like Ivo, are harder to categorize, but they emerge in response to their elder sibling. If the older child is good, the middle child may be naughty to attract attention. I hadn't worked out how this had shaped Ivo, who seemed both erratic and successful, but it raised this question: how would it be to rear a child you knew wasn't genetically yours yet keep it secret?

Mark knew Ivo was innocent, but looking at him must have ignited a cocktail of feelings, ranging from fury, jealousy and outrage to disgust. No wonder he chose not to look at him. Henry and Camilla would undoubtedly have picked up on that, and might have been distressed by it, but there was such a paucity of parental attention that they probably interpreted it as a bonus.

Camilla interested me. Last-borns can "get away with more" than their elder siblings, as their parents relax the rules. They tend to be affectionate, funny and easygoing, but they are often trying to catch up with their older siblings, who are bigger, faster and know more. *I* needed to know more but I would have imagined that, on one level, Camilla, the youngest, had an easier time. However, she had to deal with the patriarchy, privileging men and undervaluing women. To counter this context, Camilla took up her father's interests in botany, literature and family history. She was rewarded with closeness to her father. But, as I understood it, it had not worked particularly well for her either. She wasn't the funny, loving child: she was brittle and nervous. As I drew the genogram of their family, looking at the relationships and context between them, I hypothesized that Camilla's brothers had knocked her confidence. The impact of aggressive sibling rivalry, in effect bullying, is as harmful as it is in a school but often goes unchecked.

★

Given this had been his experience since childhood I asked Ivo what he wanted from coming to see me now. "I've been really good at burying it." He paused and smiled. "I'm not my mother's son for nothing. She is the Queen of Denial. Over the years I've had or heard conversations that made me question if Dad was my father. It was always sitting in the back of my mind. I would turn up to see Dad and he'd be awkward, and very distant. I felt I didn't belong. Henry and Camilla were cruel to each other but would enjoy pairing up to turn on me. They'd tie me up and beat me with a hairbrush, cover my face with mud, which felt like excrement, in my ears, up my nose, and countless other attacks. They'd tease me for being ugly, call me stupid—I remember Camilla saying to me, 'Just looking at you makes me feel sick.'"

Again, I was shocked by the brutality of the picture he painted, and the lack of emotion he displayed as he spoke—but I felt it, a twisting in my chest. It was very hard to see in my mind's eye the defenceless boy being attacked like that.

It occurred to me that their parents' neglect had metabolized within the siblings into anger, then self-disgust, which they acted out with each other. Ivo had slowed down now, which allowed more space for his words and emotions to connect. I wondered if he'd picked up mine from reading my face. Feelings are contagious.

"I wouldn't have known how to say it then, but looking back, all I wanted was to be safe and to belong, but I never did. The lack of care and attention we received from our parents would put us on the at-risk register now, but if you live in a castle with a moat and titled parents everyone assumes you're lucky, living the dream."

I saw the hurt and pent-up rage in Ivo's face: he was clenching his jaw at the discomfort his memories caused him. I guessed this was the first time he had properly voiced the many layers of distress that were sitting in his body. I told him how shocking his experience was: I had disturbing images of him being physically abused by his siblings and felt fury with them and protective of him, while acknowledging that they must all have been suffering to behave in such violent ways.

The level of neglect while the children lived in such luxury was confusing. I wondered with Ivo about how our collective blindness prevents us from seeing that class and privilege do not protect against suffering. As a society we tend to judge people from how they look, not from how they might feel. A big car represents wealth and assumed happiness but its owner's sad eyes tell a different story. I suggested Ivo had internalized that view. He nodded, holding his breath as a way not to take in my words.

From a psychological perspective, none of the siblings received reliable, secure love from their parents. They all carried negative coping mechanisms to manage their insecure childhood, but the scarcity of love meant they turned on each other to fight for the little that was available. That was the cruellest part. Healthy families use fighting to learn the difference between being clever and hurting: they discover from the trusted adults around them what they can and cannot say when arguing. This family had learnt to attack intending to wound, with no guidance or mediation from the adults around them. I thought of young birds in a nest, pecking each other to get to the worm first.

I could see Ivo was exhausted, but he wanted to continue. "My first girlfriend had been told categorically that Mark wasn't my father by a close family friend. She asked Henry, who swore it was a false rumour, and they had a stand-up fight about it. I believed Henry and put it out of my mind. Mum came to see me once at university, the only time she ever did. She brought up the usual social banalities of her life, and then, as she closed the car door, just before she drove away, she said, 'I know you think Mark isn't your father, but he is. I swear that's the truth.' Basically, I have got on with my life since then and totally buried the question. But that same girlfriend emailed me a month ago with a photograph of a man who looks like me—she saw it in someone's house. But more than looking like me it's like looking at a clone of my son Jethro."

I was racing to catch up with all that Ivo was saying, which was particularly hard as, the more distressed he felt, the faster he was speaking. I was in a dilemma as to whether to ask him to pause for us take in the story so far but decided to let him get it out in a rush. We would deal with it in the following session. Ivo spat out, "I was furious with her. How dare she just send that to me out of the blue as if it was trivial information? But much, much worse, she sent it to Henry and Camilla too. Without checking with me! I literally couldn't believe she was tearing my life up with one light-hearted email. Henry rang me to discuss it and we had a huge blowout. As usual all our old grievances were rolled out. We were both competing for who could win with the knock-out blow of nastiness. It was horrible. I slammed the phone down on him, as I have countless times, thinking how much I hate him and never wanted to speak to him again, but the fight tipped me out of my denial.

"From that moment everything I read, saw on TV, listened to was about fathers and sons . . . I couldn't sleep, concentrate, eat, and I've been drinking a lot . . . Again I'm not my mother's son for nothing . . . The last weeks I've wallowed in my melancholy. Every day has been hard. I can't face it . . . can't face the day . . . I do what I must do, the bare minimum, but I'm existing, not living. That's a long way to say I'm not coping. I want to know how to be with it, what to do with it. If it's true, who am I? How does it change me? I look in the mirror and I see the same face, but I feel different. Is that my father's nose? I'd thought it was. I've always liked that link to him. I'm good at math, like he was. We didn't have much of an emotional relationship, but I didn't realize until now how much of my sense of self I anchored in my parents—their genes, their history coming down to me. Even bloody places. My father's family made their fortune through politics and farming, and built their estate in Norfolk, so Norfolk has always been my roots—the whole county—its smell, its topography, going to my family home, the portraits of 'my' ancestors. Do I have to let that go? Maybe my father didn't believe I was his child, but he brought me up as his child. If I'm not biologically his, is he still my father? Do I lose half my family? All my cousins from that side of the family, are they suddenly lost to me? Where do I belong now?

Who do I belong to? What about my children and their biological inheritance?"

That was a lot of questions. I could feel how profoundly disturbing it was for Ivo, a tightness in my throat signalling concern for how best to support him. We agreed we might not find answers to all of his questions, but perhaps over the weeks ahead we could begin to face together what they meant for Ivo.

I research my clients' issues to be well informed and offer optimal psychological support. I learnt that knowing where you come from is developmentally important. In the 1990s Dr Marshall Duke and Dr Robyn Fivush (see Appendix, page 269) developed a "Do You Know?" scale to ask adolescents about their family. They found those who knew more of their family history showed higher levels of self-esteem, lower levels of behaviour problems and more self-efficacy—they trusted they could influence their world. Ivo had been unsure of his roots all his life. Now half of the bricks that had built where he came from had been pulled out. I knew we had to tread carefully.

I also needed to assess the level of Ivo's childhood abuse and neglect, and fully understand his coping mechanisms. Stress and trauma in early life impair cognitive, social and emotional development. They also indicate potential health problems in adulthood. The research shows a direct link to depression, addiction and suicide as well as a whole raft of physical ailments from cancer to heart disease. I decided to use the "Adverse Childhood Experiences" questionnaire, developed by co-researchers Dr Vincent Felitti and Dr Rob Anda (see Appendix, page 266). Ivo's answers would indicate to me how fragile he was.

The ten questions range from "Did a parent or other adult in the household often push, grab, slap, or throw something at you?" to "Did you often feel that you didn't have enough to eat, had to wear dirty clothes, and had no one to protect you?"

Every "yes" scores one point; the higher the score, the higher the risk factor. Ivo's score was five. That indicated to me that we would need to go slowly, build safety in our relationship to help stabilize him. We also had to develop resources for him to manage his emotions before we began on the disturbing question of his paternity.

Ivo had developed his defence mechanism of numbing to protect himself from painful emotions like shame, anger and guilt. If he was thrown into experiencing those feelings without a new way of coping with them it might precipitate a breakdown or even suicide. At this intense early phase of our relationship, I was grateful for my years of experience: they gave me the confidence that I knew how to support him, however fragile he felt. I wasn't in control of his outcome, but I could meet him at his point of need and that might be enough.

Importantly, when Ivo had answered the questionnaire, and I had helped him to recognize there were other ways of dealing with distress, he began to see that I was on his side, and that I took him seriously. Historically his feelings were trivialized or ignored. Sometimes I could see from the way he looked at me that he was expecting me to say something nasty; when I didn't, he'd sigh, partly relieved, partly putting down his sharp words to fight back.

Ivo had said he was "good at denial" and I felt that in every session. Denial is the first stage in the grieving process: it had been necessary to protect him as a child and it signalled the significance of his loss. His loss had not been the death of someone, but a "living loss": the loss of trust in his identity as his father's son. It had happened in an environment that was not safe, which meant his grief could not be expressed. The "Safe Place" helped to calm Ivo: he imagined somewhere that gave him a sense of calm and peace and would breathe deeply while imbuing it with memories of what he heard, saw and smelled. We also developed within him an image we called "The Container": it was a psychological steel cabinet, which could hold his frightening images when he wasn't with me.

The tools we developed together gave him an alternative to shutting down. It allowed him to experience the discomfort of his feelings, express them a little, then use self-efficacy to soothe himself. It may not sound markedly different from shutting down, but it is. Ivo's method defends and keeps alive the painful feelings in his system; the other allows him to release, which changes them, and supports his capacity not to be overwhelmed by them.

These tools were important as Ivo began to open up. He'd find the words to express how he felt, and then he'd shift in his seat, cross his long legs and switch into a completely different subject. Or he'd bow his head and not speak. I could picture Ivo using that exact behaviour as a small child. It evoked gentleness in me: I wanted to comfort him. We'd use a stabilizing technique to allow him to return to painful memories, the focus of which was his first term at boarding school—his earliest memory of suffering. It was of him as a small boy trying not to cry in his bed in his dormitory, a large white-walled room with twelve beds in it. I shivered: he was seven! Far too young.

There is little research about the impact of boarding school, and the research that exists is contested. But some, like Nick Duffell, believe that "boarding-school syndrome" tends to emerge in "boarding-school survivors" in their twenties and even their thirties. It proposes boarders have an identifiable set of responses, learnt as a protection against their abandonment at school, which plays out with the people and events they encounter in their life and can lead to serious psychological distress.

Ivo's memory of his prep school was that it was always cold, and he particularly remembered the chill of stepping out of bed on to the freezing stone floor. As he described it, he switched between openness and distancing himself, which allowed him to have some control over his capacity to bear his distress. In therapy we have a term for this: the "window of tolerance." We want to support our clients to reach to the edge of their tolerance—out of their comfort zone—where they learn that they can feel pain, express it, and it doesn't kill them. Instead it can release them, even lessen the pain. They can then move away from the edge to a more tolerable place and feel calm, even relieved.

★

Many sessions later Ivo and I agreed that keeping the question of his paternity to himself was not only overwhelming but toxic, as family secrets often are. He was close to his wife, Suky, who had been informed from the beginning and she was very supportive. An American, Suky had a healthy scepticism for the British class system, while recognizing it was a valued aspect of Ivo's identity. They agreed to talk to their two children: Jethro and Lottie. After all, it was their ancestry too. As it stood, the photograph Ivo had seen was not definitive proof: he would need to have a DNA test with Henry and Camilla. That would tell him precisely whether they were full or half siblings. Neither of us was sure if it was better to go down the testing route or live with the uncertainty. I had always believed the truth, however difficult it is, is preferable to a lie. But Ivo had lived for the last fifty-one years without knowing: could he face the psychological consequences of not being his father's son?

Finally, the weight of not knowing was greater than knowing. Henry and Camilla wanted a definitive answer as well, and they all sent off their samples.

It was a long three-week wait. One cold November morning Ivo received an email from the genetic testing lab. He didn't want to open it. He told me that when he read the result—that he was his siblings' half-brother, with 23 percent shared DNA—he'd felt his stomach drop. With rage in his eyes he turned to me: "So it's definitely true. F***, f***, f***. I want to scream against it . . ." Then his anger lowered in tone, becoming more intense: "I don't know what to do with it. I've lost something that is fundamental to me, a core part of me, but it's invisible and yet concrete . . . It is a hammer-blow of loss." He put his hands over his face, his body shaky, as he whispered repeatedly, "What do I do with it?"

The best I could do was sit with him in his distress. I felt the swirl of his storm in my stomach. I breathed slowly to hold my equanimity and said how sorry I was. It was a stormy, painful session.

Despite our stabilizing techniques, the news sent Ivo into a spiral of binge drinking and chaos. He started smoking again, even though he suffered from asthma. Sometimes he didn't turn up for appointments, at others he was still drunk from the night before. I turned to my supervisor, feeling guilty and extremely worried. Obviously, we had found out the truth too soon: Ivo hadn't been ready to hear it. I'd learnt from Babette Rothschild, the pre-eminent specialist in trauma, that therapists don't always stabilize their clients enough and go to processing too quickly. My supervisor agreed that this was probably what had happened, and suggested there might be a parallel process in which I self-attacked as Ivo was doing. She helped calm me, encouraging me to focus on what we could do to help him, rather than criticizing myself. Create a network of friends, and a set of soothing further behaviours, like yoga or meditation to support him in the intensity of his distress. We agreed I needed to check if he was suicidal, ask for consent to speak to his GP and his wife. Suicide might seem a big leap from severe distress, but his mother had attempted it: that increased his risk, as did his adverse childhood experiences. I wanted to cover every possibility for his safety.

I voiced my concern to Ivo about his drinking and asked him if he had suicidal thoughts. He flicked his hand angrily at me as if I was an annoying schoolteacher. While I felt the sting of his response, I knew I needed to stay connected to him with compassion. He was turning on himself and it was crucial he felt I was beside him in this, for me to let him know that I was extremely worried but without alienating him. We both knew he was the innocent victim of his mother's actions, but somehow he felt ashamed, wrong or defective. And that his family, everyone around him, would look at him differently.

The storm had a life of its own: it raged through Ivo and, thankfully, eventually subsided, leaving him spent. A more peaceful Ivo surmised that it had been sitting in him for decades. Perhaps all those years of denial had built up in him, like layers of sediment, and had needed to be blasted out. He was still drinking and smoking but he slept, he was able to concentrate and, touchingly, he felt closer to both of his children. In the end it was their love that stabilized him, not my tools.

Ivo had built a wall of defences that had kept them at a distance, and now they just burst into his heart, mainly through hugs. The power of embodied love. They just kept hugging him. Jethro had said Ivo's biological father was "a sperm donor," and Lottie had told him, "Nothing has changed, Dad. You are one hundred percent the same person you were before you got this result." They laughed, properly laughed, at his questioning of whether Norfolk was his roots—"Don't be an idiot, Dad! Of course it is! All the memories and time make it yours as much now as ever." They were smart, and it was fascinating for me to see that their vulnerability had allowed Ivo to open up properly to them.

Ivo was particularly touched by Jethro. He told me, "When Jethro was fifteen, he gamed behind the locked door of his bedroom for two years. We were so worried about him. He told us life wasn't worth living. We tried to get him help but he refused to see anybody, shutting himself off from everyone. What was miraculous was that when Suky suggested we watch *Modern Family* together, he agreed. We watched it most nights for all eleven seasons—250 episodes. We didn't speak much but he'd sit in the middle between Suky and me. It gradually drew us together. That, and growing eight inches in a year, he's now five ten and that's a good height. He went off to university last year and he's a changed boy. He's got a great group of friends, friendships he's never had in his life before . . ."

No one can predict what is curative. *Modern Family* gave them a framework to be together that wasn't emotionally demanding while offering a shared focus and connection.

I wasn't surprised that Ivo hadn't mentioned Jethro's teenage angst before: although it had concerned him, I don't think he'd felt it deeply. A protective layer had been blown off him, and now he was more open to all his emotions.

Henry, still angry from their previous argument, had decided to visit Ivo and demand he return some Wynne family chattels: Ivo was no longer a Wynne. I was shocked yet Ivo wasn't. He'd said to Suky he was sure one of his siblings would do that. He knew how his family operated.

It was particularly ironic coming from Henry, who had inherited the bulk of the family fortune. Ivo laughed that Henry could insist all he liked, but he had no power to enforce it, so it gave Ivo some pleasure to refuse him. He was annoyed with Henry, but he wasn't a victim. He knew they would be distant for a while, but in the end they'd talk again. That was the family pattern. Blow-ups and fights, then silence for several months until one of them made the first move. Nothing would be discussed or resolved; that last fight would add to the pile of resentments, and they'd carry on.

Ivo continued, "But for the first time I can ever remember in my life with my family, Henry wrote me a heartfelt apology and we have reconciled. I feel closer to him . . . which is good, pretty amazing, actually."

I translated Henry's behaviour as his wired default response, his attack on Ivo coming from a place of deficiency. Chattels were their currency of love when so little love was available. Henry was triggered into getting what he could. He'd inherited a great deal but that hadn't protected him from his inner feeling of deprivation. I couldn't know what had influenced Henry to apologize, to change the family pattern, but I imagined his wife had talked some reason and empathy into him. Perhaps that communication had built an important new bridge of connection for Ivo. Through DNA he was more distant from his siblings, but maybe he could become emotionally closer.

When Ivo and I reflected on this a few weeks later it was clear that the trappings of their family—the title, land, money and status—were valued highly while its members were not. They viewed "things" or "stuff" as more reliable than people—but, as the journalist Art Buchwald wrote, "The best things in life aren't things." You could display them, or cash them in. The family viewed people as a potential danger: they could hurt and leave you. A much riskier commodity.

I compared that to an immigrant family I was working with who had no "stuff": their family members mattered more than anything else. They were prepared to sacrifice everything for them. People were their riches, their security and vital to their survival: they knew they couldn't live alone in a foreign land. None of us gets through life successfully without close, loving bonds.

Ivo and I concluded that, as humans, we need to be able to put our trust in something, and if it isn't the people around us, we move it to things. To me, it is one of the traits of a dysfunctional family, when the people in it are secondary, and everything else matters more.

After much debate Ivo decided to ask his mother to come to a session with us and his siblings. Alongside that, I suggested Ivo find some photographs of Mark and write to him as if he was speaking to him. Because, as we came to see it, he might lose the biological father he had, but he could never lose the presence of and his relationship with the father he had known from baby-hood. His father had been far from the perfect dad, and obviously knew that Ivo was not genetically his child, but he had, never-theless, brought him up as such, given him his name and paid for him. In his father's later years Ivo and he had formed a better bond together.

It became clear that our work was to grieve the father Ivo had had and for Ivo to internalize an updated version of him. Ivo seemed to look at his father from a different perspective: "As I got older, and left home, did well in my job and needed less from him, we got closer. We saw the point of each other. He never actually said it, but I think he was proud of me. He felt differently towards me from my siblings, but I know that, in his way, he loved me. He just didn't know how to show it."

This picture of a benign but largely absent father was familiar to me, and to many people of my generation. He was a man of his time. He had no language or understanding of emotions; feelings probably frightened him. I could imagine that he was utterly confused by Ivo, who was living proof that his wife had been unfaithful to him, who was innocent, who had done well—and there were all the feelings that evoked: fury, shame, love and pride.

To my surprise, and somewhat my trepidation, Ivo's mother, Penelope, and sister, Camilla, agreed to meet with us. Henry was willing to come but, after discussion, the siblings felt all three of them would threaten their mother too much, and she would go on the attack.

I wanted to clarify with Ivo what he hoped to gain by having a session with them. As usual it took a while to get beneath his defences but, speaking in a voice that seemed distant and young, almost beyond his conscious control, he said, "I want to sit in a room with them and not feel like I'm drowning even before I open my mouth."

I nodded, thinking: There's a lot in that sentence alone, but we can go back to that.

He continued, "I want my mother to tell me the truth and give me an explanation. I'd like it if she apologized but, much more importantly than that, I want to know the full story . . . And Camilla, I don't know. She is unhappy. Troubled people make trouble, so I get why she's mean. I'd like it if we could talk about this without her attacking me, taking pleasure in my suffering. If she just offered a little understanding of what it's like for me it would be a win, but honestly I doubt it."

The morning came for our group session with Ivo, Penelope and Camilla. I was nervous. I felt protective of Ivo and fearful I might not be able to facilitate the conversation to give him the outcome he wanted—and needed.

When Penelope walked into my room, leaning on her cane, making loud puffing noises, smelling of gardenias, I saw she was small. Ivo had described her to me as "very beautiful, very serene, very natural-looking and always laughing." Swathed in silk shawls, a large crucifix hanging on a heavy gold chain and no make-up, blue eyes glinting at me, she was certainly powerful.

Camilla was taller and had heeded her mother's view that make-up was "hideous." She was also natural to the extent that I couldn't stop myself thinking she hadn't taken care of herself. Her greying hair was tangled in a ponytail; a baggy jersey and trousers covered a large frame. She was pale, with broken veins on her cheeks, and startling blue eyes. She didn't ask where to sit, just sat in the chair nearest the door, for a quick exit.

As Penelope spoke, her cut-glass vowels reminded me of a bygone era: "Ah. What a palaver to get here. All that traffic, and I had a nightmare parking." Ivo, who had gripped his left thumb, turning it like a corkscrew with his right hand, looked between his mother and the floor, with a brief pleading glance at me, which I read as "Please don't f★★★ this up." I felt the pressure, my breathing shallower than I'd have liked. Camilla was nervous too: as the "mean sister" I'd expected her to be confident in her position of genetic superiority, but she sat on the edge of her seat, making no eye contact with anyone.

I started the session by naming what I understood. The genetic tests between the siblings showed unequivocally that, biologically, Mark was not Ivo's father. Ivo had questioned it in his childhood and been lied to, but now his question was clear: what was the truth of his paternity? I asked Penelope directly: "Who was Ivo's father?"

We all turned to her, and Camilla, in a strong, deep voice, said, "Yes, Mum, you've lied to us for decades, tell us the truth."

Penelope stared at her. "You've always been a bully. You're still a bully."

I was about to step in to try to turn the conversation away from a full-on fight but Penelope continued: "Allington [Allington Hall, their childhood home] was wonderful. You had a fun youth. Miss Barrett came and I knew she'd be useful that first morning. You used to bounce around and make a noise waking us up but that first morning when you woke up you had an apple and a glass of lemonade by your bed . . ."

Camilla and Ivo sent each other a knowing look, as if to say,

Every Family Has a Story

"This is who she's going to be today." I repeated my first question and Penelope said, "I don't remember," then went off on a tangent, totally unrelated, referring to her childhood home, the number of servants, and memories of her time in Paris as a young woman. Sometimes she'd mutter, as if she'd lost her way, and fallen into a ditch, but then she'd go into yet another vignette of her past life.

Ivo tried intervening: "Mum, I'm not cross with you. I don't think you're bad but I do want to know more." Her response was to scratch very hard at the sore-looking rash on her arms.

Camilla said, "Mum, stop scratching. You're making it worse." Penelope paid no heed.

I came to see that Penelope's defences were so embedded in her that she simply couldn't hear what any of us said. It was as though she was inside a fortified turret, with tiny windows at the top to protect against invading forces. At eighty-seven, a hardened drinker, her lifestyle habits meant her coherence was inevitably faulty too.

The breakthrough came when Camilla said to Ivo, "I wasn't allowed to tell you but I knew it was Robert."

Penelope heaved herself up, threw her scarf over her shoulder, patted Ivo's thigh and said, "Oh, bugger [in a French accent, an affected way of swearing, a typical defence of someone with Penelope's background]. He is," and walked out.

We'd had half an hour of our ninety-minute session and I felt like I'd run a marathon without making any progress. Ivo said, "Oh, God, that was weird [his all-encompassing term for everything he didn't understand and couldn't overcome]."

Camilla sat back in her chair. "Well, at least she admitted it." That was true: Ivo now knew who his father was. The mood in our room had shifted: it was lighter. Camilla and Ivo fell into what seemed a familiar banter of how impossible their mother was, and with dark humour listed a cast of other possible fathers, who could have been a lot worse, for Ivo.

At one point Camilla's tone twisted, suggesting that Ivo had dodged a bullet in not having *her* father's genetic history of cancer and heart failure. Ivo just said, "Don't."

With her response—"What?"—it felt like a familiar riff of mini attacks and defences that had been played out between them since they were small.

It must have impacted Ivo that Camilla, not his mother, had revealed who his father was, but I decided now wasn't the time to go into that.

Whenever I'd asked Ivo about his mother he'd painted a picture of the siblings' formal upbringing and his parents' busy social life, how they hadn't eaten with them until they were teenagers. Apart from his strong capacity for denial—he'd learnt from his mother to self-medicate unbearable feelings—I had no insight into how his mother had actually parented him.

Camilla was more forthcoming. She was angrier. "My mother was, and still is, you've just seen it, this terrible sort of hysterical drama queen, who always needed to be the centre of attention, having tantrums. She could be very entertaining. She drank a lot. She was an emotional storm—a pretty useless mother. She was beautiful, of course, which gave her more opportunity to be unfaithful. She was and is horrible to me. She never said, 'You're pretty,' she made me feel fat and ugly. She had a particular look she gave me when I ate. As a result I've got a food thing, a control thing. I can't let go of stuff. I never cry. I never sweat. I don't poo. I've never been sick . . . You could say I'm repressed . . ."

I was about to say something when she added, "I don't want you to feel sorry for me, or in any way think I'm playing the victim."

That sentence stopped me in my tracks. I didn't know how to respond so I resorted to counselling 101, or basics, and reflected back what I'd heard her say. She nodded, with some satisfaction. "Yup, that's about right."

Ivo chimed in: "I think she was awful to you. And I don't remember cosy times. Maybe she was a bit old-fashioned and I don't ever remember Mum saying, 'I love you.' She didn't hug you, but she used to hold your hand and stroke it between her finger and thumb. I remember reading my book on my own for hours."

Camilla responded, "You felt she didn't see you, that you existed to amuse her. Otherwise you were a chore." I noticed the objective "you" Camilla had used to describe herself, rather than the subjective "I," which gave the impression of the distance that seemed to imbue their every interaction.

Ivo had a more sympathetic picture of his mother. She had been nicer to her sons than to her daughter, whose looks disappointed her. He'd had a "different" mother, albeit the same person. I couldn't help but muse on the hypocrisy of this beautiful woman, who believed in natural beauty and left her daughter feeling fat and ugly.

I knew from Ivo that Camilla had had a closer relationship with her father but asked her to tell me about him. "He adored me. OK, he was awkward, but when we did things together, like wild-flower spotting, we didn't need to speak. We just had that joy of being alongside each other, and all the rituals around it, like pulling out our reference books, pressing the flowers. He was a surprisingly gifted sketcher too. I have many of his treasured notebooks. If it was wet, we'd come back muddy, eat crumpets with hot chocolate. Or if it was boiling, we'd drink home-made lemonade." As she was speaking she showed more vitality than I'd seen before.

While Ivo nodded a little forlornly, he smiled in agreement with his sister as she continued, "No one ever talked about anything. My father was terrified of upsetting my mother. If she was upset everyone would pay, and he'd long ago learnt to keep his head down. We used to have this family saying, 'Let's change the subject.' We could talk about politics or the cat or the weather but never about anything that mattered." They agreed that their mother's tantrums ruled. Their father had been weak.

I used the tone of my voice to let them know I really felt for them, and recognized how, in their different ways, neither of them had had a secure childhood. Quite the reverse.

★

It seemed important to put the parenting they'd received in context, not to diminish their suffering but to help them recognize that their parents had done the best they could, given who they were and where they'd come from. I suggested that most of that generation did not have the least idea of how to manage relationships with anyone. Their stiff upper lip was a necessary survival mechanism as the generation who'd been brought up by veterans of the First World War, then lived through and fought in the Second.

I asked them to tell me about their parents' childhoods. Camilla and Ivo softened as they described the difficult childhood their parents had faced. Their Wynne grandfather had returned from the First World War shell-shocked, a broken man. Mark's brother was killed in 1944, and Mark had been a distinguished RAF pilot. He must have been brave, yet he was frightened of his wife.

Penelope's father had died when she was six. When she was twenty-three, her mother's neighbour had rung to say she'd found Penelope's mother dead in her bed. I guessed that had brought with it a whole world of guilt, as to why Penelope hadn't visited and been the one to find her mother. But her mother had been an alcoholic: the post-mortem cited cirrhosis as cause of death, making three generations of the family dependent on alcohol. There were probably many valid reasons as to why Penelope hadn't visited her.

As a child, Penelope had been evacuated to Wales, where she'd had a horrible time: the family spoke Welsh, and they appropriated her rations, so she was always hungry and cold. Both Ivo and Camilla agreed that she often lied, so they weren't sure how much to believe, but what was definitely true was that, once she'd married Mark, she was estranged from her two brothers. They believed Penelope wanted to escape everything from her childhood, to keep it as distant from her present life as possible. I assessed that Penelope had arrested development: her tantrums were those of a young child who had not been heard. I hear often about parents who are still children and inflict untold damage on their own children.

I told Ivo and Camilla that they had described two families with multiple traumas through the generations, none of which had been recognized or dealt with. Trauma is defined as the emotional response to a terrible event that is experienced as overwhelming. It imprints in the brain beyond where language can reach so cannot cognitively be processed. Additionally, and understandably, those who endure trauma want to forget, so they don't talk about it. But it alters the brain and sufferers see the world differently, viewing it as a dangerous place. The most common defence mechanisms in unprocessed trauma are psychological shut-down, which was Mark's reaction, or using drugs and alcohol to self-anaesthetize, like Penelope.

With Ivo's heavy drinking in mind, I turned to the research on inherited alcoholism. Finding the direct genetic contribution to addiction is complex, involving a combination of inherited variants in multiple genes. The view now is that addiction in families, as with all things genetic, is the interplay between environment and genetic predisposition. It is useful to look at the history of addiction through the generations in our own families and recognize our own risk factors—if, for example, you have an uncontrollable desire to drink that overrides your other relationships and priorities.

Mark and Penelope had had the additional dimension of their class: they believed expression of any feelings, other than humour and jolliness, was slightly disgusting or "common." Expressing hurt was seen as weakness. We learn to manage difficulty by mirroring the coping mechanisms of our caregivers. It was therefore no surprise that Ivo turned to drink and nicotine to assuage his distress.

I suggested that Henry, Ivo and Camilla had been born into the security of wealth and status on the outside while their relationships with their parents were based on the traumatic unpredictability of an alcoholic, tempestuous mother and an absent father. Both parents had, no doubt, loved their children, even had moments of being affectionate and expressive, but were ill-equipped to provide the secure foundations for a functioning family.

Briefly, and voiced in a way that sought no response, Camilla said, with a raucous laugh, "Maybe that explains my splintered heart. Maybe I shouldn't be shocked to find myself in this situation, divorced from that c★★★ and living alone. I always thought I'd live in the country with a lovely garden, a husband and children. I'm really surprised people I trusted have left me [her ex-husband and one of her best friends no longer spoke to her]— not helped by my bitch sister-in-law [Henry's wife] who locks me out of Allington." A long pause followed. "I do want to be different but I don't know how . . ."

I could see even speaking out her pain shocked her. She had a kind of febrile energy that was constantly on the look-out for danger but paradoxically meant she couldn't turn towards warmth or nurture. She habitually rubbed her nose for something to do with her hands. I acknowledged it must be tough living alone without children while her brothers' lives seemed happier. It was obviously difficult if she didn't like her sister-in-law. She nodded, and gave the familiar mirthless laugh. "It underlies what I think, the randomness and pointlessness of existence blighted by mass unemployment, climate change and everything else."

Ivo also laughed, "Thanks, Cami, for the good cheer," but I could see he felt the wrench of her heartache.

Reminiscent of her mother, Camilla then shifted the conversation and asked us what we thought the next steps could be. She suggested Ivo meet his biological father, Robert. Ivo grimaced, as if the mere thought of Robert made him feel physically sick. "I've done my best with Mum. Got a kind of truth. I just want to get on with my life." Camilla didn't agree, yet they left the session committing to have a slap-up lunch together. I was a little worried as to how that would go once alcohol was involved, but reminded myself they were middle-aged adults, not teenagers.

Somewhat relieved to see them leave, I took myself for a stomp around the park to let off some steam. I thought a lot about Camilla. I hoped the session might spark an impulse in her to find new ways of getting her needs met that would give her more happiness.

★

Ivo met his mother soon after our session and she never alluded to their conversation. He couldn't extract from her an explanation of what had happened. Penelope had stepped out of her well-built fortifications for a few minutes but was walled up again. Ivo knew there was nothing further he could ask of her. There was a relief in that knowledge. He had learnt who his biological father was. What he did now was up to him. Ivo turned to work as an escape and a place to have control. He showed me with pride a set of dining-room chairs he'd made. I thought of Sigmund Freud: "Work and love, love and work is all there is." Ivo worked to give himself a sense of agency, an important aspect of well-being, and he turned to his family.

The support Suky and their children gave him was crucial. In a tentative voice, with an edge of shame, Ivo said, "I've not been easy these weeks. Perhaps I do have some of my mother's bad things, like her blowing up and having tantrums." I asked if he felt he could change. He believed he could but "the more deeply embedded it is the harder it is." True. We decided it would be worthwhile if his family joined us for one appointment.

In traditional therapy it is unusual for different family members to pop in and out of the central client's sessions, a practice I'd followed for decades. In the last years, though, my understanding of the interweaving connectedness of every part of ourselves, our families and the natural world has shifted my perspective. Ivo's capacity to integrate the news of his true biological father depended on those closest to him holding him up when he fell down. We agreed a time for us all to meet.

Recalling that session is like pulling sunshine from my memory bank, despite its moments of trickiness. The difference in the quality of the conversation and the atmosphere in my room from the appointment with his mother was remarkable.

Ivo came in gleaming and shy, a little nervous. Suky followed. She picked up and dropped her thick blonde hair from the front of her shoulder to the back as she sat down. She beamed warmly into my eyes, styled casually in a fitted shirt, jeans and ballet flats. Jethro and Lottie looked a little wary, but were smiling and curious. The sheen of youth and uninjured openness is particularly heart-warming for me to see, when most of the faces I look at in my job are full of heartbreak. I tried to stop myself assessing which parent they resembled, but failed. Jethro looked like his dad, and Lottie had his eyes, with the slim athletic build of her mum.

I asked them to tell me where they'd got to since learning Ivo's news. I could see Suky longed to speak but turned to her children. Jethro spoke first: "I can't even tell you how it isn't a thing. Clearly you got the best genetics. You're funnier and cleverer than the others." When asked if he felt differently about his cousins he gave another emphatic no: they loved each other, it made no difference.

Lottie spoke quietly, looking between Jethro and her father: "Pops, I love you. It's so confusing and mind-bending but for us nothing has really changed. I feel a bit cross with Grandma."

Ivo's face was flushed with the love they had infused in him. He wondered with them whether carrying the family surname, Wynne, when their biological surname was different mattered to them. They were young people of their time, less binary in their views than their parents: they felt it made no difference whatsoever. Their dad was a Wynne, had always been a Wynne, had brought them up with that surname and nothing had changed.

Jethro added, "It's all thanks to you that I have the musical bug and you got that from your father, Grandpa Mark."

Ivo smiled proudly. "My father was passionate about music. I could sing very well when I was little and that's become one of my great things in life. It's very important to me . . . I realized I got that from my dad. I'm grateful for it." It was touching to witness how Ivo came alive as he remembered this, and how it lived on in Jethro.

Suky, who worked as a documentary producer, exuded balance and warmth. Ivo had not married his mother, a mistake often made. It's hard to explain that energy, but she could fully listen, with her whole being. A kind of fierce attention that was also comforting. I could see she brought Ivo a capacity for connection, with affection, that had been missing in his life.

I'd been talking about my understanding and she reflected back to me what I had said: "I think what's really interesting is what you're saying is Ivo's identity. His sense of himself and the internal structure of himself is made up of the DNA of his parents but much more than that. It's made up of the interconnected and interweaving relationships of the people and the family in his life. How we have all been to him and whether we've been loving or cruel or indifferent or forgotten him or been unreliable, as well as his daily experiences is what has built him." Ivo nodded. He was much happier but still nervously moving around in his chair.

I asked them all if there was anything further to discuss. Lottie rather reluctantly said, "Dad, is there any way you can be less explosive?" Suky stroked Ivo's leg and asked Lottie to be specific. Lottie listed a number of examples, small domestic spats, when Ivo would get angry and storm around the kitchen shouting at anyone who was present.

Ivo sat rigidly in his chair. He was hurt and raw and looked angry, but he was in a therapy session. Having me there forced him to swallow the first words that came into his head. He turned to Suky. "I know I fly off the handle . . . I want to be different but I don't know if I can."

It was my turn to be useful. I wondered if they could agree a deal. Given that no one can stop what they feel, could they as a family try a new way of coping? Create a moment's space between the feeling and the words or actions that want to erupt. Use that moment to take a breath, slow down, reflect. Walk away and have a glass of water, then come back and find the words you want to say: words that acknowledge what you feel and what you need but without the missile of attack. It is a simple but effective strategy for defusing explosive situations, often used for children.

Now that Ivo's anger had had time to subside, his hurt showed. He looked past his children's faces to the wall behind them and spoke slowly, to stop his tears: "Good God, I'm like my mother.

Oh, God. I don't want to be like her . . ." He pushed his fingers into his temples. "If you're patient with me I'll work on it." Lottie jumped across the room to give her poor dad a much-needed hug.

Jethro moved on to the next thing. He wanted to be in touch with Robert's family, to find out who they were and hopefully discover lovely new cousins. Ivo, rather beaten down but as adamant as before, did not want that. Suky gently suggested that they were his children's family too: did he have territorial rights to stop them? Ivo conceded that he didn't but simply said there had been enough chaos and change and he couldn't face any more. Jethro and Lottie understood that, and they agreed they might revisit it in the future.

I summed up what I'd understood from them all. They were a strong, functioning family who loved each other and had been through a hiatus. In some ways it had brought them closer.

I learnt later that Suky had put a star chart on the wall for every member of the family who managed to control their temper. It was a source of humour but also a mild reminder to keep it in check. Coming to see me had enabled them to name their disagreements as well as their deep bonds and, hopefully, not repeat the mistakes of their forefathers.

Lottie and Jethro grinned, their optimistic energy carrying their rather exhausted father and wise mother out of the door to go for a pizza. This family correlated therapy with food as a just reward. Others might want to journal to embed what they had learnt, or perhaps to talk about it with a partner or friend. The Wynnes didn't have a script for that in their memory bank, but they did for eating together.

Ivo had come to me in crisis. Learning that his biological father was not the father he'd been brought up with was a hammer-blow. He felt that something integral to who he was had died. His distress was exacerbated by the fact that this was information he had never wanted; others had insisted on finding "the truth," ignoring his feelings or wishes. I remember he said, with such intensity, "It leaks into every corner of my being, leaving no centimetre of

space for any other feeling, particularly not love or connection."
Working through that is the pain of change. But the natural pull
and push had to run through him, which allowed him to adapt.
His new sense of identity was in the process of emerging: change
takes longer than we'd like. But it allowed his biological father a
small place beside Mark, the father he'd known and loved all his
life.

Ivo was certainly coping, functioning better at home and work.
His relationship with his mother and siblings reverted to old patterns of connection and disconnection. But, importantly, he felt
he belonged to that family, dysfunctional as it was. He didn't feel
an outsider. Ivo had told his friends: quite a few had taken his news
seriously; others had laughed; some were fascinated by the age-old
question of nature versus nurture, but none felt differently about
Ivo. That helped his confidence.

Plenty of issues resulting from Ivo's childhood had remained
untouched—he still smoked and drank too much. The theme of
numbing unbearable feelings using alcohol, work, cigarettes, food
and busyness ran throughout our work together. He had learnt it
well at his parents' knee. I think if most of us looked at our families or ourselves we would find these familiar defences. I believe
the reward of emotional richness makes it worth changing an
entrenched pattern. But Ivo told me, "Frankly, I just can't face it."

To be fair he didn't have the internal mechanism to do it, not
having learnt from his parents how to process painful emotions.
He was a product of his upbringing. Now he'd learnt many better
ways of dealing with difficulty than his parents could offer, but he
had limits. I'd recently read a theory about what conditions people
are more likely to change: Professor Richard Beckhard suggests
that resistance has to be less than the Dissatisfaction, Vision and
First Steps of change. In other words, your belief that the change
you make, your picture of it, is worth all the effort to make it happen. I think if Ivo could have found the words, he'd have said he
didn't trust that he could be any different.

Crisis had opened Ivo up. He'd shifted, but doing a whole lot more was not for him. He couldn't see the point of making the psychological effort that change demands. To feel the pain in overcoming deep-set hurts and the trail of injuries left in his psyche was beyond him. He'd done enough to see him through his crisis and that was plenty.

In their Stages of Change model, the American psychologists Dr James Prochaska and Dr Carlo DiClemente picture a wheel, which turns from pre-contemplative to preparation to action to maintenance and exit or relapse. The model highlights that behaviour change is a six-stage process. Ivo seemed to be in the "contemplative" stage where he was weighing up whether the benefits of changing outweighed the suffering that results from present behaviour. But this conflict was not resolved so he was not yet prepared to think about making further changes. Some people can be in this stage for many years—even a lifetime—on the edge between considering and not wanting to, sometimes even oscillating back to a pre-contemplative stage of denial.

The nature-versus-nurture question rages on, with most experts believing that both biology and environment influence our character and outcome. Maybe that isn't even the right question. There is no simple way to disentangle the multiplicity of forces that exist and shape us, not forgetting the randomness of life and luck. It seemed to me that the greatest life-shaping choice Ivo had made was marrying Suky. Which part of genes, luck, environment and upbringing had influenced that?

For me the question is, given where we came from, who we are, the challenges and opportunities we face, how can we best support ourselves to have optimal outcomes? The evidence is unequivocal that our relationships fundamentally influence our health, wealth and happiness. It is a responsibility of our society, our community, our family and ourselves to prioritize them.

The Singh and Kelly Family

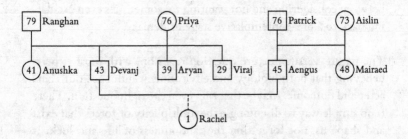

The Singh and Kelly Family

How to process big life events: becoming parents through adoption

Case conceptualization

Devanj Singh, aged forty-three, was a solicitor, who was married to Irish-man Aengus Kelly, aged forty-five, a graphic designer. They had been together for fifteen years and married as soon as it was legal to do so in 2014. They had made the decision to adopt a child and wanted support to process this big life-changing event, for themselves before the adoption took place and after the adoption of their daughter, Rachel. Although Devanj had had some difficulty in coming out to his family, they both now had good, loving relationships with their parents and siblings. There had been no significant traumatic losses or deficits in their history, which predicted good outcomes for them and their daughter.

When I started thinking about this family before I met them, I experienced a moment of self-conscious ignorance, and feared my lack of knowledge implied prejudice. I had rarely worked with a same-sex married couple before. New territory for me as a therapist holds the excitement of learning and the fear I might make a mistake. I was surprised that one of my first thoughts was what seemed a trivial question about their surname. Since their marriage had they hyphenated it? Or kept their own surnames? If they successfully adopted, whose surname would their child take? Whether or not these were the right or wrong questions to be asking myself, I decided that to meet the couple confidently I needed to be better informed. Also, I am not a specialist in adoption issues in families, and agreed with my supervisor that I needed to learn more and keep an eye open to see if I was working beyond my expertise.

I spent time immersing myself in research papers, adoption organizations, LGBTQ+ books, and memoirs like Mohsin Zaidi's *A Dutiful Boy*, his story of self-discovery and the obstacles he faced in being true to himself as a gay man in his loving, religious Muslim family. Research shows that the number of same-sex couples in North America has risen sharply. According to the 2016 Census in Canada, "From 2006 to 2016, the number of same-sex couples increased much more rapidly (+60.7%) than the number of opposite-sex couples (+9.6%)." A 2019 US survey found that 58 percent of couples in the nation's 980,000 same-sex households were married. Same-sex marriage and adoption is relatively new territory in North America. Same-sex couples have been legally able to adopt in the US since 2016 and in Canada since 2015. Year on year the number of children adopted by LGBTQ+ couples has grown, with more than 16,000 same-sex couples raising an estimated 22,000 adopted children in the US.

On seeing the dates and the data, I gave myself a sharp dig. I had been too immersed in my own heterosexual world, and although I knew these laws had been passed, I had not recognized the meaning of the huge transformation they had worked on LGBTQ+ individuals and families. I was now better informed, which gave me a stable ground from which to welcome Devanj, or Dev, and Aengus to their first session.

Dev and Aengus walked into my counselling room in a relaxed manner, discussed where to sit and dropped into their chairs as if they'd sat there many times before—unusual confidence for a first session. Dev's tall frame was immaculate in an elegant suit and crisp blue shirt, his black hair swept back. He had brown skin and a chiselled, handsome face that smiled brightly.

Aengus, dressed more casually in T-shirt, chinos and trainers, as his profession might predict, had pale skin and a freckled complexion, a well-trimmed beard and gleaming auburn hair. I noticed that now he was seated, he turned his head sharply, almost surprised to realize where he'd arrived, his striking blue eyes looking nervously at me.

He said, "So, what now?"

Perhaps we start, I said, with what they hoped to gain from coming to see me. Instinctively I warmed to them. I couldn't know how the work would progress but they transmitted an energy that gave me confidence that we were going to have an interesting time. I sensed we would build enough trust for us to go into uncharted territory. I was keen to learn what they wanted from the therapy.

Aengus spoke with a faint Irish accent, which filled me with warmth due to many happy childhood holidays spent in Ireland. I'm aware that our reactions to each other are ignited by our lived experience: our responses, good and bad, may have absolutely nothing to do with the person in front of us.

Aengus was telling me that, as a couple, they didn't do anything in a hurry. They had been together for fifteen years, married since the law changed in 2014. It was a gradual process but over time they had come to the decision that they wanted to be parents.

We agreed that this wasn't an area of my expertise, and if it became beyond my level of competence I would refer them on. It was important that I had an understanding of their decision-making process, but first I needed their back story. We carry our past in us, like a dowry of gifts and burdens that influences our present and every aspect of our lives. It is rare for people to enter therapy because of wounds of the past: they come because those wounds are hurting the present. To be able to attune to them accurately, I needed the context into which they were making this life-changing decision. They had recognized this was a major transitional event that would need processing, a predictor that they would flourish. It is often people who most need support who don't choose to access it.

Dev smiled at Aengus as he gave me a brief outline of their relationship. They'd met at a Pride dinner fifteen years previously: "When I met Aengus it clicked into place." Up to then he'd had a terrible time dating, meeting someone and thinking they were "the one" but they never messaged back. He'd been single for a long time. Aengus had been in a few committed relationships but none that felt "this right." Dev was wondering whether to text Aengus or not when he received a message from him: "Do you fancy coming to mine for food?" Simultaneously they had felt "No games," and that there should be no "Shall I wait a week to reply?"

Very quickly Aengus rented a place on the same street as Dev, and they moved in together not long afterwards. Although apparently so different, they had a lot in common: family was very important to them, their values were similar, they had a friendship of respect, mutual interests and humour, and they understood that they needed to work on staying close to each other through talking and pragmatically solving problems. Relationships don't just fix themselves.

This was particularly interesting to me since they came from two diverse cultural backgrounds: Indian and Irish heritage; Hindu and Christian faith. There was potential for clashes of beliefs, and such questions as "What are the norms for us?" "Who holds the power?" Aengus chuckled as he said, "We do sort things out." I could feel the hum of their connectedness and was reminded of the first of the psychologist Professor Anne Barlow's ten questions couples can ask each other to explore their chances of enjoying a long-lasting, happy and healthy relationship: "Are we a good fit?" Their score would have been high, which was fortunate because the journey to adoption requires a deep, supportive bond. As Dev was to say later, "It's like a mind experiment."

I asked them if they'd had therapy before. Aengus shook his head, saying lightly, "Nope."

Dev pushed his hair back as if to give himself the impetus for what he was about to recall. He told me of the crisis he had been through ten years ago: "I woke up one morning crying. The thought of going to work was too much to handle. Aengus made me call in sick and go for a swim. Looking back, it wasn't work that was so stressful but the pressure in my head to be something else. I didn't confide in or talk to anyone except Aengus for many years. It was a pretty horrible experience. You don't know how awful it is till you go through it. When I was working I was struggling to make decisions, I couldn't even reply to an email. Things piled up, I got into a pattern of working more at home, and I ended up doing long hours and thinking about work all the time." I said it sounded like he was drowning. He nodded, and I could feel his sadness at remembering how troubled he'd been. "Increasingly I realized it's hard to make a decision when you don't know who you are. I didn't know what I felt. I'd lost sight of me."

Dev had experienced an internal schism between who he was and who he thought he should be. It wasn't played out in his relationship with Aengus, only during those times that asked him to show himself to the world.

I asked him what the origins were. Dev described his upbringing. For a number of generations his family had built a successful business trading in silks in India. In the 1960s his father, Ranghan, a teenager at the time, had come from Mumbai to the UK with his parents. His grandfather and then his father had expanded the business into Europe. Being financially secure was a significant protection in their acculturation process. As I understood it, Ranghan had had to negotiate his Indian heritage and Western lifestyle through battles with his parents. It meant that although Dev still had challenges, cultural assimilation was not as complex for him. He held his Hindu faith, an important aspect of his identity, from a non-dogmatic perspective. Ranghan was extremely hard-working, travelled a great deal and engaged with many global issues and ideas. He was a committed, dutiful father, wanting the best for his four children, three boys and a girl, of whom Dev was the eldest boy. But his father was quiet. He didn't say very much in the home. As Dev described it, "He had 'All I want is a quiet life' tattooed on his forehead."

His mother, Priya, who also worked in the family business, was in charge of everything at home. Dev's crisis was more associated with his mother than his father and had led him into therapy to work out what was going on.

Dev said, "We all grew up in a way where our task was given to us by our mother. 'You do this exam. You will get an A if you work hard.' It was the same with university and our jobs. It was like 'You follow life's steps on this path.' Joining the family business was my designated career, and I had to fight to become a lawyer. But although I was able to hold on to being a solicitor, most of my decisions were made because I was trying to please someone else. They were not based on what I wanted. I operated on a system of shoulds, always aiming for perfection, which, of course, I could never reach.

"If a big life stressor happened at work I would freak out inside and couldn't make any decisions. My automatic response was to get advice from my mum. Of course, her advice didn't help me because she didn't live in my shoes. She wasn't me. I realized through therapy that I self-censored . . ." he took a breath, pain in his eyes ". . . all the time." He explained how conflicted his internal world felt, with what was asked of him externally, as he grew up and developed into adulthood.

He told me that although he had come out after university, there remained inside him a huge amount of unexpressed emotion from hiding his sexual identity throughout his childhood. Dev described the shame he felt: "I'd lived in an entirely heterosexual world where homosexuality did not feature. All that performance as a teenager, having to impress people because what you are is *not normal*. Even hiding it from myself for such a long time."

I couldn't fully imagine what it would be like to have to hide an essential part of your identity. The word that came to mind was "poison." I said, "It sounds like it poisoned you. That performance you put on, the mask of shame of being different for fear of being judged, it's very moving and painful to hear." I could feel the intensity of it sitting in my chest.

When Dev spoke he had been looking out of the window or at the carpet, accessing the rawness of his memories, and in hearing me acknowledge how tough it was, he looked at me, then turned to Aengus, as if to his sanctuary of stability.

Aengus gave him a warm nod, imparting the message, "Yes, that is how it was and you're all right now." This was momentary. A few seconds, but powerful in the transmission of security: we can't risk going to painful places in ourselves unless we feel safe.

It gave Dev the confidence to describe his mother's adjustment to him being gay. It had taken a long time. He told me, "When I was born Mum thought, My son is going to be a successful CEO, go to Oxford, live at this ridiculous pace, and I ended up not knowing who I was. Initially, Mum was not supportive of me being gay. She was not harsh, but we lived in this kind of Limbo Land of her not accepting it. I'd say something, we'd fight. Then nothing was said. She hoped I'd grow out of it—'It's a phase you're going through.' I remember saying once that I'd get a Saturday job working in a hairdresser. She said vehemently, 'No, I don't think that's a good idea.'

"All our conversations were about what is suitable and unsuitable for her boy. I know part of that is being of Indian descent, wanting to fit in, not to be judged. We are already different, and being more different frightened her. She wouldn't budge. For instance, when we were on holiday and I told her I wanted to tell my youngest brother, she said, 'You can't, not yet, he's too young.' But I did tell him. I was sick of it. He was old enough. It stemmed from her version of who I should be, what she could tell family and friends, what she felt would make her proud, but it did not include who I actually was."

We discussed the importance of his Hindu faith and the tension he was aware of. For some Hindus homosexuality is unacceptable: it goes against the teachings of it being "natural" for men and women to marry and have children. Others believe it has a place in the community, stating that ancient carvings in temples show men and women having homosexual sex. As in all religions, some are opposed to it, others actively for it, and many simply neutral or, as in Dev's father's case, silently for it. Dev knew he couldn't control other people's judgements, and for him it was important to turn to himself without judgement, to hold his faith and beliefs with compassion.

Dev was in the flow of his memories. "Of course, my dad never

ever talked about it. That was difficult in itself, but despite being traditional by nature, on this, surprisingly, I knew he had my back and didn't really care. If it bothered him he would have said something. We never ever had a conversation, that father–son chat . . . It might have been horribly awkward . . ."

Dev turned his attention to his mum. How much she did for him, her loving affection, but he always had a queasy sense of failure—"Almost nothing I did was good enough"—which arose from having to conceal a key component of his identity. A fundamental aspect of our identity is that we feel we are loved and we belong. Dev felt the opposite. "My being gay did not fit in with her plans for me, and her resistance really wounded me." It meant he didn't take boyfriends home and it blocked his ability to have a relationship: "I never really liked anyone enough."

Meeting Aengus changed everything. It gave him the confidence to challenge his mother. He gave her the choice: either she had to meet Aengus or Dev would not come home for Diwali or at any other time. That was too much for her to bear. Priya loved her son deeply. One winter's day she met Aengus and "She was blown away by how amazing he was. We never had this issue ever again. She loved him and wanted to spend all her time with him."

As I listened to Dev I imagined there were thousands of versions of that response of parents to their children being gay, not because they didn't love them but because they did. It was a fierce protectiveness to shield them from the prejudice they imagined they might face. It would, of course, perpetuate the stigma of being gay and same-sex relationships.

As importantly, a principal tenet of developing confident children and young people is knowing your own child, discovering and supporting who you find them to be, not who you expect them to be. Dr Michele Borba's *Thrivers: the surprising reason some kids struggle while others shine* details the research and expert opinion that underpin this point.

Dev's history shaped who he was now, which meant he was vulnerable to criticism and being an outsider. It was not all of him.

Now he was older, he felt proud of being gay, and stronger because he'd come through it. He'd also cultivated ways to deal with stress, to exercise regularly, take time to relax, and express openly what he felt. He had come to know himself better through being in therapy and his self-esteem had grown. He demonstrated that it isn't what happens to you that matters but how you respond to it.

Aengus had been listening closely, giving Dev encouraging signals. I shifted my attention to him and asked where he was with the LGBTQ+ community and discrimination. I was surprised to hear that Ireland had been the ninth country in the world to support gay marriage.

His parents were of the generation who had transformed attitudes to LGBTQ+ issues from overwhelmingly conservative to some of the most liberal in the world. They had not struggled with his sexuality, and had expressed their opinion by voting to change the law on gay marriage. Aengus was proud of their openness and courage in helping change the world for him and the gay community. He was impressed that Dev's mother had dared to shift her view. By the time he was married, he said, he and Dev were really close to each other's families. "I remember saying in my wedding speech, I could never relate to mother-in-law jokes. We slotted into each other's life and each other's family so contentedly."

This led us to their presenting issue: adoption. Unlike some couples they had not automatically assumed they would have children. Aengus told me, "As a gay person, having children wasn't an option . . . Although the polls suggest acceptance of homosexuality in general, my personal experience was that it used to jar people when you said you were married. Gay was bad and embarrassing when it involved being a parent." Ouch. I was taking on board that although they lived happy, openly gay lives, with close family and plenty of friends, there is still an innate barrier and judgement against being gay, and a greater one against being a gay parent. It shows how slowly cultural attitudes change, how entrenched our view of "normal" can be. Those of us outside the LGBTQ+ community need to recognize that they suffer from our prejudice.

Dev looked me in the eye, as he described the discussions they'd had over a number of years. Their earliest conversations began, "Do you see yourself as a parent?" When they agreed they wanted children, they asked, "How would you do that?" They had looked at all the different options and, without judgement, knew that surrogacy or co-parenting (when a woman has their child and they share the parenting) was not for them.

Their views were very much in sync. Neither partner had a particular urge to pass on their genes to their child, probably because it hadn't been thought of as a possibility when they were young. They did a great deal of research, went on many courses and seminars, and their thinking evolved until they knew they wanted to adopt through the local authority. They discovered they had to have a suitable house for a child, to show the stability and strength of their relationship, prove financial security through their jobs, and their availability to parent. All those boxes had been ticked.

Despite some fears and a little procrastination, they had recently contacted the local authority and had been given a social worker, Candice.

Their families were delighted. "Both sets of parents were ecstatic we'd pressed the button," Aengus said. Their parents had to be told that it would by no means be plain sailing, that there would be bumps in the road, and they had no idea if they'd be approved. If they were, they couldn't predict who they would adopt: they might have siblings or a child with disabilities. The chance of adopting a baby was small, and if they held out for that it could mean they'd have to wait up to five years, which they didn't want. They knew they couldn't adopt a child with pre-existing anger issues, and had sorted out their capacities and limits, an important step in adoption.

We acknowledged that their relationship with me was more a reflective space than intense therapy, and we agreed to meet monthly, always with the possibility of increasing our sessions should there be a crisis.

In the past four decades adoption numbers in the US have dropped from approximately 175,000 in 1970 to around 125,000 children annually in recent years, despite the growing number of children in care: more than 400,000 in 2020. The reasons are varied, one being the increased success rate of IVF from 7 percent to 30 percent. Figures on the success and failure of adoption are hard to measure, so any statistics are an approximation. Only 1–3 percent of infant adoptions fail, but for older children failures are much higher: up to 30 percent of teenage adoptees go back into care. The abuse and neglect these children have often suffered can result in their difficulty to trust their adoptive parents, and their consequent behaviour can be unmanageable.

As Dev and Aengus were talking to me I realized they were actively positive about adopting as their first choice to make a family. It was a gift for them. They had negotiated their own losses around identity and sexuality when they had come out. At that point they had believed they had no chance of becoming a parent so had no expectations.

Meeting our expectations is a predictor of well-being, and unmet expectations are a source of pain. To many couples and individuals adoption is the Plan B after having failed to have a child biologically. They have had to face multiple griefs in not getting pregnant, having miscarriages or stillbirths. Men and women have had to come to terms with the reality of not giving birth to a healthy child, which they had initially expected was their right or the norm. It is a tough journey. Specific aspects of self-esteem and identity can be severely wounded, bringing a raft of emotions, like fury, failure and envy.

I remembered a visit I'd made to Adoption UK a few years ago to discuss the emotional availability of bereaved parents to adopt. We explored the merits and impact of a prescribed time-lag between a child's death and the parents' suitability to adopt. This was by no means a judgement on their ability to make loving, happy homes through adoption, simply that grieving for their initial dream of a family requires time.

Through that first year I was impressed and a little intimidated by the thoroughness of the vetting Dev and Aengus had to undergo. I couldn't help thinking that perhaps all parents should go through a version of that experience to reflect on their ability to parent, their capacity to create a loving home, their access to robust support from others and their reasons for wanting a child. The process of reflection, where they looked back at their childhood, took from it what was positive and left behind aspects they felt had been less so, seemed a simple but revealing exercise for any future parent.

Each month I learnt of a new hurdle Dev and Aengus had had to overcome. Dev, with echoes of his childhood need for perfection, found it anxiety-provoking, constantly weighing up their need to be honest against sabotaging their chances if they were too honest.

Both men developed a good relationship with Candice. Over that year, she became the most significant person in their lives. In every meeting, as Aengus said, "I felt I had to be on my toes. I didn't know exactly what criteria they were looking for, what their thought processes are and how they compare adopters. Every meeting is like an exam."

Some months when they came in I could feel the intensity of their not-knowing butting up against their longing. In one session Aengus thought he'd blown it because he'd been asked to give an example of his parents' stress response: "When my sister and I had been really annoying, my exasperated mother drove us to a children's home and said, 'You are going in there if you don't behave.' We sobbed all week and were as good as gold."

Dev looked at him, twisting his hands: "OMG! A children's home! I'm dreading the next meeting. Have we f***** up?" Every month there was another landmine when they feared they'd blown it, sometimes when they were submitting completed in-depth questionnaires, others when they were unable to access proof of their work abroad to show that they didn't have a criminal record. All was eventually resolved.

In one session they described the surreal day on which Candice came into their kitchen and spent hours going through all their bank statements, asking in detail what each item meant.

Aengus kept rubbing the back of his head as he spoke, sparks of his tension visible. During each session I acknowledged the weight of what they were going through, suggested behaviours that could hold them steady. At times, in parallel, I felt powerless. I didn't want to transmit that back to them.

I recognized I was hugely invested in their success, as I often am with my clients. I am never an unbiased screen reflecting back an interpretation of their experience. I aim to have one foot firmly planted on their side, the other on mine. I wanted to let them know how much I believed in them while remaining separate enough to be able to support them effectively. I had to check that I hadn't lost sight of the balance and recalibrate myself through supervision and my usual medicine of exercise and meditation.

Within eleven months of their application Dev and Aengus skipped into my room. Grinning from ear to ear, they hopped into their respective chairs—always on the same side: we pick our spot and stick to it for a sense of security. They outlined the terror of the fifteen-strong panel they had sat in front of: the chair, former adopters, observers and Candice. Dev recounted his elation: "It could have been the most hellish day of our lives when someone behind a desk was saying, 'We aren't approving you for this and this reason'—it could have meant we wouldn't have a child."

Aengus was too excited to let him focus on the negative. "We were approved! I feel this sense of elation—I'm utterly delighted. We can't tell anyone because we have to work out how we're going to be actually placed with a child."

I could feel my joy too. It had been a long, emotional and

difficult journey and our collective relief was almost palpable. I wondered if approval for adoption was similar to being told you're pregnant in a wanted pregnancy: you have reached the point at which becoming a parent with a living child is a real possibility, but it still isn't certain. There is another raft of not-knowing, lurches of fear and time to endure.

In searching for a child to adopt, Aengus and Dev described how they had the surreal experience of signing up to what looked like a Facebook page with hundreds of children on it, sifting through the profiles. They had already put their names forward for several children but heard nothing back from the local authority.

Six weeks later, they told me they had expressed interest in a three-month-old baby, R. It is rare for such a young child to come up for adoption. She was a relinquished child—her mother had given her up for adoption. They knew many other families had applied for her but Dev and Aengus had been chosen as her adopters. I expected to see their joy, but the stress from their meeting the day before was in their bodies. It had been ninety minutes long, and they were gritting their teeth. Aengus's voice was tremulous: "We've seen three photographs of this little person. She's gorgeous . . . It's miraculous . . ." Tears stood in his blue eyes. He was overwhelmed by the enormity of the event. Dev's and his future was changing for ever. It was by no means easy for them to assimilate all that was happening.

Dev and Aengus had been told that, at first, they would foster little R. Ten weeks later they would apply to adopt her. Candice told them they needed to have everything ready in two weeks.

I was relieved that they had learnt and integrated good coping mechanisms to keep themselves emotionally resilient. Dev had his regular yoga, swimming and meditation sessions, Aengus his journalling, running and visits to the gym. Those mechanisms would be tested in the weeks and months ahead.

As a couple new to parenting they noticed that many friends and colleagues offered authoritative advice, certain of their views. But they were both comfortable in not knowing: their flexibility would allow them to be sensitive to baby R's needs. Crucially, they had a fantastic network of family and friends they could call on for support. In addition they had asked eight family and friends to be their team of advisers as new parents, each person having particular skills or knowledge. They felt confident to ask them for help or advice: it was a reflective, informative team. Perhaps all of us should have our support team. As the proverb states, "It takes a village to raise a child." It really does.

Since I'd been working with Dev and Aengus I'd noticed that my attitude and openness to same-sex parenting was going through a transition. I had thought I was unbiased, but I can't have been because I was now drawn to reading articles I hadn't "noticed" before. I was particularly interested that my emotional response was heightened. I was no longer vaguely interested: now I was hungry for more stories to read and programmes to watch. I was open to a whole vista of learning that was new to me.

It led me to mull on difference, why it causes such a barrier to connection. Our first response to difference is often fear, and the antidote is exposure. When we look at a person from a distance and label them, we may judge them negatively. As we step towards them, though, see what is actually going on, the threat is diminished. Our psychological make-up, for evolutionary purposes, sees difference as a potential hazard—"stranger danger": to our ancestors, being outside the tribe was a threat to life. In the last century there has been high-speed change in society: we live in a world that is exceptionally connected through globalization, technology and travel. We are confronted with a quantum of diversity and difference that was unimaginable even seventy years ago. Our internal systems have not adapted as fast as these changes. We can still be triggered by difference. We often choose to stay in our comfort zone, behind the walls of our own "normal," which is diminishing and creates judgement through ignorance. I know it is vital for me, perhaps all of us, to remain curious, to explore and learn the myriad different ways of living and being: bearing the discomfort brings growth. I was certainly grateful for the expansion and energetic reboot this couple gave me.

Dev and Aengus cancelled the next few sessions because they were focused on adopting their child. I missed them. They had texted me brief updates, which kept fear at bay, but it wasn't until I saw them via Zoom, due to the pandemic, sitting side by side on their sofa, baby paraphernalia in the background, that I learnt of the drama they had been through. We smiled broadly at each other, and I kept looking at the playmat behind them. I wanted to hear their story, and I was thrilled to know that a baby girl was sleeping in the next room. Their baby girl, Rachel.

On the day they were due to meet baby Rachel, Candice had rung: the foster carer wasn't well and had cancelled. It was a massive let-down for them. They had been on tenterhooks, barely sleeping, but had managed to buy the crib and the rest of the kit. They were also worried. Immediately they thought something was wrong. As with all of us, they took out their distress on each other, having fights about small domestic irritations, walking off in huffs as they endured the terrible wait for news. The anticipation of giving birth is stressful, but there is no doubt that the baby will be born. As Aengus pressed his finger to his chin he told me, "The local authority takes the baby's needs first and foremost, then the birth-mum's, and we are some way down the list. If the birth-mother had had second thoughts, it would be over for us." It was this that had fomented their deep fear over the next week.

Dev joined in: "We were utterly powerless. We had to make sure we remained completely rational with Candice, not lose it on anyone, just say thank you for the update and then wait . . ." Their hard-won coping mechanisms were well and truly pressed into service.

Finally, they were called to the office for a meeting with baby Rachel's social worker. To their surprise and joy, they met Rachel. Unlike established practice, Rachel was not with her foster carer: she was with a friend. Aengus remembered, "At that moment all the chaos disappeared. Rachel was in a stroller, and we just focused on her. It was the most amazing thirty minutes."

Dev added, "We fell in love with her at that moment. She smiled at us. She gripped my finger." Now we were in tears at how fast and deeply she had travelled into their waiting open hearts.

Aengus spoke for them both: "Holding her and playing with her was wonderful, and we genuinely felt there was a connection between her and us. It was love, although that love has grown—and continues to grow—deeper and stronger, unlike anything either of us has felt before." That was real parental love, the heart-bursting love of a parent for a child. I'd felt it personally, heard and read about it for birth-parents, and was immensely moved to hear it was just as huge for adopting parents.

The next day they met Rachel again and were a little disturbed by her wet nappy and sickly-sweet smell but overjoyed to be with her for another fifty minutes. Aengus said, "I felt I was a parent," and longed to take her home. A senior social worker took them aside to tell them that the usual transition period had been cut: they could take Rachel home the next day, but they weren't to tell the person who had come with her. They thought that was strange but were buoyed up by the news.

Dev and Aengus arrived at the contact centre ridiculously early with the new car seat, stroller in the trunk. "It was the biggest day of our lives, as important as our wedding." But it turned out to be traumatic. The foster carer did not arrive and could not be contacted. They waited with increasing anxiety at the office, only going home at nine o'clock that night when they had been told that her case had been escalated to "missing child" and the police were looking for her. In effect she had been kidnapped. Dev and Aengus were distraught, their worst fear voiced by Dev, that "The foster carer might jump off a cliff with her. I felt utterly hollow. This child was not legally ours, we hardly knew her, but she felt like ours." We all shivered at the thought of what might have happened. I could see the shock in their bodies. I looked at the mat to remind me she was alive and well.

At midnight two policemen arrived at their door. They were kind and realized the meaning of their presence. Smiling, one handed Rachel to them, saying, "Come and get your baby."

Over the next weeks two scenarios played out at the same time: parenting Rachel and legally becoming her parents. She was a happy, smiley baby, who responded to them. They believed she made it easy for them. I was chuckling. When they aren't driving us mad, we all believe our children are spectacularly special! They learnt over time her signals for hunger, tiredness, and how to manage the juggle of sleepless nights and bottle-feeding. Parenting her contained a layer of complexity: she felt like their child but legally she was not. They were in a liminal space where they couldn't have loved her more yet feared she could be taken away from them if the birth-mother changed her mind.

As Aengus said very solemnly, "We are parents but not parents." They tried to protect themselves from the potential hurt "by reserving our love," but none of us can measure out our love to match possible injury. Loving is a risky business. They had to show their social worker everything they did: noting every feed, length of sleep and nappy-change. New parents usually feel inadequate. They are learning a new language and set of skills, but as new adopting parents, who are being observed and assessed, that process is heightened, and as I was to understand, Dev and Aengus longed to prove their legitimacy to be parents. As Aengus said so eloquently, "Being evaluated makes you feel other. You get a prod—you aren't a real family . . . It's exhausting."

Adopting is a profoundly challenging enterprise. In its unique way it required of them huge reserves to remain robust, sensitive and loving. Alongside their parenting was a court case from the foster carer, who had gone against all the rules and applied to adopt Rachel. Fortunately, Dev and Aengus succeeded in their claim. Later Aengus went to court, successfully winning their application for Rachel's full adoption: "I stood on the viaduct and cried a dam's worth of tension, all the worry, the sleeplessness."

They grinned at me across the screen. She was now legally their baby, "But it took a long time."

As someone who had navigated early parenthood within the traditional framework, in which no one asked intrusive questions, I was perturbed by the level of insensitivity that Dev and Aengus were subjected to when they went out with Rachel. Dev told me, as he twisted his finger, "We noticed it more and more, two men with a baby. People would stare at us, and we live in a diverse area . . . An old man's jaw literally dropped when he saw us. He just kept watching us. It felt uncomfortable. It could have been positive but it's not where my brain goes . . . The odd millennial smiles at you. It's all slightly strange."

Other incidents were equally troubling. A leader of a playgroup asked Rachel, "Where's Mummy?" without looking at Dev, as if he didn't exist. A pharmacist enquired where her mother was and, when they'd explained she was adopted, said, "What a shame." Referring to her brown skin asked, "Is she English?" It was bizarre. As they recalled their sense of alienation, I could feel the tension in their bodies even through the screen: Aengus, jaw clenched, looked at the floor while Dev pressed his hand to his chin as he gazed out of the window, each occasionally glancing at the other.

I felt they had to distance themselves from the memory. Their experience of being stared at for being different was particularly disturbing for them because they were "straight passing." Aengus explained, "The way I was brought up was never to express public displays of affection, so we weren't obviously a gay couple. We don't hold hands in public. With Rachel it's like coming out again. I feel visible in all sorts of different ways." I was taking in the meaning of their words, and for the first time had a clear picture of what it meant to be a gay father in today's world. How, as a society, we stare and sometimes judge what we categorize as abnormal. I could see it had hit an exposed nerve in Dev and Aengus, and it would take time for them to come to terms with the sting.

Being gay fathers in a world that has worshipped at the altar of mother and child, from the Virgin Mary on, is an expansion of our perspective on parenthood. Our behaviours have not caught up with the changes in many aspects of life. Even though about half of the workforce is composed of women, mothers are still doing most of the parenting. Dev and Aengus's professionally successful friend said, "My husband does a job share and we agreed to be equal parents, but the stuff he doesn't see, what he doesn't do to keep it all going, is unbelievable. I did not sign up for this."

Aengus noted, "There's no one I can see who's like me for miles at work. It's quite alienating." When Aengus said to his colleagues that he didn't want to have meetings on Fridays so that he could be more available to Rachel, it was forgotten. He wasn't assigned the role "parent." His female colleagues were annoyed when it was assumed they couldn't make five o'clock meetings because they needed to be home for their children.

Finding a balance between parenting and working is the Holy Grail that remains elusive. And it is still gender-based. Working mothers are less likely to be promoted as they are seen to have responsibility for their children—which may partly account for why the percentage of women in senior leadership roles has remained low. Men with children are seen as competent in handling work and family life, often because they aren't doing the juggle, except, of course, parents like Dev and Aengus, when they are not seen as the parent who parents. There is still a lot of work to be done by employers and government to enable both parents to work and parent. Dev nailed it when he said, "I don't think people understand the issues we're going through. I understand what regular families are going through, but people don't understand what gay adopters are going through."

There were two aspects of becoming Rachel's parents that they had to come to terms with, their internal acceptance of themselves as rightful parents being the most important. We had all enjoyed a moment of illumination when we watched a documentary that showed a gay father's brain develops like a mother's when they had a new baby, producing more oxytocin, the bonding hormone. Dev and Aengus excitedly described their experience, which matched the research: their hearing had heightened to alert them to Rachel's cries. I wondered if knowing this gave them confidence or legitimacy—and "legitimacy" became the word they grappled with for the rest of our time together.

The second aspect was what kind of parents they were going to be. Dev described their position: "We have the benefit of not having that role model of how it's done, no formula. There is a formula for straight marriage and parenting—so for us it's fantastically liberating but scary. If we need to break it down I'm more boisterous, and Aengus is very gentle, but the differences are marginal. A neighbour asked me who Rachel goes to when she's ill, and I said both of us. He said his child always goes to her mum. That 'norm' doesn't exist in our household."

They were also shifting their perspective about control. To adopt Rachel, as Dev clarified, "We controlled it to a T. There is a legacy of that control, which is highlighted by our inability to meet our need of perfection in reality." Now she was their child, they had to find a new balance. As Aengus said, "I'm not going to micro-manage. I want to protect her, but I can't always do that. It's the normal parenting worries, and that's quite a nice realization." He sighed, with a smile.

They were right. These were the transitions of parenting, the holding on and letting go, the wanting of control for protection and recognizing their limits, the lifelong dance of holding close and allowing space.

Reflecting on all our work together led me to wonder about "normal" and "abnormal," and if there is a line between the two. I felt a spurt of anger at people's ignorant insensitivity, then realized that had been me before I met Dev and Aengus. I also thought about the right many people believe they have to ask intrusive questions about others' children. Dev and Aengus's experience showed an additional layer of intrusion with adopted children:

people felt they could say things about Rachel that they wouldn't about a biological child. The couple had people say to them, "I'm going to take her off you," or "Can I share her?" as if Rachel was a commodity that was up for grabs. It was difficult to explain, and Dev said, "It's micro-aggression, which is always hard to nail down. If you challenge it people say you're being difficult, that they were only joking." Aengus described it as "a strange sense of assumed community or ownership." They'd discussed it with other adoptive parents, who all recognized it in their own experience. It sounded tough—and very annoying.

Through our discussions, over a number of sessions, Dev and Aengus were able to reflect and set a clearer boundary in responding to people that was polite but protective. Aengus told me, "At one point I was about to over-share and I caught myself. I thought, No, we're just standing by the slide. I'll never see them again. It's a small thing but it feels like something is shifting and changing in a really good way." It was a signal of their growing confidence as Rachel's parents: they did not have to justify themselves or answer to anyone. Rachel was *their* child.

What of their future with Rachel? The biggest issue for Dev and Aengus was to support her in flourishing. They wanted to set her up for success. Aengus voiced their concern: "How can we make sure we do everything possible now for her future self? What are the issues she might have to deal with that we can take steps to support her in now?"

They understood that adopted children may live in two families throughout their lives. The first is the reality of their present life and the second a fantasy life, with their "real" daddy and mummy, who are idealized. For adopted children there can be an ongoing negotiation between being abandoned or relinquished by their biological parents and belonging with their adopted parents. It takes high-quality thinking and psychological intelligence for the adopted parents to participate in and support their child throughout this turbulent process.

I have heard many a tale of adopting parents' hopes that love-bombing their child, immersing them in love, will push away the pain of adoption. They are shattered when it isn't enough. Love cannot fill the space of loss. We need love to support us as we feel and express our pain. Paradoxically, that can free us to dare to love again.

This was by no means the case for Dev and Aengus. They had made a big canvas bag, with a photograph of Rachel on her mother's knee. She carried it around, saying, "Tummy Mummy," so she would have a muscle memory of this as her birth-mother. They wanted to be able to show they had done everything they could to stay connected to her biological mother. They kept asking the social worker to contact her and were continually told that she did not reply. It bothered them that they had no information about Rachel's father. They wanted to be able to respond truthfully to her questions when she was older. But they did not have answers.

We were going round in circles: they would imagine possible scenarios of Rachel being "triggered in her future," then hit the brick wall of what they didn't know, which served only to ramp up their worries for her. I asked them to name what they did know. Her birth-mother had written a third of Rachel's life-story book, with photographs of her and her own parents: they looked like "a regular family."

Dev and Aengus hadn't been able to continue with the book themselves because, as Dev said somewhat anxiously, "Rachel's birth-mother had written, 'Your dads can explain more about this,'" and they knew they couldn't. However, they had written Rachel a letter on her placement day and another on the day her adoption was legalized. I told them firmly that they could drive themselves mad with imagined storylines, that they had to find a way of being at peace with what they did and didn't know about Rachel's background. Immediately they looked revitalized.

I was impressed by how open they were to new ideas—often, as parents, we resist other people's thinking, believing it belittles our own. They were different. They had done so much work on themselves through the decades of coming out that they were confident and not defensive. I suggested they create a ritual that represented Rachel's story of adoption and marked the moment their relationship with her began, just as we observe rituals for all of life's other transitions—blessing a new-born baby, a marriage ceremony, an eighteenth or twenty-first birthday party. I saw their energy shift. Aengus said, "We could show Rachel our ritual when she's older, and perhaps she could do her own . . . If her mother is off the grid all we can do is hold our heads high that we did everything we could. We are also powerless. We can't predict how Rachel's going to feel." That was a big relief. We agreed they could support her in her grief for her birth-mother: she wouldn't have to hide it from them.

The following session was one of liberation. It was as if the week before I had planted seeds in fertile ground. Their smiling faces looked at me from the screen and they made a few jokes before we started. Dev began, practically bouncing on his chair: "Something happened last session, about answering questions on her past, and realizing we had to let her go through the bereavement process. We can't give her solutions. We've been thinking about her a lot. We even have a ritual—something to symbolize that and bring into the house."

I was excited to hear what it might be. Dev continued, looking straight at me, as he always did when he wanted my full attention: "It goes beyond just giving her answers. It's somehow letting go of her past story to move forward, and not protect her to the hilt, doing things our way. Yes, we've come out again. We *are* looked upon as different. But instead of spending so much time thinking about that, or bowing down to those things, we need to park them. We need to create, shape and own our story."

I was smiling in agreement. Perhaps all of us could do a version of this, shape our own story rather than believing there is some perfect narrative we have to fit. We could trust in our own beliefs and values as parents, not compare ourselves to others, which is the route to misery. We could give ourselves permission to be "good enough," create our own family rituals to signify our bond and special times.

They spoke excitedly together, taking turns to express how the scales had been unbalanced. Rachel's past had weighed heavily on them, and they thought continually of ways to promote it. They didn't want to pretend the past hadn't existed: they were living with it, but they didn't want to live looking backwards. Aengus said, "We thought a crystal because it's—"

Dev jumped in boisterously: "It's a marker: light, magical, spiritual."

Aengus continued, "Being spiritual has significant connotations. This object [the crystal] is special. It brings something into the house and we are living with it, so we will have a ritual around it. We will verbalize it." Dev continued his thought—they were truly aligned: "We will finish with a poem at the end of the ceremony. It is a full stop. We are parking something, marking the end of it. Placing a boundary. An impermeable one and an important one."

A further small mark of Dev's shift of perspective was that he posted on his private social-media account a lovely picture of him and Rachel singing together. He had been wary of doing so and this small act demonstrated his recognition of his position as her father. Now that he had internally integrated her birth and adoption he could bridge it and mark that he and Aengus were her legitimate parents who would shape her future.

The experience of witnessing their development as parents was for me the most touching and illuminating aspect of our work together. My perspective was that for them, as it is for everyone, becoming a parent is one of the most challenging elements of life: longed for, meaningful, important, full of joy and love, and incredibly hard—all the worry, exhaustion, not knowing, missteps, fears and frustrations. And there was the dance they had to do as a couple to work out what kind of parents they were together, what kind of family they wanted to be, influenced by their upbringing, personality and environment.

For Aengus and Dev there were layers of complexity for them to integrate. Rachel was adopted, which had meant they were continually assessed and had to edit their behaviour as her parents when being observed. But once that hurdle had been overcome, there was another process, as Dev said, "to liberate ourselves to parent her," of recognizing that they loved her and they were her *legitimate* parents. They were enough.

When I thought about it afterwards, I wondered if a version of this progression exists for all parents. One of the greatest gifts parents can offer a child is confidence, and surely that confidence has to be transmitted from the parents in words but also in what they model in the unvoiced messages they transmit. Most parents are likely to be their best selves when they know and trust themselves with all their strengths and vulnerabilities.

I checked with Dev whether he felt his distress was still in his body, and he shook his head happily, saying their experience had been enough. He hadn't realized how much he had held tightly inside him, but telling their story, connecting with their emotions, he felt lighter. That is satisfying for a therapist to hear: it shows that the therapy is working.

Dev and Aengus reflected on our time together. Being supported to hold steady during the first part of our work had been important, and the second had given them the opportunity to reflect on themselves as parents. It had allowed them to find themselves as a team. They wondered about what it meant to be family, that it was much more than blood: when Rachel was with her cousins, they believed she felt a deeper connection with them than she did with friends. They felt increasingly liberated to be themselves. Smiling broadly, Aengus said, "My mum's looking at me, so proud of me, seeing Rachel love me. She gets such pleasure in seeing that. It's so lovely . . . one of those moments, almost out-of-body, when you see yourself through someone else's eyes." She believed in him as a parent.

Belief in another person is a powerful magic. It is a propagator of confidence and aids the growth of strong roots in the person on the receiving end.

Dev smiled into my eyes, brimming with confidence. "It's a good feeling, our own growth and how we're changing, and at the same time to see her changing. She's full of energy. She's totally our daughter. She's adopted our mannerisms. She walks with her arms behind her back like I do, and my dad does. That's beautiful."

My last words to them were that Rachel was lucky to have them as parents. The future would not be simple, but it would be joyful and loving. I had confidence they would all thrive.

The Thompson Family

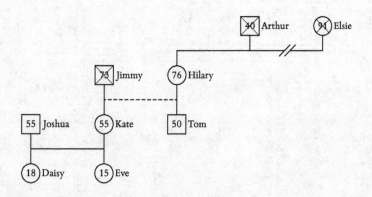

The Thompson Family

How to hold on to our children while letting them go

Case conceptualization

The maternal line of the Thompson family comprises Hilary, seventy-six, Kate, fifty-five, and her daughters Daisy, eighteen, and Eve, fifteen. Hilary had been married for thirty years when her husband, Jimmy, came out as gay, and they separated. He died five years ago. Hilary has retired from her work as a continuity director. Kate was a successful journalist, but stopped work when she had children. She is married to Joshua, fifty-five, a successful barrister who travels a great deal. Our work focused on the relationship between Hilary, Kate and Daisy, in their adjustment to Daisy leaving home to go to university.

I think of a child leaving home as a living loss: it has the qualities of grief, but its complexity is often unrecognized. I have a personal aversion to the term "empty-nest syndrome" for its blunt insensitivity. The development of a child into an adult impacts everyone on a spectrum from mild to intensely difficult. Problems surface when the trickier aspects of separation in families are left to fester underground, unvoiced and unacknowledged.

Parents are often assailed by anxiety, sadness, loneliness and anger in missing their child, while feeling a sense of relief for the reduced daily tasks and care. There can also be an underlying worry for the child's safety and happiness. Close, meaningful relationships, particularly with a partner, finding other sources of self-esteem, financial security and good health protect parents from falling apart during this transition. Their relationship with their child needs to be supportive without being overbearing, assisting their development and discovery. Research shows that intervening early in critical life transitions protects against long-term risks for mental health and life outcomes.

Kate had come to me because she wanted help in understanding herself now that her daughter, Daisy, was leaving home for university, and she was interested to see if intergenerational family patterns and beliefs were playing out. Although in most cases I like to involve the whole family in the therapy, the process of change is a collective business. With the Thompsons, this was mainly an issue for the women—about mothering and letting go—so they were front and centre for our sessions.

We agreed that, if necessary, Joshua and Eve could join us. They would certainly be kept updated as to what was going on: even if they didn't participate in our conversations, they would be impacted by them. When the dynamics of a family system are reconfigured by a number of members, it affects everyone in the family. It would be counterproductive not to inform them: secrets held in therapy could create tension between them all. I met Joshua and Eve informally through the sessions, his technical skills sometimes called on, or waving as he walked past, and Eve popped in to say hello. I felt I got to know them through the others, and it seemed they benefited from the therapy without having to participate.

The three generations were striking in their likeness. Hilary's hair was thick and wavy, cut into a bob and allowed to grey; she was pale-skinned, remarkably unlined, wearing a dramatic dash of red lipstick. Kate, her blonde hair worn long with a fringe, was stylish in a crisp white shirt buttoned at the neck and long silver earrings. Daisy, sitting between her mother and grandmother, looked a little uncertain, often throwing her hair away from her piercing blue eyes. She wore no makeup, little diamond studs in her ears, and her nails were black and manicured.

Their sparkly eyes and sense of fun drew me in—I could imagine wanting to spend time with them as friends—but I needed to hold the boundary: I was their therapist, which meant that although I hoped to create a level of openness and intimacy between us, the relationship was in the service of them and their needs.

They had chosen to embark upon a short-term, focused therapy as a sort of preventive medicine. They wanted to use the sessions to ensure they understood each other and their differing ways of coping in order to guard against taking out turbulent feelings on each other.

In the theatre of life, whether a woman works or parents full-time, motherhood is never part-time. Daisy growing up and leaving home would be a major life transition for Kate, as well as for Daisy, and would affect all members of the family.

This transition tends to hit at the same time as many other changes. A mother is likely to be going through the menopause, and dealing with ageing parents, while working out a new shape for the couple relationship at the heart of the family. Full-time mothers can be stripped of their daily structure and purpose; the loss can be no less profound for working mothers. Fathers tend to express their emotions less but can feel them as much. They may later regret what they have missed.

For the young person the significance of leaving home, hoping for a new phase in life, is also two-sided: thrilling and scary. They have to learn to juggle academic and social pressures, which include dating, while finding their way to becoming an adult.

Kate Thompson had seen me when she was in crisis ten years before: her much-loved younger brother, Tom, was a cocaine addict—what she called "his terrible addiction." It had been a good piece of work, allowing her to be furious with him for the horrendous fallout from his addiction: debts, broken friendships, the powerlessness to stop him using, and the toll on her parents, who feared he might die. In the end, he'd come to live with Kate, spending much of his time sitting on the sofa watching cooking programmes and eating until he became obese.

It had been a difficult time, but Kate was proud to have come through it. Her dogged love for her brother, calling him out while loving him, combined with the innocent joy of her two daughters, had helped to heal him, and given him a picture of a future he wanted for himself. Together, she and her husband had steered Tom to Alcoholics Anonymous (AA). Ten years on, he was still clean.

I remembered from those sessions that Kate had great insight into her own process, and an ability to form trusting relationships. She often underestimated her strengths, which meant she was surprised to discover the depth of her courage, and her capacity to manage difficulty.

I started by asking Daisy how she felt about leaving home. She seemed hesitant, not about what she felt but about talking to a stranger in front of her mother and grandmother. I over-smiled, in an attempt to make her feel comfortable, but decided that if I said, "I guess it's odd talking like this with me," she'd feel even more self-conscious. On reflection, I would have done better to start by talking to Kate, thereby letting Daisy find out what I was like by observing me with her mother and grandmother.

Daisy said that, because of Covid, she'd had a crisis the week before about whether to delay going to university for a year. She spoke quietly, finding her way through her thoughts as she gathered confidence, telling us that, although she was excited, she wanted to keep her expectations low. She would be in a bubble of six people, so a lot would depend on how well they got on together. Her greatest worry was loneliness, because there wouldn't be any of the usual gatherings and frosh events, and all her lectures would be online. She'd had bouts of anxiety—once when she walked round and round Ikea. I nodded vigorously: I've always thought there should be free therapy pods at the exit to every Ikea.

Hilary, confident and energetic, stepped into the conversation, telling me that Daisy going to Oxford University was an arc of achievement her mother and grandmother would never have dreamt possible. I was fascinated to hear Hilary's story. We learn who we are from stories, and unless we take time to examine them, we may miss nuggets of wisdom. Hilary's grandmother was a cleaner from Glasgow who had died when her daughter, Elsie— Hilary's mother—was five, at which point Hilary's grandfather disappeared, leaving Elsie to be brought up by her elder sister.

Elsie fell in love with Arthur at the beginning of the war and hurriedly married a man she hardly knew. He was of "a different class, he spoke differently," and they never set up home together. Hilary was conceived when Arthur was on leave—but by the end of the war the relationship was over. Hilary said, "I knew of my dad, but I didn't know him . . . I've been affected by him, though. When he registered my birth he put the wrong date down: my actual birthday is the twelfth and he put the fourteenth." I clocked then that not knowing her father must be more significant to her than his getting her birthday wrong, and determined to dig deeper when appropriate.

Hilary continued her narrative: even after her mother's fruitless attempt in court to get a pound a week in maintenance from him, she'd never felt bitter towards her husband. Hilary told me, "She held on to her romantic illusions about him for the rest of her life. On her deathbed she was talking about that man . . ." Arthur had lived with them briefly when Hilary was ten years old. She said: "When he left my life for ever after two or three months I never felt sadness. I was relieved."

By then he was an alcoholic. As Hilary described it: "My poor dad was grasping hold of something that could never have been . . . I learnt much later from his death certificate that he'd had a job as a barman in a hotel in Portsmouth and had killed himself in a gas oven, the preferred method of suicide in the 1950s."

Kate chipped in, "His family were all drinking and killing themselves—his mother, his father, his aunt. They were posh and my grandmother took some pride in his poshness."

I pointed out that both Hilary and her mother had had absent fathers, at which she nodded. It was as if the paternal void in two generations was a space that Hilary could not name. But Kate found the words, turning first to her mother: "My grandmother was able to hold on to the romantic memory of your father while she kept you from him." She faced the screen: "Her need to love and protect my mother was stronger than her fantasy. It meant she didn't let Arthur have a relationship with my mother."

Hilary noted, rather like a full stop: "I couldn't have saved him. I was only eleven when he died."

I could see Daisy listening with interest, although it was a story she'd heard before. I was wondering where Hilary's sadness for her father had gone, when she returned to her mother's story. Elsie had remained single until Hilary married Jimmy, at which point she found herself a husband. I didn't explore why Elsie had been single all that time, but hypothesized that she did not have the emotional energy or need for someone else until she found herself alone; husbands seemed secondary to her primary purpose in life of being a mother.

Ten years later, Hilary and her family had left England for Sydney for Jimmy's work, at which point, Hilary surmised, "My mother's life was stripped away . . . a whole chunk of her had gone. She had lots of friends in her community housing complex, got on the bus to get to her job as a personal support worker, but over the next eight years she slowly dissolved . . . For those years she had kept dreadful disappointment and loss at bay, but finally she lost her marbles—she was diagnosed with paranoid schizophrenia."

Elsie's psychosis had had two characters: a wicked working-class woman who shouted at her, saying things she found shocking—for example that she was a lesbian—and a colonel who was very kind to her. Hilary and Kate described the force of those characters and Elsie had personified them, putting on their accents and, although they laughed now, it had clearly been a worrying time.

Hilary stated empathically that her mother's relationship with Kate had brought her back from the brink of madness. Kate agreed, but they disagreed about how that had come about. Kate believed that, aged eighteen, she'd been sent by her mother from

Sydney to London to look after her grandmother. This Hilary vehemently denied, maintaining it had been Kate's choice to do so. Daisy leant back in her seat to avoid the crossfire—but it passed as quickly as it had started. I noticed that the importance of telling Elsie's story overrode their conflicting viewpoints; it felt as if this was an argument they'd had many times and which they saw no benefit in prolonging. With smiles, they agreed on the outcome: once Elsie had Kate to look after, "she just got better. She made a story about her madness, put it in a box and off it went, never to be referred to again."

I pondered to myself that being needed—as a parent or grandparent—gives us purpose and meaning, a tenet of well-being. Maybe Elsie's madness had left her when she had someone for whom to be sane.

The three generations of women lit up when they remembered the woman who preceded them. Kate said, "You couldn't keep Nanny away." She had more memories of her than of her father. They all noted feeling safe in her physical presence, utterly adored by her. Kate became very energized as she conjured up a vivid image of her grandmother: she worked as a caregiver, lived in community housing, but had "huge glamour, the way she dressed. She wore red lipstick until her death at ninety-one . . . She always turned up perfectly dressed with lipstick, headscarf, beige mackintosh and beautiful little bootees. We'd watch *Coronation Street*, which was a real place to her, she loved it so much."

They both laughed. It reminded me of the saying: "Heaven is being a memory to others." Elsie's love for them was alive in them decades after her death. They agreed the message she transmitted through the generations was that, for mothers, family is a sacred institution.

Daisy's presence had been thoughtful and quiet, but she said: "I like Grandma stories. She had such a broken childhood. Nanny [Hilary] and Mum were her whole life and when they left it literally drove her mad." She paused for a long beat. "Mum, you won't do that, will you?"

Kate smiled into her daughter's eyes as she said, "I'm stubborn. I'll make sure I'm OK. You don't need to worry about me. It's taken me many years"—she gave me a nod to acknowledge our therapy—"to let myself know I'm more powerful than I think."

Hilary chipped in, "I'm not like my mother. I ruminate. I wish I could put things in a box. There's something to be said for wrapping things up and storing them away." Kate disagreed with her, telling her they both had a capacity to overcome difficulties and remain happy and optimistic. That she never became bitter. She added, "You can go awfully dark, but you come through it and reset. You don't do it through fantasy, like Nanny." Then, turning her attention to herself: "I'm a survivor without a shadow of a doubt. I am one tough cookie, I have to say . . ." The belief that she was part of the line of strong women was a very important statement for Daisy to hear.

She also needed to know that her parents were in a strong relationship. Young adults can be kept tethered to home by the fear that their parents won't manage without them. Divorce in couples over fifty has doubled in the last twenty years in the UK, often precipitated by their last child leaving home, dissolving the glue that has held the family together, the noise and busyness that can mask a moribund relationship. On this, too, Kate could reassure her.

Unsurprisingly, working therapeutically with three people is a bigger psychological juggle than one-to-one therapy. It throws up more information, while the different relationships and the additional perspectives need to be managed. That may mean I miss important points. It wasn't until the next session that I remembered to ask Hilary where she had put her grief for her father, and why Kate had more memories of her grandmother than of her father, whom she'd missed terribly since his death.

Hilary treated my question lightly, saying she didn't miss him because she hadn't known him. Kate, on the other hand, described her grieving for her father as "a terrible loneliness, a terrible bleakness."

We were without Daisy, who had left for university. I raised the question of absent fathers and how that had affected their relationship with men. Kate stated, with some force: "I come from a long line of women who have been disappointed by men. Starting with my mother's mother, they were all abandoned by men. My mother is more positive about men than me—she loved her uncle—although she was quite bitter after Dad left."

Hilary responded that she was always fascinated by men, whom she termed "the other," but that she'd felt murderous when Jimmy had come out as gay: to force the break-up of their thirty-year marriage, he'd been bitingly cruel.

For Kate and her brother, Tom, the difficulty wasn't that their father was gay, but the pain and awful fury the separation ignited in their parents and not having their familiar home to return to. Hilary nodded thoughtfully, not at all defensive, allowing the truth of it to be voiced. She pushed her hand on to her forehead as she spoke deliberately, allowing the words to land: "I had to give up all the justifications I'd given myself for years. I had asked myself, Is he queer? I'd even asked him if he wanted to live another life—and he'd said, 'No.'"

It's interesting that Hilary ended up with a husband who was as emotionally elusive as her father—albeit for different reasons. This is a paradox I often witness: as long as people are unaware of the impact of their past, they often find themselves re-enacting elements of it, rather than making conscious choices that would work better for them. Hilary continued: "So on we went for another chunk of time. He didn't leave me till I was fifty. It was hard. I didn't want to give up on being a family—I didn't want to be a single parent like my mum."

We were silent as her words sank in. That in itself helps to keep families healthy: allowing each member the truth of their own subjective experience—and having that truth acknowledged by the others.

They continued talking about Jimmy. I could hear the emotional croak in Kate's voice. The loss of her dad was especially raw in this session because she'd spent the last few days unpacking his boxes, which she hadn't been able to face for years. Our conversations about fathers had given her the strength to move towards him in memory, bringing him closer, which was heart-breaking for her. I began to get a picture of Jimmy. He'd been brought up in a brutal, poverty-stricken household, where fury and violence were everyday hazards. He had worked hard not to inflict that on his own family, but every now and again he would erupt and, as Hilary said, "We all tiptoed on eggshells not to set him off."

Kate said, "My father was self-educated and it was baked into him, and us, the desire to move forward. He was always chasing opportunity. He never stopped but I don't think he ever got the success he wanted." On top of that, they agreed it must have been hard for him to battle with his sexuality for all those years. I heard that Jimmy had got to a point where he couldn't hide being gay any more. Kate believed it had brought him a new community of people and a new way of living, but it had never filled the hole of abandonment that he'd felt since he was a child.

In those first years after Jimmy had come out, he went on a solo journey to discover his new way of being. Thankfully, once his new identity was established, he'd grown closer to them all for the few years before his death.

How did this impact their relationships with men? They giggled as Kate said: "My mother is very flirtatious, still now, and that's not something I do. I don't have very many male friends. I often don't understand Joshua. I think it might be English men, as I grew up in Australia. I am more comfortable with Aussie men, where I can be more myself because I can read the signs." She continued that Joshua was similar to her dad, in that he was a searcher, always looking for attention. He would be absent for a while, then come back needing more attention; that he was tremendous fun and a brilliant provider, would "drive to the South Pole for us, but there is a feeling in him, like my dad, that something is missing. A restlessness."

On the rare times they were alone, he lavished her with attention, which kept them bonded. Looking out of the window, Kate reflected, "There is something addictive about those personalities, but I can't quite get him."

She's right: variable reward, never quite knowing when you'll get what you long for, keeps us hooked—looking, wanting, wondering. And those moments of satisfaction set the cycle off again. There is also an interesting psychological perspective, which suggests a repetitive unconscious behaviour: the theory advanced by the couples therapist and author Harville Hendrix that we seek in our relationship the hope that we can complete the unfinished business of our childhood. Often we don't succeed. We just repeat the same pain.

I found this family's perspective on gender particularly interesting. Hilary was emotionally intelligent and seemed to have known that her husband was gay and hiding himself. But his denial of it for so many years might have undermined her confidence in her ability to judge men or read people. Perhaps it was the way her husband turned on her, which then made him seem unknowable. Or maybe she didn't want to know. Seeing men as "other" also seemed to be her way of sidestepping the more challenging mode of engaging with them. Men have done this to women throughout history, seeing them as "other" in order not to engage with them as fellow humans. Othering comes from fear—fear of difference, powerlessness—but can be bridged by curiosity: wanting to know, being fully known for all of who you are, including the mystery. This had eluded Hilary and, to a lesser extent, Kate.

Hilary put her head on the table, shaking it from side to side. When I asked what was happening, she just said, "Men!"

Kate leant into the screen. "Yes, men! I couldn't survive without my girlfriends. My marriage is maintained by the intimacy I have with my girlfriends."

She was recognizing the truth that one person can never meet all our needs. Girlfriends, work, life outside the marriage are all essential components of a successful relationship. Mother and daughter looked at each other as they wondered aloud how their relationship with men would live on in Daisy, and agreed that, although they didn't know, they trusted she had more awareness and confidence in getting her needs met than they'd ever had. I nodded, smiling: that was their gift to Daisy.

There is a fine balance between what is helpful and productive for family members to share together with a therapist, and what needs to be spoken about individually. This is particularly true between the generations. Openness and honest communication are the foundations on which to build trust in a family—but that does not mean promiscuous honesty at all times. How does a parent know what crosses the line? This is incredibly hard to define. For example, it's important for a child or young person to witness a parent in distress—so that they know it's all right to show distress—but how much is too much? Letting your child comfort you when you're sad is lovely—but leaning on them for emotional support is a step too far. Parenting requires constant calibration, teaching and modelling behaviour, rather than reversing the child/parent role.

Kate and I discussed whether it was wise for her to talk in front of Daisy about how upset she actually felt at her leaving. We agreed that Daisy needed to know—and would like to know—that her mum would miss her, but not to be burdened with the full extent of how thrown Kate was by it. I agreed: in many families the parent takes the victim passive-aggressive position—*Don't worry about me*—which signals, *Please worry about me*.

Kate and I had a couple of one-to-one sessions. As she logged in, she said a weak hello and immediately started to cry, deep, racking sobs. She intermittently wiped her nose, looked down, fingers pressed into her eyes, and muttered, "Oh, God," until the wave of sadness passed through her body. She was quiet for a moment, breathed and looked up with a shy smile. "Oof, it's exhausting."

Yes, it was: allowing her sadness to travel through her was a physical and psychological dive, but it opened her up to find out what was going on beneath.

Kate took time to find her words, sometimes looking me straight in the eye, often to the side. I learnt that Kate and Joshua had driven Daisy to university, trying to be cheery in the car, listening to an upbeat playlist. Kate fought back tears; Joshua talked incessantly; Daisy sat quietly in the back. Their goodbyes had been hurried.

On the return journey, Kate had been stonily silent and Joshua had oscillated between understanding and annoyance. He'd emphasized his pride in Daisy being at a prestigious university, how brilliant it was for her, what a wonderful time she would have. Kate didn't argue with that, but couldn't help feeling it as a bereavement. She was angry that he didn't feel the sadness as intensely as she did.

She found herself blasting at Joshua: that she knew they had been gradually releasing their control of Daisy through her adolescence, the tricky times when Daisy had pushed for her freedom, the fights about screen time and when to come home, but that her leaving now was of a different order of grief. It was about more than the last few years. Kate felt keenly the loss of her dependent child, an overwhelming hollowness that it marked the end of her hands-on parenting, when she'd felt validated and powerful in the role of mother. Then she had known her purpose: "I believe the most important thing I could do was to grow my child. There is nothing as important as that, and in my life nothing compares to it. As Mum said to us both, to raise one's child is a sacred task."

I could feel in my chest the import of what she was saying, and had to push away my own self-critical thoughts that I had never fully dedicated myself as a parent in that way.

For a moment, she sat back in her chair and found her anger, which she was reluctant to discover. Shaking her hands in front of her, as if they were hot and she wanted to cool them, she said fiercely: "I didn't know that was there . . . I'm angry. Maybe that's a bit too strong. Cross, yes, and also envious that she's going out into the world and will discover and explore new things while I'm at the other end of my life . . ."

I was impressed by her ability to let herself know what we often try to deny, that we are envious of our wonderful young adults. But revealing it to herself meant that she wouldn't take it out on her beloved child. This wasn't a feeling that could be "fixed"—but one that needed to be allowed, even befriended, so that it could convey to her the preciousness of her own life.

As we talked, Kate alternated between the depth of her loss, then her pride and sense of achievement in being the parent she had been. She told me that, when she looked at Daisy, she knew she'd done a good job, that she was an extraordinary child, sensitive, curious, bold, loving and clever. Wiping away a tear of happiness, she said, "I look at Daisy and Eve with astonishment that they are individuals who have gone and will go out into the world, and are more rounded and balanced than I ever dreamt they could be. They will make the world a better place for being in it."

I found myself looking at her with pride too. I've heard so much guilt from parents: it was refreshing and a delight to hear that a mother really believed she'd done a good job. I thought that, if we heard more voices like hers, perhaps we'd all be more open to celebrating the wins of parenting.

The balance of parenting between mothers and fathers is rarely equal. In a later session, Kate acknowledged that Joshua had been a brilliant father, but that "he was never as close to them [both daughters] as I was. He couldn't be as deeply involved as me: he was out earning the living to pay for us all. He had a huge commitment to the idea of a family, but chafed under the yoke of it—the day-to-day slog. He can't feel the same loss—though he feels sad." Sometimes, she said, he looked at her as if she was mad—when he found her on her bed racked with sobs, or driving beside her in the car when her tears would suddenly descend. He wanted to make her feel better, and was somehow irritated that he wasn't enough, that she wouldn't let him fix her.

Traditionally, it's fathers who encourage their children to leave home—it annoyed Kate, as it does many mothers. They would talk, and spend weekends together with Eve, but there was definitely a corner of each other that didn't meet when it came to their children growing up. Kate was also trying to focus on her new identity. It was an internal push-and-pull. On the one hand, she needed to acknowledge what she'd achieved: "I had the honour to be that person to them, and now I have to have a different relationship with them. I will endlessly search for a role as vital as that one, and I know I will never find it. I'm completely uncertain as to who I am." And she knew it wouldn't be long before Eve left. She hated the cliché of the empty nest—yet the house *was* more silent and she felt lost. On the other hand, she had moments of hope: "I have an idea that whatever it is will come—some people seem to seamlessly redefine themselves, but I'll take my time. There will be a renewal of some sort," and then, laughing, she said, "F★★★, it won't be gardening." We both chuckled.

Many grandparents and parents today look at this generation of young adults and say things like "When I was your age I had a job, was married . . ." But Professor Jeffrey Arnett, an American psychologist, believes that young people are not fully adult until their late twenties. The intervening period he termed "emerging adulthood." He proposed it as a new phase of development, brought about by the enormous social changes that have taken place in the Western world in the last seven decades: the feminist movement, the diminishing power of the institutions of marriage and the Church, the extended lifespan, the growth in university education to support the shift of the economy from industrial to technological and, of course, the ever-increasing cost of housing. Arnett believes that young people are right to spend these years enjoying the freedom they are unlikely ever to have again: trying things out, exploring their identities, being in a state of flux before settling into more secure adulthood.

I wanted to understand whether the Thompsons fitted the norms of development between the generations. In the UK, a woman in the early 1960s would expect to be married and have children by the age of twenty-one. Hilary, like most of her generation, had left home at seventeen. She had started life tap-dancing and doing "incredibly frivolous things," with no plan of what she wanted. She had married at twenty, and given birth to Kate at twenty-one. Feminism had taken hold by the time Kate was a young adult, broadening her possibilities.

According to Hilary, Kate had always been independent: "When she was a baby I gave her rosehip syrup, and I will never forget the look she gave me, telling me 'I'm my own person' from very young."

Kate argued that she felt her mother would act as though she was powerless at inappropriate times, and could be passive-aggressive—which prompted an "Ouch!" from Hilary. They did their usual dance: a show of steel, naming their irritation, expressing their feelings and ending up laughing. But Kate's was an important point: parents need to hold their power; handing it to their children overwhelms them, even reverses the parent role. Hilary acknowledged: "I've let you down badly a few times, which I regret."

Kate nodded vigorously. "Yup, you weren't great then, but I don't think I would have been a good parent at twenty-one."

It had blown through in minutes, and was such an embedded pattern of "rupture and repair" that, until I pointed it out, they hadn't noticed the security it gave them. "Rupture and repair" is the psychological term that describes what often happens in relationships: there is disconnect and then, through acknowledgement, reconnection. It is not the ruptures that cause lasting wounds but the lack of repair, particularly from a mother towards a distressed child. Kate grinned at her mother, and gently jabbed her in the arm, saying, "It's true, we've never fallen out."

Kate returned to the story of her transition into adulthood. She had left home at eighteen and gone to London to help her grandmother, while living with her boyfriend in a squat. Mother and daughter looked back at that with some shock, Kate realizing she had gone to the other side of the world without a thought for how her parents felt, and had had no contact with them for months. Hilary commented: "God knows she was at risk. I was very lucky."

Kate described those years as chaotic, when she had met with real danger, mainly from men, but she'd also been protected in some way by not thinking too deeply. She hadn't worried too much about who she was and, rather, had made it up as she went along. This is an interesting but complex point that I didn't see at the time. Not thinking too deeply had defended her from the destabilizing fear of the danger she was in, but came with its own inherent risks. It might have reflected a lack of internalized self-protection and care. There are no easy answers: life is by no means simple, and the balance between risk and safety is tricky. In some way it requires us to negotiate individually our own route between the two.

They both wondered if millennials worried too much and didn't have the "balls" just to jump into the cauldron of life. Kate's job as a journalist had been scary: she was on a rollercoaster, dealing with difficult bosses and fighting to find her place, riding dips in confidence to moments of triumph. She often felt she only just got away with it. But she was happy to acknowledge her success, wistfully looking back at herself as if at a virtual stranger: "I've lost that identity of success. I've loved motherhood but it's eroded my confidence to do other things."

Research shows how much harder it is for women who have completely stepped out of the workplace to get back into it later. It's easier to start again part-time before picking up full-time work. But for Kate this had not been an option. She hadn't wanted to juggle, or have the bad-mother-bad-worker diatribe circling in her head—though she recognized that she was fortunate enough to have the choice. As she thought about it, she saw anew that redeveloping her work identity would be a big mountain to climb, which would call on her courage.

Hilary finished the session with a quip—I wasn't sure if it was a kick or a nudge of encouragement: "If I did it, you can too."

Kate retorted, "That was decades ago, Mum. It's a completely different world now."

It's not just parents who are affected when a child leaves home:

the whole family infrastructure is jolted. Kate had noticed that, after Daisy left, Eve wanted to redefine herself as separate from her sister—to change schools, take her own route. It's interesting how siblings' identities can be forged in relation to each other, whether as rivals, opposites or disciples, and how they can get locked into them, even when they no longer fit. Kate paused. "Maybe I'm like Eve and want a change . . . I've suddenly thought it might be nice to have a different environment."

I was a little uneasy as to what would come next. I pictured her taking off to New York, following her father's path. It showed my bias: my instinctive response is to want families to hold together.

I need not have worried.

"From both my parents I saw how to change," Kate went on. "They had periods of depression—which is perhaps what I feel now—but they had this enthusiasm for life. There was always a resetting to a very sunny disposition, which was very protective for my brother and me. They went to the dark and came out in the light, and I know I can too."

Kate spoke with as much confidence about this as she had about her sadness—and at that moment we both knew she would find her way through. It would be painful, and probably take longer than she wanted, but she had a future she could see, based on the picture her parents had modelled for her. It is how parents live, far more than what they say, that becomes embedded in their children. I have often witnessed parents saying to their children, "All I want is for you to be happy," but how would the child begin to know what "happy" looks like if they haven't seen it?

Kate was in a better place, but there was still work to be done in reconfiguring how the family operated together. I saw Hilary and Kate without Daisy, who was caught up in her university life. They had gone up to Oxford to visit her, and Hilary said, in a tone of reverence: "I felt all my ancestors walking behind me, my grandmother the cleaning lady from Glasgow, my mother the caregiver from Tooting, and I said to them, 'Look, look.' I could sense that

Daisy had changed in some way. Within three weeks she had changed. You could tell she'd begun her life on her own."

As she spoke, I felt the import of what she expressed, and Kate, nodding, said: "It was slightly unnerving. She was definitely looking at us differently."

I noted that, as Daisy was maturing, her mother and grandmother knew they were smaller in her and that she didn't need them in the same way. Yet strength was imbued in her from the previous generations. Kate agreed, acknowledging, with sadness and joy, that they had to figure out a different way of being in a relationship with each other. Kate played with her rings, as if testing the thought that, in some fundamental way, she was also released, a big part of her job done.

But she felt confused—which is, of course, the definition of the process of change: it is a back-and-forth between releasing and holding on. The last weeks had not been straightforward. Daisy had rung in tears at times, worried about her work or needing something—which Kate had immediately resolved. But then there would be days when they heard nothing from her, and Kate, imagining disastrous scenarios, had resorted to her iPhone tracker to make sure she was still in the city. To me, this was an intrusion into Daisy's privacy—but it had been previously agreed between them, and gave Daisy the security of knowing her mother could find her.

With evident excitement, Hilary commented that Daisy had telephoned her. She had been outside a shop and wanted advice as to what to buy. "It was one of my proudest moments."

I assumed that Kate would have been jealous, hurt even—rivalry for love and attention between as well as within generations can be a secret destroyer of family life. Not so with the Thompsons. Kate responded: "It's a sign that she knows how to look after herself. She turned to my mother because Joshua and I are more complicated, but Mum is still an anchor who loves her unconditionally. I feel good about that."

As Hilary smiled, I could sense her chest expanding. Then she was able to ask Kate whether her mother, Elsie, had been important in the same way. As much as Hilary had delighted in Daisy's connection, she didn't make it all about her: she turned to her daughter with interest and warmth.

That tiny moment showed how patterns in families can be reconfigured, while the depth of the love between them can remain. Kate laughed, as they both tended to when Elsie was mentioned: "Nanny was as mad as cheese, but I did feel a comfort in her. I loved going to her house. I can see retrospectively how great it was to have her . . . even though I couldn't talk to her: she talked a lot!"

Hilary frowned, worrying about whether she talked too much as well. Kate let her know she didn't. The exchange demonstrated that we really don't need to be perfect—far from it: we can be "mad as cheese," as long as we are fundamentally loving. When that love comes from a place of goodwill it is trusted, and withstands many missteps.

As the weeks passed, Kate turned to Eve for comfort, enjoying being able to mother her. They watched TV together, and cooked cosy suppers—but as she described this, tears sprang to her eyes as she remembered that Eve, too, would depart. Hilary stroked her arm and they momentarily connected in mutual understanding of what it is to have daughters grow up and leave. It was as if that touch had lit a new network in Kate's mind. With a burst of energy she turned to me and talked about doing a counselling course, which she felt wasn't such a big leap from her job as a journalist. Within minutes, she had allowed herself to express her sadness, feel supported by her mother's love, then look to new ways of being.

It is too easy to underestimate how sustaining and joyous the relationship between parent and adult child can be. Interestingly, Daisy's behaviour at university echoed that of her mother. She'd ring in tears, be comforted and perk up. Kate wondered how Daisy would manage her intellectual confidence surrounded by so many clever peers. Hilary believed university wasn't just a measure of Daisy's academic capacity but also of her ability to be disciplined enough to match its standards. They talked energetically about their social mobility from impoverished roots to Oxford's "dreaming spires." Kate bent her head towards the screen, as if to emphasize this important message: "My grandfather on my dad's side was adopted, illiterate, a miner who lived in miserable poverty his whole life. But my father had this desire to move forward and had the guts to do it. He overcame his fear. He was self-educated, built a business from nothing, and took us to Australia in pursuit of that. My parents, although complicated, always provided security and they have this extraordinary life force, and . . ." she hesitated, tears in her eyes, as she looked at her mother, who was smiling at her ". . . you're the same . . . You've given it to me and Daisy has it too. She has that force." They gave each other a hug.

Hilary, expressing that force of character, talked about her addiction to online Scrabble, and that a man who was a year older than her was to become one of the most powerful leaders in the world: "What if Biden needs a little afternoon nap?"

That was her way of raising what was preoccupying her: "My next chapter is my death." She found it annoying that people said, "You're only as old as you feel," as if ageing was an illness. She resented people like Jane Fonda: she wanted to see old faces, not have them banished as if there was something vile about them. She said emphatically: "I want to feel my age. I've lived many a year and gained some wisdom. There must be something you can haul out of me."

Kate, looking extremely sad, began to speak, but her words were blocked by tears. Hilary stroked her arm as she went on with her own thoughts. She pursed her lips, and put a hand on her chin. She said she had no fear of death, but perhaps a fear of dying. She was a member of Dying with Dignity, and did not want a slow, unbearable Alzheimer's death. She wanted to be cremated, her ashes buried with her mother's and their dog's (both of which she kept in pots in her kitchen—you'd be surprised how many people don't scatter ashes) under a tree in a woodland burial site.

She turned to Kate with some impatience. "You know all this, and you've got all my stuff, like power of attorney, the funeral," as if she was discussing the details of a chicken recipe.

Her face flushed, Kate told her, "I can't bear for you to die. You can be annoying, but you're the only person I can be myself with. We have a shared language, we laugh a lot together. My whole life history is with you."

Hilary looked chuffed, but also a bit uncomfortable. Sometimes hearing what you most want to hear is painful, and can only be taken in afterwards, where I knew it would warm her. It seemed to me that although Hilary was emotionally available, she came from a generation that contained its deepest feelings. It was a difficult conversation, but it was important, for it helped to protect Kate from future regrets of what she wished she'd said, and opened the way to future conversations.

When Daisy returned for the Christmas break we had a number of sessions. Covid was surging. Having felt herself released into adulthood, Daisy was then shut down at home. There were inevitable tensions between Joshua and Kate about the rules. Joshua was anxious, constantly checking the news and statistics; he had loud meetings on Zoom. Daisy found it hard being with them. When Kate and Eve had some symptoms, Daisy went to her grandmother's house. Hilary was delighted to have her.

Kate's emotions showed in the nervous twisting of her earring. "I love having her back, seeing her face . . . when I get her."

Daisy looked directly at me, then spoke gently, with confidence, to her mother: "I told you I felt neglected when term ended and I came home. I'm over it now. It made me angry at the time. I could have stayed on at university, which was more fun."

Kate flushed. "You didn't seem to want to communicate with us much. I'd be anxious when you didn't text. It was weird. I spent eighteen years knowing exactly where you were, what you were doing, day and night. It was difficult for me. Now I keep my phone on at night, worrying about you."

Daisy interjected that Kate had always kept her phone on. "No," replied her mother. "I did when you were out but never otherwise, and now you're out for the rest of my life . . ." Kate's face dropped. Daisy softened. "I can see it's sad for you."

I was aware that the more anxious Kate felt, the harder Daisy had to work to hold her boundary between them—but then Kate would balance herself and they'd be back on track. More confidently, Kate stated that, without Daisy, they were less coherent as a family: they didn't sit down and eat together any more; they missed her fun and vitality. The bonus was that, although Eve missed her sister, she loved having her mother to herself. As Kate noticed, "Once all that sibling-rivalry behaviour went, she became easier."

I could see them picking through the new family dynamics, talking about how they felt, openly and honestly. The importance of how we communicate what we feel and need cannot be overestimated: when it's done clearly, pain and resentment dissolve. Resentment is the silent poison in families. I have witnessed it most often between mothers and daughters—"I've given you my life, and now you just don't care about me," the mother says, in a dramatic voice. The child responds angrily: "I didn't ask to be born. You wanted me!" As that pattern embeds itself, in all its tricky hues, the rift widens and love turns to hate. It is truly painful for all.

The Thompson women, in airing their views, found a new balance. Kate learnt that, next time, she would communicate in different ways, with cards and packages. She was getting across her message: you need your space and I am always here.

The psychological aspect of holding on and letting go for parents is intense, forcing adaptation, their emotions invisible but turbulent beneath their words. Learning to live apart but stay connected, to hold boundaries and allow difference is a complex business, as is re-entry after separation. Daisy wanted to leave home, to flex her intellectual muscles and find her new identity without being someone's daughter or sister. At the same time, part of her wanted to be celebrated, cherished and, most importantly, kept in mind. For Kate, Daisy's leaving brought up a sting of abandonment, a trace of the fear of not being loved any more. Perhaps this made it difficult for her to show her joy on Daisy's return.

On reflection, it seemed right that Daisy went to stay with Hilary, who could cosset her in a way that might have seemed infantilizing had it come from her mother. The relationship with a grandparent is less intense. As Hilary put it, "I've done the parent job, made my mistakes. I think parenting is an enormous responsibility, which is often taken too lightly. Kate took it seriously. I'm so proud of her. Now I have the hindsight to be a good grandmother. Being a grandmother involves less anxiety, less responsibility, much less work. It's less painful."

Yes, parenting is painful: where we love most we hurt most. Hilary's home was the place for Daisy to be at that moment. Having the secure love of a grandparent is an often unrecognized gift for the grandchild. From an intergenerational perspective, Kate had adored her own grandmother and took real pleasure in seeing her daughter benefiting from a similar relationship.

As lockdown continued and Daisy returned home she became more anxious. She was finding the intensity of her academic work increasingly difficult without the support of her peers, and felt emotionally confused about her identity—hanging between her new student self and her old self as a child at home. Her new wings had been abruptly clipped. She sounded small as she told us, "I feel sad a lot of the time. I feel suffocated at home . . . and safe." She apologized for crying, wiping away her tears as soon as they appeared, saying: "I'm lost. It's like looking at the world through coloured glass . . . and I know I'm lucky."

Hilary and Kate reassured her that her feelings were normal and healthy. They held her safe while she felt wobbly. Their relationship couldn't fix the consequences of the pandemic, but by supporting her, they did the next best thing, confident that, when the world opened up again, she would be in a good place to pick up the reins of her life.

As the physician Dr Gabor Maté wrote in *Hold On to Your Kids*,

"Adults who ground their parenting in a solid relationship parent intuitively . . . They act from understanding and empathy." That was what I observed between the three generations of Thompson women. It was epitomized by Hilary's words: "Family is the strong centre of gravity. They know they're ours, and we're theirs." It was the definition of belonging, a vital part of our mental health.

The Thompsons did not come to me with a family crisis to manage. The three generations of women I met have loving and resilient bonds with which to explore the bittersweet change of a child leaving home and finding their adult identity.

The therapy revealed much of the work that needs to be done when confronting this living loss. It's the tricky balance the parent needs to hold between giving the young adult space to breathe and experiment, while allowing them to feel securely rooted and not burdening them with guilt or worry for their parents or their relationship. It's the updating of the contract between parents, and with any remaining siblings: what will our new relationship look like now, as our family dynamic re-forms? And the change in identity for the parent(s) who must work hard to fill the gap within their own lives and find a new sense of purpose, pride and self-esteem.

In the Thompsons' case, this latter issue was Kate's biggest challenge. To equip herself for it she needed to remind herself of the touchstone of female power that came from her mother and much-remembered grandmother, to gain the strength and courage that would free her for a different future, as well as allow her daughter to move forward without constantly checking over her shoulder.

Perhaps this explains my aversion to the phrase "empty nest." The nest in a healthy family is never empty. It is filled with the spirit of past parent–child relationships, which allows each new generation to take wing and fly.

The Taylor and Smith Family

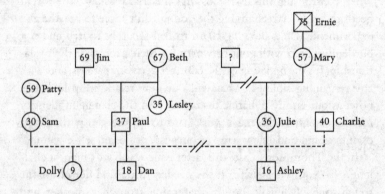

The Taylor and Smith Family

*How can stepfamilies find harmony when their relationship
is built on pre-existing conflict?*

Case conceptualization

The Taylors and the Smiths comprised Paul Taylor, a butcher, aged thirty-seven, his ex-partner Julie Smith, a personal assistant, thirty-six, and their two sons, Dan, aged eighteen, and Ashley, sixteen. They had been separated for ten years. Julie had custody of the children, and they visited Paul at weekends and for holidays. Paul was living with Samantha, and they'd had a daughter together, Dolly, aged nine. Julie lived with her partner, Charlie. There had been difficult financial issues causing extreme stress, but they had largely been resolved as the children got older and Julie could work. The reason for counselling was that Ashley had "lost it" when spending Christmas with Paul and Sam. It was the breaking point of years of conflict and distress between the two families. Dan had gone to live in Berlin: Paul and Julie feared if they didn't find a way of resolving these intransigent conflicts Ashley would leave too.

Every family has a story. Every family has its history of love and connection as well as wounds and hurt, yet some families' stories are more complex than others'. The Taylors' and Smiths' story was at the complex end of the spectrum.

At our first session the tension between the three people in front of me, who avoided looking at each other and me, sat like a block of iron in my chest. I needed to remind myself to breathe. Paul Taylor scowled at me. He had broad shoulders and a big frame with bouncy auburn hair that he frequently pushed back behind his ears. His ruddy face filled the screen. I intuited that beneath the scowl there was a sweet boy who often felt out of his depth and whose physical strength belied his sensitivity. As he spoke, I realized his boyish smile and quizzical green eyes held a certain seductive charm. I asked him what he hoped for by coming to see me. He told me he'd been separated from Julie for ten years: "It's as bad as when we separated, and it's Christmas that's done me in. I hate Christmas."

Julie nodded, her lips pressed together, and muttered, with a rather intimidating glare, "I bloody hate Christmas." Her many necklaces jangled as she spoke. Paul swallowed his response. (I couldn't quite hear his words, but I guessed it was to the effect that that was the only thing they agreed on.) I found myself thinking that hate is a heavy burden to carry: it blocks every other feeling. I felt for them and hoped we could at least reduce its intensity.

I learnt there had been a big falling-out over Christmas lunch at Paul and Sam's house, when Ashley had been very upset that he had been treated as "invisible" by Sam's mother. Julie bit her nails, and I noticed the beautiful tattoo of a butterfly on her thumb and wrist. Her jet-black hair was in a single plait, which showed off her angular jawbone and ivory skin, multiple silver earrings adorning her ears. She was striking, her swish of black eyeliner completing her very particular style.

When I realized she was only thirty-six, with two sons aged eighteen and sixteen, I did a double-take. It's not something I've seen very often: when I'm working in a hospital maternity unit I see women of thirty-six yearning for their first baby.

I hoped that, as Paul and Julie were relatively young, they might have a greater capacity for adaptability than a relatively older couple, a key tenet of good outcomes in people's lives. I knew that I would need to hold steady in the face of Julie's apparent ferocity, be empathic and not judgemental towards Paul's seeming "weakness." I needed to check my assumptions. I knew I had a bias against the type of men I perceive as delightful to be with but who take the path of least resistance. They don't accept responsibility for the consequences of their actions, in the hope things will "work out." Of course they don't, and more damage ensues.

I acknowledged how much they had all suffered and said I hoped to create an environment that would foster a less painful way for them to operate together. At this, I saw them both sigh: a small release of tension in having their pain seen. I am ceaselessly surprised at how powerful it is to have your feelings allowed. There is still pervasive shame in suffering. As if it is a personal failure.

My further hope was that in using me as the person through which they told their story, they could begin to be less defensive and more open to each other's experience. The only way Julie had learnt to express her feelings was through embedded negative patterns, being hurtful and name-calling. Similarly, Paul's learnt behaviour was to shut down. It meant that the experience of each was invalidated by the other, and necessarily excluded whole aspects of their narrative. There was a possibility of repair: they could co-create a shared narrative that allowed for all the difference and complexity between them. By not making the other the "bad guy," they might be able to forge a new collaboration as parents.

Since Dan, their elder son, had gone to live in Berlin six months ago, he'd had almost no contact with either of his parents. He'd left hopeful of building his music career, despite his persistent marijuana habit. I noted that in his behaviour he had found an emotional and physical escape. Perhaps his departure from the family so young had helped them decide to do something different to improve their relationships.

His younger brother, Ashley, was pale and dark, like his mother, and dressed in his pyjamas. It was 11 a.m. and he'd just woken up. Ashley's darting green eyes, like his father's, expressed his nervousness, or maybe he was unsettled. The set of his mouth told me he was angry. I imagined a world of disquiet inside him.

We'd like our emotions to be simple and identifiable but more often than not we feel lots at the same time. We know we feel awful but can't describe what is going on. Ashley was probably still hurt by his parents' separation, despite the ten-year gap: angry at what it meant for him, confused by the crossfire, furious at his powerlessness to have the family life he wanted, competing for attention with his half-sister, Dolly, all while trying to grow up and find his own identity.

I'd discussed in a preliminary session with Paul and Julie whether it was to Ashley's benefit to be part of this process. There was a risk he'd be reinjured by witnessing his parents' fights. But Paul and Julie particularly wanted him to be present. After the big falling-out at Christmas, it was Ashley who had asked for therapy. Influenced by his peers, he understood the importance of mental health and knew he needed things to change. He couldn't stand his parents still being hateful to each other.

Although his parents recognized Ashley could have individual therapy, they knew his distress centred on them. They wanted him to be part of the repair. I thought their response showed an impressive level of emotional intelligence. I sought advice from my supervisor, and we agreed that, as long as we established good boundaries, it might well be curative for them all.

We discussed Sam, Paul's partner of ten years. Paul and Julie agreed they could have therapy without her: they needed to work this out between them and, hopefully, she would benefit from it. Charlie, Julie's partner, was clearly important too. He got on well with Dan and Ashley, and as he and Julie had no children together, a complicating factor, he wouldn't need our attention right now.

From Paul I surmised Sam had initially been on shifting ground to find her place. As stepmother to Dan and Ashley, she was not only negotiating her new relationship with her partner but finding out how to be with them. What role did she have? She couldn't parent them directly as they weren't hers, yet they were in her house, all around her, making a mess, even if only at weekends. Sam probably felt they intruded on her relationship with Paul: Sunday was his only day off and she had to share it with them. Once Sam had given birth to Dolly, the threat from Dan and

Ashley would have felt even greater. As with Julie, the scarcity of money and Paul's time were very real challenges.

While we frequently find ways to accommodate ex-partners and step-relations, there is probably a part of us that wishes to annihilate any threat to our relationship. We are animals and, in the wild, a new male mate kills his female's progeny. The Max Planck Society reported new research, stating that "Across mammals, females are more likely to commit infanticide when conditions are harsh and when having offspring is particularly costly to females." That reflexive response is, I think, buried deep in our biology. We block it, then act it out in unconscious ways.

I often start an initial session by asking my client, "When you were upset as a child who was your go-to person, and who is it now?" I also ask them what they do to soothe themselves when they're stressed.

Julie sounded annoyed when she spoke. She didn't want to go straight to her vulnerable place. "The person I didn't go to much, but who I really loved was my granddad. Now it's my partner, Charlie. My dog Raffa is also my comfort, having him on my lap, stroking him and taking him for walks. I'm a dog person. I spent hours and hours with our dog Ghillie when I was a child."

For Paul: "I don't think I went to anyone when I was a kid, sometimes my mum and dad. It would depend on what was going wrong. Now it's Sam. When I'm stressed, and, if I'm honest, when I'm not, I still play games online, which I did when I was a kid."

I was curious as to what Ashley would say. "My mum and Raffa." I felt he was afraid that if he let himself speak more, words and feelings would cascade out of him that he didn't know what to do with.

Their answers, though brief, were a portal through which I had an insight to their inner world. We are wired to connect to others: when life is good, connection helps us thrive, and is needed especially when life is tough. Never underestimate the importance of pets to console distressed owners. In most cases that silent companion, their predictable affection, good mood and lack of complexity, sustains and comforts. Although they all had one or two people and a dog to rely on, theirs was the bare minimum of support.

Julie spoke with vehemence of what had precipitated their appointment. Ashley had walked out from the Christmas meal at his father's house.

I turned to Ashley and asked him what had happened. He didn't speak for a long time, head down as he played with his sleeve. Julie watched him with frustration, letting out big sighs. Finally, he spoke haltingly, so quietly it was hard to hear him, but I didn't want to make him self-conscious by saying, "Speak up." I noted that his difficulty in finding his voice might reflect how silent he'd been all these years, swallowing words and emotions that no one had been willing to hear.

He said, "It sounds silly, but Nan didn't give me any money at Christmas, and I saw her give money to my half-sister, Dolly. I don't know . . . I had to get out." Nan was Sam's mother, Patty.

Julie couldn't sit any longer on what was bubbling up inside her: "That nan's a mean cow, just like her daughter." Julie pointed across the screen at Paul. "Why can't you sort this? You only have the children every other year and every bloody time Sam and her mother treat them like second-class citizens. They're your kids, for God's sake. Do something. They've known Dan and Ashley since they were young—what's wrong with them?"

Paul was silent. Stony-eyed. His silence stoked more frustration in Julie, who swung her head sharply as she hissed, "Oh, God, you're always the same. Nothing, nothing, you do and say bloody nothing."

At this point in their story, I was interested to notice how the different family members dealt with uncomfortable feelings. Julie got angry and demanded that Paul sorted things out, rather than helping Ashley to process his emotions. This left Julie feeling powerless, with nowhere to go but blame. Ashley acted out his emotions, because his mother wasn't showing him how to process them, by getting angry or shutting down, therefore relying on

Julie to speak for him. Paul went silent. Perhaps he had learnt from Julie that this was the least inflammatory option, or as a child from his parents.

Paul and Julie hadn't found a way of communicating successfully when they were together, and their capacity to do so had thinned over the years, making co-parenting strategies non-existent. Their relationship was reduced to name-calling, fury and distrust before any conversation started. It was clear to me that what was playing out between Ashley, Patty and Sam was not just about them, but an extension of Ashley's parents' conflict, and the painful loyalty bind in which Ashley found himself: if he was close to Sam he felt disloyal to his mother, yet if he showed himself to be against Sam he got on badly with her.

A family's health relies on the quality of relationship between every member, whether they live together or not. Parental conflict in separated families, and how it affects co-parenting negatively, is the biggest predictor of bad outcomes for children. As I took that on board, I realized that this was unlikely to be therapy that included moving expressions of feelings with big psychological shifts: there wasn't the emotional safety, or even necessity for that. If we could simply improve how Paul and Julie communicated together—making decisions with and for their children, without huge blow-ups—that would be a big step in the right direction. It was essential that they free themselves from their own blame, and blame of each other. My mind was turning to how best we could achieve that.

Julie was an enigma. Her emotional foundations laid down by her parents were fragmented and insecure. Her father had left the family when she was young, and her mother was a binge-drinker. One of the coping mechanisms Julie had developed was to be tough and attack, not allow herself to express her vulnerability. That was the side of herself that she'd shown me so far. Her relationship with Paul played out in exactly the way her childhood had predicted: she had picked someone who couldn't give her what she wanted and lived in a state of constant and precarious drama. I wondered whether at some point Julie would need to address the trauma: it had left an indelible wound of abandonment in her, but family therapy was not the place.

And yet she had, to a great extent, overcome that adversity as she'd matured. She wasn't an addict, a common way of coping with a traumatic childhood, and very likely in Julie's case, given her mother was an alcoholic. Furthermore, she'd had the determination and even confidence to train, then get a decent job. Now she was with Charlie, a partner she loved.

I started the next session by disclosing my puzzlement. Julie giggled, an infectious, rather raucous cackle, and I saw Paul and Ashley smile in response. "Ha, I had a lot of shit, like you said. I don't really know . . ." I asked whether there had been significant people or experiences in her life that she saw as positive. "Well, like I said before, there was my granddad. He died when I was seventeen. He lived miles away but I went to him some of my holidays . . . I loved that. He was ex-military, strict, he smoked a pipe, but he was a real softie. He loved his vegetable garden and I'd putter in it with him, digging, weeding. I still love the smell of earth on my hands."

A new tenderness showed in her face as her whole being travelled back to those happy memories. It reminded me of how many versions or parts of ourselves there may be: the loved grandchild was often hidden behind the fierce version of herself, which she'd had to develop to protect her vulnerability. But it was still there. She could access it and, in doing so, her openness and emotional availability. Mini lights went on in my head: that was the source of her capacity to dare to love her children and Charlie.

It takes only one person in our life to be a vital and protective factor in our outcome—a teacher, a boss, a mentor believing in us. More is better, but one is enough. The other person who had shaped Julie was the manager at the supermarket where she had worked. He had seen something in her, believed in her, and encouraged her to go back to college after Dan's birth, then again after her split. He had been persistent in his call for her to progress her life, and fortunately she'd acceded to his belief in her.

Being a stepchild is difficult. I had a vivid memory of a young woman telling me, "I had to live with a stranger I didn't even like, who watched what I ate and wore, and stole my dad from me! Then my dad told me to be nice to her." That sums up Dan and Ashley's experience. While Julie, as the ex-partner, had had to let her children go into another household, had suffered their weekend absence, and perhaps consciously wanted them to be happy, she was probably unaware of the impact on them of her needing them to be loyal to her, and thereby against Sam, which caused conflict for them.

I knew this as familiar territory in stepfamilies, where there would always be someone who was excluded and furious. I wanted to shift the toxic patterns between them and recognized it would be hard: interventions that occur later are less likely to succeed. I hoped they would develop a new way of behaving together, founded on a better understanding of what was going on, to allow permeable boundaries and mutual respect to facilitate cooperation between the households, rather than battles.

Fortunately, I didn't see anyone as good or bad, which is the basis of my training but not always the case! I am informed by my own subjective experiences, too, which bring with them biases and strong responses. I wanted to get beneath the mythologized representation of stepfamilies, a trap I could sense I was falling into, in which the father is weak or absent, while the mother is both a victim and a hounding harridan. A stepmother is personified as an evil witch, and a stepfather is feeble at best, a bully at worst.

Their difficulties to some extent were the problems we all face when we feel under threat, the painful emotions that that engenders, when at heart we need to be loved and to belong.

I thought it might be helpful for us all to avoid going straight into the crisis, but to step back, and for the family to give me the background to what had led them to me. I hoped that telling their story would give them space to build trust with me and perhaps the opportunity to hear each other in a way they hadn't before. Sometimes the open discussion of what has happened is as important as finding answers to questions. Most of this family's experience was hidden beneath unspoken rules and beliefs. I hoped the collective listening might clarify what had been invisible.

Relationships tend not to work if we can't see things from the perspective of another. Julie, for instance, stuck in her suffering, couldn't hear anyone else's view. Knowing they had been heard and understood, at least by me, if not each other, interrupted the family's usual patterns of listening and interacting. It would have given them a felt-sense, meaning an experience in their bodies of being heard, and also modelled what I'd hoped they would be able to do for each other.

To begin with it was hard for me to piece it together because Julie interrupted Paul with such ferocity. She had ten years' worth of anger she wanted to get out, and he was forced to face what he'd spent ten years trying to avoid. I regularly had to pause them as their talking across each other escalated, and gave them basic listening skills: I asked them to reflect back what they'd heard the other say. They didn't like it but learnt quickly and the tension eased.

I understood they had met and started dating when Paul was nineteen and Julie eighteen, not long after the death of her grandfather. There was a touching moment between them when Paul spoke wistfully of their early days: "I couldn't believe she was my girlfriend. I was head over heels in love with her. She was stunning."

Julie nodded and bit her lip as he spoke. She'd accidentally become pregnant with Dan and neither of them had wanted an abortion. Paul had moved into Julie's mother's house and they had "muddled along for a few years." On hearing that sentence I had an image of a family house built on scant foundations. As a couple they'd had no time to put in solid ground, with being so young and the speed of her pregnancy. They didn't have the experiences to find out who they really were, what they loved doing, their differences, their similarities or, crucially, were they a good fit?

Julie's mum, Mary, did a lot of the childcare, which enabled Julie to return to college and work in the supermarket. Paul worked in his father's butcher's shop. It was a family business, in which his mother worked full time, running the accounts, and didn't look after her grandchildren, an early source of strife. Paul described his family as "Traditional. We like to follow the rules. For my parents, marriage and family is everything . . . My dad has taught me how to be self-sufficient and work hard."

Difficulties arose when Julie became pregnant with Ashley. Her mother was furious at the added burden in expense and care that another baby would bring. In a fit of drunken rage, she yelled at them, "Get out of my house."

Paul and Julie found a tiny flat to rent, where Ashley was born. Having another child and no mother to help her meant Julie had to give up work. As Julie described that time her jaw hardened. She began to speak: "That's when I lost my . . ." She saw Ashley's startled glance and stopped, shrugged and went on: "I lost who I was then . . . I lost the me of me. Paul was working all the time, but only earning just above the minimum wage. I had no money and two small kids who sucked the life out of me . . . literally." I heard a brutality in her tone that sent a shiver down my spine. I doubt there is a mother who hasn't shared Julie's sentiments, but hers had not shifted over time: they were a fixed lens through which she viewed Paul.

Paul stepped in, trying to make it better, half a smile on his face. "It wasn't so bad."

Julie snorted, "For you it wasn't. You still had a life." This was an interesting moment, which illustrated an aspect of the dynamics between them. Julie was simmering with righteous resentment: she'd had to sacrifice so much to be a parent, and although she loved her children she had paid an unfair price as their mother, much higher than Paul. It wasn't just the repetitive boredom of childcare, it was the "always" element of parenting: the invisible labour stealing years of her life, the loss of her work identity, and the inability to earn her own money.

Julie is by no means the only parent who feels this. The online forum mother.ly's *Motherly's 2019 State of Motherhood Survey Report* found "The majority of mothers (61 percent) report handling most household chores and responsibilities themselves and 62 percent report having less than an hour to themselves in a day in which they didn't have some kind of obligation to take care of."

For Julie the powerlessness pinched her every day, each pinch building a source of distress. Paul couldn't let himself face the force of her feelings, and in ducking it wanted to make it better but, of course, heightened her resentment. Meanwhile Ashley absorbed their battle, feeling hurt but also entangled in it, which gave him no place to go. The psychological toll on Ashley, who rested his head on his elbow, was something we would need to focus on in the weeks ahead.

As I understood it, the fights increased over the years, never being resolved, and the distance between Paul and Julie grew. Paul's version: "I was always at work by six thirty a.m. Every day is busy, particularly Saturdays. I'm on my feet all day and it's a physical job. I do most of the lifting as my dad is getting older. I would get home about six p.m. and Julie would expect me to help with the kids . . . I did my best. I worked six days a week and I was exhausted. Nothing was enough for her. I didn't earn enough, I didn't help enough, I didn't give her enough attention. She wanted my parents to give me some of the business . . . All the while her spending was out of control. I'd come back and see she was wearing something new, which I knew we couldn't afford, but if I said anything, she'd go for me."

As Paul was speaking, I saw Julie turn her head away and press her hand on her mouth, physically having to restrain herself from expelling the shout that was sitting in her chest. She managed to condense it to two words: "You're pathetic."

I find raw aggression hard to deal with: as a therapist it is not my happy place. Yet it was my job to find a way to acknowledge what I saw was going on and respond with empathy so that they could begin to be empathic to each other and themselves. I told them Julie saw Paul as weak and, the other side of that coin, Paul saw Julie as a bully. Consequently, physiologically, they were always on alert, fired up to fight or defend, which blocked their ability to feel safe enough to trust and connect. It meant they had never found a way to cooperate together. Good communication, which really means being able to listen effectively, as well as speak, is at the heart of good cooperation.

The very real challenges of parenting, their duties, their time and their money became the weapons they threw, rather than mutual difficulties they needed to face together. They didn't talk about it honestly; they didn't find ways of budgeting, look for solutions or express kindness when they were wrung out. I went so far as to say it was hard to hear how two people who had fallen for each other initially had grown to hate each other. What had attracted them—her force of character, his softness—was the root of their split, and their circumstances had wreaked havoc on what was left.

After years of battling and mounting misery they had separated. As Julie spat, pressing her thumb into the palm of her hand to push away the pain, "We split."

Paul dropped his head. He was not a man who found it easy to say what he felt, but his sense of failure still cut into him, and was pulsating through his body language. The separation ended their daily contact but by no means ended their fight. Mary-Kay Wilmer, former editor of the *London Review of Books*, summarizes: "Marriages end but divorces never do." Because Paul and Julie weren't married, the children had to be legally provided for by him but not Julie. To add to the complexity, Paul had fallen in love with Sam almost immediately, and they had moved in together. Within a year she was pregnant, and Dolly was born. Now Paul was being pulled financially and emotionally between Julie and Sam.

Julie took her turn to voice her distress. "He left me high and dry when he shacked up with Sam and had another kid. Gave us virtually no money. I was alone with both the boys and we were desperate. They'd go and see him when he finished work on a Saturday, but Sam was a bitch . . . There were times I'd shout at him, 'You do it, you try and live it,' and he'd nod, and say, 'Well, anyway, I'm off.' I remember nights I'd seethe, not be able to sleep with my fists in my mouth."

I felt that fury cut into me too. Her rage versus her powerlessness stung my chest.

Julie was at that point living alone, looking after eight-year-old Dan and six-year-old Ashley. She could work some shifts at the supermarket during their school term but not enough to pay all her bills. Julie's mother Mary helped occasionally but was unreliable.

Ashley, whose silence had been powerfully present through all these discussions, now spoke a truth I hadn't heard so clearly before. "We grew up poor. My mum struggled to feed us. I remember days when we couldn't do a food shop. We were always broke . . ." He looked at his mother, tears in his eyes. "You were stressed out all the time . . ." Behind those words I could see images of Julie exhausted and worried, trying to keep it together, but constantly bewildered by the responsibility of parenting alone, the chill of poverty haunting her.

British poet and lexicographer Samuel Johnson's definition of "bewildered" is "to be lost in pathless places." Julie had no one to hold on to, nowhere to go and no idea how to cope with where she was. Occasionally she was able to hug and be emotionally present for her children, but more rarely than she'd have wanted. Paul reddened further, looked ashamed, and said, "I'm sorry."

At that moment I felt the possibility for a shift in his connection to Julie, but she hadn't taken in his sincerity and was still burning with anger: "So you should be." Paul retreated.

To protect against splitting between good and bad, I reflected in as compassionate a voice as I could muster, how they had both suffered deeply during this painful time.

★

Separated couples hope that life will be more harmonious once they are apart. But the tug of war for the diminished resources of love, money and time can be overwhelming. The evidence from the Tavistock Institute of Human Relations report highlights the critical role the quality of the relationship plays between a separated couple and how it influences the financial support that is agreed, and the difference it makes to whether separated families live in poverty or not. The overall relationship and the financial support shape the outcome for parents and their children.

A US Census Bureau population survey states that in 2021 there were 19 million single parents, nearly 70 percent of whom were women. Mothers are more likely to be tipped into poverty after separation simply because they cannot work when they are looking after their children. The same findings indicate that children living with a single parent were three times more likely to live in poverty than those living with two parents. And the poverty rate for single-mother families (35 percent) is nearly twice as high as that of single-father families (17.5 percent). The division between non-paid caring duties and paid work for mothers is a problem that has not been solved despite the decades women have struggled with it.

Beneath that statistic is the unshifting reality that requires systemic and policy answers, but they are absent and individuals end up believing they are failing. Often a separated couple will try to get on amicably for the sake of the children, which is valid, yet they ignore the fact that it will improve their own lives. Hating your ex, fighting with them in your head, and in reality, is exhausting and destabilizing for everyone.

I told the Taylors and Smiths about this data: I wanted them to know they were not failures. In my experience clients feel validated when their experience is backed up by research. I spoke slowly because I wanted them to take in what I said: "You were all doing your best in a system that is weighted against you. I think if I'd been in either of your positions, my response would have been the same." I don't often bring in my subjective view, but I felt in this case it would ease their default self-criticism.

Julie was blinking a lot. She was used to defending herself against attack, and being valued unconditionally shook her, in a good way. Paul sighed. "Hmm. I hadn't thought of it like that." Ashley was silent, but more of his face popped up in the screen. This was a small moment of alignment, which I hoped to build on.

Now I shall fill in the gaps in their story. I learnt that Julie spent five years as a single parent, challenging years for them all. She was regularly swamped by the demands of meeting Dan and Ashley's needs. There were ongoing fights with Paul about his visiting rights and money. For the first three years she was in temporary accommodation, moving four times, which brought further disruption. Another parent at Dan's school introduced her to Gingerbread, the charity for single-parent families, when she was at her lowest point. "It saved my life." She joined a group and, with their support, was able to hold firm and agree fair child maintenance with Paul. Their importance in connecting with Julie, empowering her, cannot be underestimated.

Touchingly, in a rare moment of vulnerability, she looked at Ashley and said, "I could never win as a parent. I had moments when I felt I was on top of it—I felt close to you both, even happy—and then something would happen. One of you would be ill and I couldn't work, or you'd be content and I would blow it by being stressed out." Ashley smiled as he lowered his head, his eyes filled with tears. I felt the kindling of their meeting: there was no need for me to say anything.

Julie, frozen in her loneliness, had tried dating occasionally without success. She had no one to look after her while she had relentlessly to meet other people's demands. "I was tired of being alone." It was at this point I asked her to pause. Could she tell me what was happening in her body? "I don't know." She sighed. "I feel a bit raw. Hollow, yes, that's it, hollowed out." I let her words sink in, and she continued connecting through her body memory: "I remember feeling completely alone, like I was on an island with me and my boys against the world. I was shut down. Oh, God, a memory of being at a parent–teacher meeting all alone, dreading it, feeling like a total failure." At that moment I had a new connection to Julie: I sensed her fragility beneath her rage. I wanted to be in the same room as her and lean towards her with warmth, but instead I tried to imbue my voice with it. "Yes, I can really feel your chilly isolation, all alone for so long. I feel closer to you. Tell me more."

Her anger had kept me at a distance, which was by no means all down to her but my issue too. I glanced at Paul and Ashley, their eyes alive with emotion.

Julie continued, "Once the children were older life became a bit easier. I was less worried. I trained and got a regular job as a PA, which gave me confidence and reliable money. I started to believe I could have a good time, and slowly I did. I was thirty-one when I met Charlie. It took me a long time to like someone enough and trust them enough to try again. But my life has changed—it's improved a lot. He loves me. He's an amazing stepdad, and my kids really love him."

Now I was curious. First, the curative power of love: had her relationship with Charlie managed to heal the wounds inflicted by her parents and Paul? Partly. His love had restored her confidence. Yet although Julie was considerably happier nowadays, the awful cycle with Paul had not abated. The wrath she wielded against him meant he ducked to avoid it, Dan and Ashley paying the price.

I was interested in how trapped we can be by poisonous feelings for a particular person, and how they can be triggered faster than our conscious mind can influence our management of them. It meant Julie's hatred and contempt for Paul blasted through her, even though she was now more settled and happier, Paul playing his part by shutting down or retreating. We are genetically wired to look for danger, to protect ourselves. Fear, like Julie's, sets off a smoke alarm in our brain to fight, fly or freeze. Julie fought and Paul flew. The problem was that they were stuck on a loop. I would need to find a way to support them to release that old distress.

Let me make a point about grief, and that overused, often mis-understood term "the process of grief." Julie was grieving the loss of the relationship and family life she'd hoped for. Remembering and focusing on the loss is central to grieving. But there are two different forms of remembering and feeling pain. One form, like Julie's, involves repetitive emotional loops that sufferers become stuck in. It is often at the root of complex grief.

The remembering that helps us to integrate experiences, accommodate the loss and move forward in our life takes place when we are supported to feel the pain of change, and let it shift us emotionally, over time, to heal. The process is the push and pull between the poles of the past and the present, which allows us to adapt to the new reality.

As I reflected in supervision about the Taylors and the Smiths, I knew that anyone who has been in a relationship will have played out a version of Paul and Julie's story. Haven't we often wanted to run away from conflict and, even more often, been furious and wanted to attack those we love most? Either as a couple living together or separated, isn't the most regular fight over money and who is not doing their share of the duties? An unwelcome stereotype, perhaps, but isn't it often women who juggle parenting and work, or don't work to parent? Many men feel burdened by the need to pay the bills and be involved fathers. This influences how couples parent, their ability to be loving parents, and may ignite competition for their child's love and attention, which naturally intensifies when they separate and bring in a new partner. It leads to those common feelings that I guess we've all had at times, fury or the low-level rumbling anger that contaminates every other emotion and blocks all possibility of connection.

We would like to believe that the age-old dilemma has been solved in the twenty-first century when half of the working population is female. It has not. Paul and Julie's central problem had been money. It wasn't an exaggerated worry but a very real obstacle. Of course, their responses were influenced and hampered by the psychological difficulties from their past that they needed to face.

When I explored with my supervisor how to work with them, we agreed that initially I needed to build on their existing strengths, which might enable them to be open to change later. I was now pretty certain that Dan's exit to Berlin had been the real motivator for them to ease their conflict. The best place to start was with their love for their children and that they wanted the best for them. Julie had a partner with whom she felt secure, which might help her to manage the emotions Paul triggered. She had overcome being abandoned by her father, her alcoholic mother, her split from Paul, and had found love with Charlie. For all her fury she was fundamentally resilient, could grow and change. Research shows the first two years of a new committed relationship after a separation are the hardest and when the new couple are most likely to break up. Paul had been with Sam for ten years, showing his capacity to create a secure relationship. For all its apparent complexity there was room for hope.

I told Paul, Julie and Ashley that theirs was a difficult story with many moving parts. We had already done an important piece of work in finding a cohesive narrative together. When Paul and Julie had started dating they did not have good strong psychological roots, or networks of support. The bitterness of their separation had intensified through lack of time, financial and emotional resources, which meant everyone suffered. To protect all of us against getting lost down rabbit holes of blame and fury, I asked them to agree with me that the focus would be Ashley and, in his absence, Dan. Ashley remained silent but Paul and Julie nodded, and I felt warmth towards them.

A predictor of good outcomes for families in transition is support and guidance, which neither Paul nor Julie had ever had. Now they had the courage to go out of their comfort zone and ask for help for the sake of their sons.

I looked for a framework that might help us create a shared vision that the four of us could work towards together. Until this point, they had had no shared goals they all valued. It was important to acknowledge they had moved away from a single-perspective "stuck" story, in which they were the angry victims, towards a more open, collaborative narrative of the family that recognized multiple perspectives and enabled their own hurt to be "seen." For me, this is the key to shifting family dynamics: it gets people out of bad habits of thought and destructive behavioural patterns, allowing the group to form wider, agreed goals. I hoped this would improve their family system, with them all recognizing it as an ongoing process not a one-off event. Perhaps it would eventually influence Dan to re-enter the fold.

I found Patricia Papernow's work helpful on stepfamily architecture. She suggests that, whether they are the biological parent or step-parent, someone is always an insider or an outsider. Children are torn between loyalty to one or other of their parents. The whole family needs to change and adapt to allow space and acceptance for the new family members to join and find their place.

First, it meant some psychoeducation for Paul, Julie and Ashley. I firmly believe none of us can begin to understand what is going on inside us until we have some grasp of what is likely to be going on. It was important they recognized that what they were experiencing was normal, given their situation. They weren't defective. I liked the term "stepfamily architecture" because it was explicit when so much of their experience was inchoate. I went through each challenge briefly, leaning on Papernow's expertise, and gave them a link to her article to explore it in their own time.

There is a real challenge in finding a sense of belonging when stepfamilies share physical space. For example, Ashley wanted to eat in the kitchen where Sam worked. Tensions build until anger may spill into an attack; not belonging triggers spikes of fear and fury. Also, when someone new enters the room, someone else is left out: this image energized me. It explained so much of the impenetrable "stuckness" between them.

The grief children feel when their birth-parents separate, and they want to be loyal to both, feels like a physical knot that is impossible to unravel. As Dan and Ashley transitioned from their first family to their stepfamily they experienced a "living loss" on every level: their trust in their love for their parents, their beliefs, their safety, their sense of a "whole family," their daily life and even their identity. Loss brings with it all the experiences of grief. Loyalty binds are normal, but parental conflict worsens them unbearably. As I saw it, Ashley and Dan were still grieving the original split because there had been no opportunity for them to express it.

Ashley nodded. "I can see it now, why I had that tightness in my chest when I was with Dad. I felt bad for leaving Mum." I was relieved to hear Ashley's anguish, which until now seemed to have been silenced by the other, louder, narratives. Everyone having an opportunity for their experience to be heard was curative.

The separated couple have to agree on how to parent their children, who does what and when, who pays for what. With Julie and Paul this had caused chaos and distress. They remained fixed in their position of "You are wrong. I am right." There was no space for agreement and it inevitably impacted how they responded to their children. Being too lenient or too strict is a common difficulty. Papernow writes: "A large body of research finds that children in all family forms do best when parents practise authoritative parenting. Authoritative parents are both loving (warm, responsive, and empathic) and moderately firm (they calmly set developmentally appropriate expectations and monitor behaviour)." From Ashley's face, I saw there had been plenty of authority in his life, but inconsistent affection, although his parents really loved him.

Forging a new way of behaving requires resolving multiple differences. I thought this would be tough. Papernow cites, "Building a new family culture is a key developmental task for stepfamilies. However, what feels like 'home' to one part of the family may feel foreign, and even offensive, to the other." I was thinking that the

Christmas debacle was a perfect example of how things can go wrong. Maybe we could unravel it and forge a better culture.

There is the perennial difficulty of ex-partners, like Julie, being part of the new family. If we managed to make that work, it would be the signal of success. It would mean that both boys had good enough relationships with all the principal adults in their life. They'd feel their whole team supported them. Conflict is clearly corrosive to children, particularly when one parent turns a child against the other, hence the UK's Parental Alienation Law Child Abuse Bill of 2020. (There is no such law defined in Canada or the United States.) It is worth the effort to work on co-parenting with goodwill until children become adults. Although the damage doesn't become less poisonous as children grow older.

That was quite enough for one session. I could feel all of us burdened by the task ahead. I suggested that it raised differences and difficulties that needed to be voiced, discussed and, where possible, resolved or at least understood. I smiled as I spoke to them, "It gives us a map, one we can use to discover new understandings." I went on, "As I see it, if we can work through the first challenges, the others will follow naturally," adding, a little less confidently, "Of course I can't predict where it will take us . . ." Ashley was in school uniform, his head to one side: this was not easy for him. Paul and Julie looked relieved, shoulders dropped, breathing heavily—maybe a bit nervous. I hoped they would read the Papernow article in the time between the sessions and discuss it with their partners, maybe write a few notes of how it related to them. I thought doing this outside the session gave them a sense of agency for themselves, to do it in their own time supported by their partners and begin to understand what had been going on beneath the surface for years.

In the next session I asked them to give me their take on insider–outsider roles. Julie was determinedly silent and looked to Paul. He was hesitant. I turned to Ashley, wondering if he had something to add. He looked embarrassed. I suddenly noticed his screen had gone blank, and called, "Are you there?" After a few moments, in which I had berated myself for focusing on him, frightening him off, he spoke quietly, telling us he had an example but couldn't speak when he saw his parents looking at him. I thought how clever it was of him to know that. Ha! "Dad, do you remember a few years ago Dan and I wanted to take you to Pizza Express for your birthday, and you'd agreed? Then when Dan and I turned up Sam and Dolly were there, smiling at us and you just shrugged . . . You chose her, not us . . . again . . . I don't know exactly if that's an example, but I know we were both upset. We wanted you to ourselves."

I intuited from previous conversations that Sam was too jealous and angry to stay at home: she couldn't bear to be the outsider and let Paul see his sons alone. I could see Julie about to speak. I asked her to pause, and waited for Paul. "Oh, God. Oh, God." His face flushed and he grappled for words at being forced to confront the dilemma he'd been in for a decade. "I was always caught between you. I don't know . . . Your mum was crazy. Furious with me." I glanced at Julie, and modelled a deep breath, hard for her, but she breathed and didn't speak. "Whatever I did was wrong. Sam told me I didn't give enough to her and Dolly . . . I don't know. I still don't know." He pushed his clenched fists into his eyes, wanting to hold back years of distress.

This was where I could come in and validate the bind he was in. I said as simply as I could that, yes, he felt the pain of being torn between the two families he loved. He had to allow the pain and the love he felt for them: he couldn't stop the pain by hoping his love was enough.

I sensed from Julie's eyes she was ambivalent. She could see his hurt but she still wanted to punch him for all his failings. At that moment I felt protective of Paul and didn't want to hear what she would say: I was worried her default fury would crash into Paul's vulnerability. But I had to let her speak. I framed it a little formally: "Julie, what have you heard from Ashley and Paul?" She shook her head, her earrings jingling. "It's a fuck-up . . ." I thought, She's going to attack him, but she didn't. She went on, "We've fucked up so badly . . . What a mess. You trying to please everyone. The years of fighting . . . What a bloody car crash. You can't handle much . . . and in a way I can't either."

I felt a swish of satisfaction run through me. Here Julie was reflecting, standing outside herself and being able to see from a bird's-eye view what was going on for herself and Paul. It would be a key agent in their reconfiguring how to be as a family.

I voiced their collective position: "This was a tough session, and an important one. For the first time you have heard how your separation has tested you beyond what you could cope with. It has meant you have both behaved in quite destructive ways. And, to be honest, so would anyone. You have all had so much to deal with. The feelings inside you are huge: abandonment, loneliness, fury, jealousy, sadness, shame, to name but a few. The ongoing rupture between you all has been unbearable at times, certainly crazy-making. Ashley, I want to give you particular credit for having the courage to speak up, and I think your parents have really got what you were saying today." He switched on his camera and waved at me with a shy smile. The session ended.

I hoped we could build on that session, but feared something would sweep it away—this was a fragile process. I started by asking them all to check in so I could see how they were doing. Paul had arrived late, looking sheepish. Julie was energetic: she was by nature a doer. Maybe a bulldozer! Ashley remained off screen for the rest of our sessions together, which seemed to work well: it was a bit like being able to listen to the adults from behind a closed door, but with the chance to chip in when necessary. It also meant his parents could focus on each other without him being caught up in the drama.

Julie looked determinedly into the screen. "I want to sort out Ashley and Paul seeing each other. I'm going to be blunt but, Paul, I'm not against you." This was significant: something had clearly changed in her perception of him. "Look, Ashley needs you. He knows you're with Sam, but he doesn't like her—or he doesn't trust her . . ."

I wished I could see Ashley's face, and wondered if he'd agreed with his mum beforehand what she would say. Were those her words or Ashley's? Was she being manipulative or straightforward? I wasn't sure, but I had to go with it.

Paul looked at his hands. I felt a tightening in my chest: I was irritated. I wanted him present emotionally. I let the feeling pass. "Paul, I can see you look a bit lost, or is it upset? What's going on?"

More silence. Slowly he said, "I can't win. Sam is angry with me. I came back full of the last session and, somehow, she felt I'd betrayed her. Julie, she feels your malevolence against her is unfair, and when she tries talking to you, you blow up."

I responded, "I imagine this is the kind of thing that's happened a lot in the past. You both want to resolve an issue, but you get tangled up in it all—you feeling torn, Paul, and Julie wanting to fight for her kids. Let's do it differently here."

I then asked Julie and Paul simply to reflect back what they'd understood the task for them both was. They agreed it was to arrange time for Paul to see Ashley. I asked Ashley what he wanted and heard the answer to my previous questions: "I'm not against Sam. I know she loves Dad, but she scares me. I'd like her if she was nice to me! But I want to see Dad on my own now and again . . ." He paused. "I was thinking, he gets to see Dolly and Sam alone, so all I want is some of what they have. I think that's fair." Ashley was mature beyond his years, probably more so than he should have been, having had to parent his mother, trying to make her feel better when she hadn't been able to cope, but his straightforward clarity shifted the session.

I modelled how I wanted his parents to respond to him, by warmly praising his clarity and the heart his request had come from—I couldn't see his face and had the surreal sense I was talking into a rabbit hole—but felt closer to him when he said, "Thank you."

Rather sweetly, his parents waved at his blank screen and said, "Thank *you*."

Julie, following her son's lead, asked what times Paul could see Ashley on his own in the next month, even being creative and wondering whether, if they met for an hour alone, to kick a football around, they could then go back and have supper all together.

I suggested to Paul that he match his time with Ashley with "special time with Sam." It could be a date night. He needed to find a way of letting Sam know how important she was to him, show compassion and understanding for her feeling of being "left" when he went to see Ashley. It might help build her trust in her importance and the value of their relationship to him. As I was talking, I could sense that Julie was huffing beneath her breath. I didn't want to open up a new line of her venting so drew the session to a close, stating how different they all were with different needs. The key was to allow and make space for their differences, rather than fight against them.

Paul looked relieved. He was fundamentally a good man who wanted to be a good dad and partner but hadn't known how.

When I was writing up my notes from the session I realized that Sam becoming distressed at being "left" was probably an early injury from her childhood. I hoped in the future, once we had Paul and Julie working better together, we could spend a little time looking at the source of Sam's vulnerability, which might allow Julie and the boys more compassion towards her, even though she was holding on to Paul with such force.

We had a number of neutral sessions in which nothing much happened: that felt to me like a huge win. Neutral was what we were looking for, using the therapy as an opportunity to check in, keep the lines of communication open and address small niggles before they became huge fights. I reassured them that I could see they all wanted to find a good enough alliance in their stepfamily system.

Some basic rules emerged: they would not fight in front of Ashley, not badmouth each other or each other's partner in front of Ashley, Dolly or Dan, talk more and text less because texts often led to misunderstandings. If they'd agreed a plan, and someone wanted to change it, they would stick to the original plan with grace if no alternative could be found. I asked Ashley to check in with himself as to whether there was residual hurt from Christmas, and he just shook his head: "Nope, that's gone." So much had been released by having the conversations.

I let them know that small steps of adaptation, accommodation for and with each other had huge consequences. They liked that. Sometimes I made a connection between what was happening and the stepfamily architecture, helping normalize what was going on and giving them a quick reminder of the checklist, the challenges I'd given them at the beginning, that they could turn to if they felt confused.

Now that there was enough goodwill and improved communication, we needed to address one of their biggest difficulties: money. It was included in Papernow's "Family Tasks" and "Forging a New Family Culture" because it was essential to find practical ways of addressing it and developing new attitudes.

I started with my take on money. Money is a taboo. It is suffused with silence. Where there is silence, limitless fear grows. We don't know how to talk about money or how it influences and shapes our identity or impacts families. Money can be used as power, status, control. It can be confused with love. We may have a contradictory or ambivalent relationship with it. There can be shame in not having money, and even in having it. We all have a relationship with it, which will be informed by our upbringing and our position in life. As an aside, I remember a client saying, "I'm not interested in money," and my sharp retort: "Only because you have enough. It's a luxury not to have to think about money." There is often the reverse when money is at the centre of everything: in a mindset of scarcity, there is never enough. In stepfamilies it is often the source of the greatest conflict. Battles take place at every angle of the insider–outsider dynamic, in which someone is furious that they are not getting what they believe is their right.

"Not enough!" is the cry. Or "It's not fair!" Money can challenge our deepest human needs for safety, love and to feel important.

I started by asking Paul and Julie what their parents' and grandparents' attitude to money had been. In their different ways, both said they had never talked about it.

Paul scratched his arm, as he was thinking. "I picked up different messages. One was that you should never borrow, always keep to budget and work hard. But it came from a kind of fear that I guess was from my grandparents, who lived through the war and had a 'Watch out, danger ahead. There isn't enough' attitude.

"We're all much better off now, but those days when Julie and I were together, and then with Sam, I felt terror the whole time. There was a kind of crazy hammer drumming in me. Julie was unreachable and I didn't know what to do about not having enough so I hid . . . Yes, that's what I did. I hid." Then, as if a network of understanding had suddenly joined up in him, his face brightened and there were tears in his eyes. "I hid and that was the worst thing for everyone. Oh, God. If only I could have spoken. But I was ashamed. As the man I was failing . . ." Tears were now running down his face. "I'm so sorry . . . I was such a fool . . . An idiot . . ." All of us felt something connect, and a release.

I spoke gently, appreciating Paul's honesty and how healing it felt. For once, Julie didn't speak. She nodded, made sighing noises, and looked at Paul with kindness.

I allowed some space for this to sink in, then turned to Julie. We needed her insight on money too. She was deep in thought as she examined her nails. Her understanding was that they had been "dirt poor," which her mother had tried to block with drink, so the toxic cycle of borrowing, fear and scarcity went on and on. "I guess money makes me angry. Yup, fear and anger . . . I turned some of that on you, Paul, and some of it was from how you were. I can still be triggered if I think there isn't enough. But thank God we're more stable now."

Ashley was interested in this and showed his face. "I am never, ever going to get into debt. I never ever want to go through what

Mum went through." Paul and Julie looked at him lovingly, agreeing with him.

From there the practical organization flowed easily. The well-known "three-pot system" finesses some of these struggles. They contribute equally to one pot to pay for Ashley's and Dan's expenses, divided between household bills, clothes, and extras like birthday celebrations and holidays. They could both afford this, but had their earnings differed by much, a government website works out the proportion to be paid by each parent. The second and third pots are for their own existing families. They would discuss extras for Dan and Ashley and come to an agreement case by case.

To a great extent the poison between them had drained. The telling of their story initially had laid a narrative we could work with. Undoubtedly scars and bruises still existed that could be inflamed again but the attack-dog nature of their relationship had levelled out.

I was curious as to how they had succeeded in their subsequent relationships. Julie answered, "I wanted it more. I wanted to be with Charlie much more than I wanted to be alone, and the big thing for me was I felt he could take care of me . . . It meant I didn't blow up as much, and when I did, he knew how to calm me . . . often by teasing me." As she said this, a warm smile shone across her face.

Research shows that someone who has attachment vulnerabilities, as Julie did, can develop a learnt attachment through a relationship with another person who is more securely attached to them, like Charlie. That he was also financially secure contributed to that. I'd also read research that suggested how you perceive and think about your relationship has a greater influence on its quality than the individuals' characteristics, accounting for as much as 45 percent of your relationship satisfaction; your partner's personality traits account for 5 percent and your own 19 percent. The study's lead author, Samantha Joel, said in the science magazine

Inverse, "Really, it suggests that the person we choose is not nearly as important as the relationship we build." I reflected some of that to Julie and she agreed, with some sadness in her voice: "Yeah, I've been able to give to Charlie, somehow been willing to share myself with him, in a way I had no idea how to do with Paul . . . and he wants it as much as me. He tells me he loves me, wants to work things out. I trust him. Paul and I, we never had a chance."

I saw Ashley's face: he looked sad, swallowed hard. It was tough for him to hear that his mum had never been able to love his dad. I also thought, as difficult as that was, it was good for him to hear her voice it. It had been his experience, but he must have kept wondering what had gone wrong. Was it his fault? Children often blame themselves for their parents' split. Now he had a clearer narrative to make sense of it for himself.

The work we did together was important, facilitated by the fact that the family was not in crisis and both sides had financial security. By choosing to see me, listen fully, their understanding of themselves and each other had grown. They had chosen therapy: their willingness to engage in it helped in allowing change to happen.

It generated mutual empathy, which allowed closer connection as they lowered their defences. We worked with their history of suffering, and they found a way to express a great deal of their distress. In releasing the stress they opened new ground to heal and rebuild their relationship as a separated couple and co-parents. With the knowledge and map of stepfamily architecture, they had a vision to build on. Dan and Dolly needed to be integrated into what had been processed.

The meaning they gave their newly configured relationships not only reflected but shaped how they would behave. We agreed that the children's relationship with their parents would be different, thanks to the therapy, and that might be enough, or there may be more sessions to come that would include them.

Our work continues. We agreed to meet monthly to check in and keep the dialogue alive, oil the wheels until they were confident that their new way of being was embedded. Then we would review and decide what they would need going forward. I believe that relationships need ongoing servicing so I could well imagine meeting every few months for the foreseeable future. It is preventive medicine, the best medicine of all.

The Browne and Francis Family

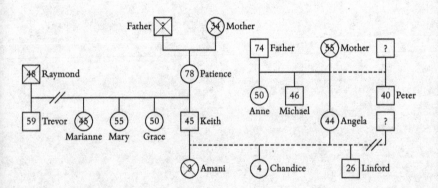

The Browne and Francis Family

*How to live with the consequences of loss, how it influences
and changes family dynamics*

Case conceptualization

*The Browne and Francis family consists of Patience, seventy-eight, a Black
woman, originally from Antigua, whose ex-husband Raymond, had died,
her youngest son, Keith, forty-five, his partner Angela Francis (also of
Black Antiguan heritage) and her son from a previous relationship, Linford,
who is twenty-six. Keith and Angela have a daughter, Chandice, who is
four years old. Five years earlier, their first child, Amani, died of a brain
tumour at the age of three. Patience's oldest daughter, Marianne, had died
of cancer twelve years ago. We met to explore the long-term effects of
Amani's death, which had caused ruptures in both sides of their family.*

Before the pandemic unzipped our lives, I decided to step out of
the comfort zone of my therapy room in Central London to seek
fresh insight. I would travel the geographical and psychological
distance from my world into that of my client.

Early one December morning, I found myself sitting on a
brand-new green sofa in a flat in Peckham, looking at three generations of a family. Patience, the grandmother, sat quietly, her
spine straight, having asked for a cup of weak tea. She was wearing
a well-fitted navy dress and polished shoes. Her eyes were calm as
she surveyed those around her. Her son, Keith, and his partner,
Angela, were moving about getting drinks for us all, chatting jovi-
ally. I knew them from the psychotherapy work we'd done years
earlier, which meant there was ease and warmth between us. Linford, tall and athletic, was munching a breakfast muffin and seemed

surprisingly good-natured, considering the early hour. Chandice was at nursery school.

Amani's death had been an earthquake that devastated the entire family, leaving lasting wounds. For most of us, families are the most important relationship we have—and the most difficult. Under pressure, pre-existing fault lines in families can fracture: tragedy often triggers defensive behaviours, causing people to pull apart. I wanted to understand how this close-knit unit had apparently thrived and grown together, while schisms had formed with their wider family: Keith and Angela had had very little contact with their siblings since Amani's death.

First I wanted to track back to the roots of both of their families. Keith explained how he and Angela had similar heritage. Keith's maternal great-grandfather, John Browne, an Irishman living in London, had gone to Antigua and never left. Aged just seventeen, John's granddaughter, Patience, made the reverse journey. Patience told us that a mere month after she and Raymond had started courting, he had told her he was going to England and, rather audaciously, asked her to join him there. Three days later she had made her decision: "I said yes, and by January 1959 I was here."

As Patience spoke, everyone giggled and I could see in Patience's face an echo of that romantic girl. "I came because I was madly in love with him. I think of the past and I think that man really did love me. I'd never been on a plane or a boat. I flew to New York then boarded the *Ormonde* to England. It took ten days to get here. I was so seasick but I got here all right. It was freezing. Raymond met me at the station with a warm coat. I'd never seen snow before. I cried night and day: 'I want to go home. I want to go home.' But then I said to myself: 'Stop talking about Antigua. This is my home.'"

Patience still lived just around the corner from the room they had first rented from an Irish woman sixty-one years before. As I learnt over time, this was characteristic of Patience's personality: she had courage, and once she had decided on something, she had the determination to see it through. But that might mean there was rigidity in her life. She built strong bonds with people and places, which in turn supported her through the twists and turns of her life.

Angela's lineage was similar. Her great-great-grandfather, Bob, was an Englishman who had prospered in Antigua. She told me, "When you say my name, people automatically assume you're a particular way. I'm sort of proud of it."

Her parents had come to England in the 1950s when her father was sixteen and her mother eighteen. Keith's and Angela's parents had known each other as young adults from Saturday-night dances. I was interested that as a couple they had such similar roots: their identities bridged Antigua and the UK, and they had a secure sense of belonging to where they lived and to each other. Humour was the music that played beneath every interaction. I had never been with a family that laughed as much. As one of them spoke, they would lean towards the others with an invitation to smile, which was instinctively accepted. Humour can be used as a deflection, a way to avoid the discomfort of difficult conversations, and can even feel diminishing. I kept an eye open for defensive laughter, but it was authentic, heartfelt and connected.

Amani's tragic early death had brought Keith and Angela to my door years earlier. I could see how much he'd changed: back then, his eyes were pools of grief; his sagging tracksuit trousers and grey sweatshirt silently screamed his pain. Now, with a closely shaven beard and designer shoes, he appeared full of bounce and cheer. He smiled, turning to look directly at Angela as he described how, as his pain and worry had receded and their lives had improved, Amani's spirit grew in them. When a child dies, parents often hold on to the intensity of their pain because it keeps the child close. For Angela and Keith, Amani was more alive in them as their pain receded, which freed them to seek more joy in their lives.

They had been sufficiently buoyed to go on holiday, a first-time visit to Antigua, and Keith believed the trip, the previous winter, had been pivotal. He was now stronger because he felt Amani urging him on, saying, "Go out and enjoy yourself." As Angela reached out to touch my arm, with tears in her eyes, I could see it wasn't quite so clear to her: "Sometimes I'm fine. Sometimes I'm guilty." At that point, it seemed to me that Keith was the central force in the family, his energy radiating to everyone else. I was keen to see if I was right, if his healing was reflected in the rest of the family.

I asked Patience what her experience had been of witnessing her son's grief while she was grieving the death of her granddaughter. Patience sat upright, her hands crossed on her lap, as she recalled her delight that Keith had finally become a father. Then her voice lowered and there was a pause: it required courage to say Amani's name, which was associated with so much grief. I noted that its origin must have had particular meaning for them: it translates as "peace" from Kiswahili.

Patience held herself still as she stepped back into their tragedy. A few months after Amani's birth, she had noticed that Amani wasn't as bubbly or alert as a baby of that age should have been. Keith interjected that his mother was a nurse. The outrage that Patience still felt, all these years later, reverberated in her voice as she described taking Amani on countless trips to their GP and the ER, each time being dismissed with advice to give her Tylenol. We didn't discuss this at the time, but it is important to note that the 2018 MBRRACE-UK Embrace report (Knight et al., 2020) found that Black women are five times more likely to die in the postpartum period than others. This disparity is also present in the US and likely the same in Canada, although the available data is limited.

Keith and Angela kept banging on doors until, finally, they were granted an appointment with a consultant who, on seeing Amani, immediately diagnosed that something was seriously wrong with her. Following a brain scan, they received the devastating news that Amani had a brain tumour. As Patience spoke, Angela, who'd been silently crying throughout our conversation, started shaking. I checked whether it was too much for her, but she shook her head: she wanted Patience to continue.

Amani's treatment in hospital over the next three years was brutal. Although there were times of remission, she never fully recovered. As most families do, they had hoped against all the odds that she would survive, fearful that any lessening of their hope and belief might hasten her death. Patience spoke slowly: "Towards the end of her life she couldn't walk or talk or do anything for herself. When she died I thought I was going to die of a broken heart. I held her in my arms and she dribbled into my cardigan. I have never washed it since. I hated seeing her in the funeral parlour. She was only three years old . . . I thought I'd never get over it. She was my little angel. I didn't want to live without her. But I had to pick myself up. In my flat I can see her sometimes, looking at me, talking to me. We always remember her, never ever forget her."

As Patience spoke, her devastation reverberated around the room. Angela sobbed. I acknowledged how raw it was for Angela and she said, "I can play back every minute as she describes it. I can see it like a film. When she passed away I thought, Who am I now? Who do I fight for now?"

When I thought about this afterwards, I was interested that Angela struggled with her loss of purpose and deep guilt. Patience was grieving not only the death of her grandchild but the loss of her identity as a protective grandmother, while still grieving the death of her own daughter. I have noticed in my clients that a mother's guilt at the death of their child can be more pervasive than the father's.

Keith spoke up, trying to tilt the conversation back to the positive, as he had when I'd seen him and Angela in the months after Amani's death. He told us how clever she was, how nursing staff adored her and how they fought to look after her. Angela broke in with pride to note, "At her funeral there were masses of staff from the hospital—four hundred people came to it." I felt the power of Keith's pride, without guilt, in their daughter and how Amani lived in him so intensely.

Throughout this discussion, Amani's half-brother, Linford, was silent, as if frozen in his seat. I suggested to him that siblings are often the hidden mourners in a family, that they can be angry that the sick sibling sucks up all the attention, but also feel guilty, as they know it's unfair to blame them. Linford said forcefully that he'd wanted his mother to focus on Amani, that he was all right being independent, but that as Amani had become sicker, "it got kinda hard. I was by myself. Mum was never home. Keith came when he could . . . The day it happened I'd just won a football match. I was on a high. I got the phone call and I dropped the phone and passed out."

Linford described weeks when he'd been saturated with grief. "I may get angry. It's pointless being angry. I call myself out. I'm not going to do anything violent." Angela interceded, talking to Linford in the present, but I intuited this was also from the time Amani died: "He never lets me in. Maybe I'm suffocating him."

Linford looked at her and shook his head. They laughed loudly. In that moment, the depth of their understanding became clear: a question had surfaced and been answered, with eyes meeting, laughter and few words.

I took Linford back to his grief. "Over time I said, 'What can I do?' And slowly I let go."

I needed to check that: it sounded a bit too simple to me. He agreed, reluctantly, and said that when he gets angry he works it out in his head and talks to his two closest friends.

I was sitting near Angela, and opposite Keith, and I noticed that, as Linford spoke, their bodies were stiffening, sadness flowing to anger. I sensed we were moving into difficult territory, out from the epicentre of grief and into its hinterland. More questions revealed that, unlike Linford, there was a bubbling anger they hadn't reconciled. Angela had two brothers, Michael and Peter (one of whom was from a different father), and a sister, Anne. Keith had a brother, Trevor, and two surviving sisters, Mary and Grace.

When Amani's tumour had first been diagnosed, the siblings on both sides had been in touch. But as she grew sicker and then died they disappeared. In Angela's case, there'd been an apparently minor disagreement with her sister, Anne. Her brother, Michael, had even said over Amani's body that he wanted the rift to be over—but Anne had blocked any reconciliation. Angela had seen them a few times since at family events, and they'd tried speaking to her—but she'd ignored them. When I asked if she wanted to reconnect, she said, "No, not really. They are meant to be your family, we grew together . . . I sent them a massive text saying everything. My father and brothers said they wanted the fight to be over but nothing has changed. Keith wrote them a letter asking for them to reconcile—and nothing. My life is good now. I don't want to waste my life being angry about things I can't change."

I told Angela I was confused: on the one hand, she wouldn't speak to her siblings, but by sending that text she seemed to want a resolution. Keith and Angela tried to explain, but I couldn't untangle their conflicting messages. I concluded that probably both were true: they were furious *and* they didn't want the rift. Later in our therapy, Angela said she believed her father to be "an absentee dad," who focused on his own needs and avoided conflict. I wondered whether, if he'd stepped in to attempt to resolve the rift, the outcome might have been different. I believe parents of adult children, if they are trusted, hold a great deal of power.

I had left them that day feeling optimistic, confident I would unravel the ambivalence in Angela's sibling relationships over further sessions—even imagining that, perhaps, I would be able to broker reconciliation. I didn't quite picture myself as a saviour, but possibly something quite close to it, which is always an error for a therapist—and particularly so here, with the complicating layer of white-saviour complex.

Over time, though, I realized I was wrong: as I write this, no reconciliation is in the offing. Angela often talked about her sister and brothers. She told me that her brother Michael had fallen out with his own daughter, and now he barely spoke to her—but also barred the daughter from being close to Angela. Angela spoke with energy: "I don't want to know them any more. They are a headache—they are rude, obnoxious and frustrating." Then, more sadly, "Since my mum's death, it's Anne who rules my brothers. They have to choose between us. She will cut them off if they are in contact with me."

Keith added, "You look like your mum and they hate you for that."

Angela responded, "Nothing I can do about my face—my sister looks like my dad."

That is one of the snares of family: it is the only relationship we cannot leave, however much we might like to. Our family is a part of us genetically and in our deepest being, whether we see each other or not. It may well be the right call for now that Angela and her siblings don't reconcile: there has been too much hurt to overcome. But she cannot be free of them in the same way she could end most other relationships. In family rifts there is always a lasting bruise.

Yet families can—and have—reconciled after terrible hurt and conflict as seemingly intractable as this one. I hoped that, when there was more emotional energy to acknowledge each person's part in the conflict, and to appreciate each other's experience, this might allow the possibility for reconnection.

Keith's family was equally complex. He was the youngest child, and Patience's favourite: "I do love them all, but you get more attached to one than the other because of who they are . . . Keith is so good to me. He's like my right hand. I don't know what I'd do without him." She didn't trust the others in the same way. Keith described different incidents of jealousy from his siblings—particularly when Patience let them know she wanted to be buried next to Amani, not her husband or daughter, and that she wanted Keith to be in charge of all the arrangements.

Keith added, "I'm the only one with the key to her papers."

At the same time, Patience said she didn't understand why there was this rift between them, that "We are all one family. We should live as one family, not 'You are number one'—everyone is number one."

I challenged her—Keith was clearly her number one: I told her that favouritism can undermine, even poison sibling relationships.

Keith wanted unity. He was sitting on the floor, in a yoga position—he'd read how bad constantly sitting in chairs was—but spoke out passionately: "There's a plinth that's big enough for all of us, but I'm the only one standing on it . . . I could help them up." I could hear his sad confusion as he spoke about them, how close they had all been, telling me: "I want to have the answer, and I don't have it." Yet, as ever with Keith, he veered towards hope. Perhaps his default positivity required less energy than questioning whether their grief had broken open and destabilized pre-existing family dynamics. That was too heavy to face right now.

As an aside I asked Linford what he thought about Keith's sibling dynamics and he said, "I didn't know all this. It's quite like . . . wow . . . but, yeah, I can see it."

A bubble popped up in my head. "We can live in a family and not know our family."

When Linford nodded, everyone laughed. I began to see their laughter was a recognized signal of acknowledgement: Aha, that's how it is.

The next time we met I saw half of Patience and Keith's faces—but all of their mirror and sofa. The pandemic had forced us on to screens. Neither of them had video-called before and, despite instruction from me—which included my exasperated "You are utterly useless with technology!"—I never succeeded in seeing their faces in full. My impatient exclamations drew gales of laughter from everyone.

I was happy to hear they were all healthy and doing well. Angela looked younger than usual without her work make-up, hoop earrings peeking out from under long braids, which lay loosely on her small frame. Chandice was chatty and friendly, prancing about happily to the music from *Frozen*. She told me she didn't miss her school, and loved being at home with her parents dancing attendance. Keith commented: "I could cry with the gratitude and joy she brings me."

Linford was wandering in and out of the kitchen playing on his phone. This informal domestic scene, the opposite of most therapy appointments, was the backdrop of our sessions to come. In some ways it gave me a clearer view of their lives and the dynamics between them, though it also gave them the freedom to be distracted from the therapy.

Above all else, a deep-seated, all-encompassing sense of goodwill for each other travelled across cyberspace. They were knitted together by warm amusement. At a time when the world felt Covid-bleak, I felt my well-being lifted by being with them.

Lockdown gave Keith the chance to catch up on DIY jobs while Angela, petite but strong, was busy in the garden, digging, weeding, planting. She'd discovered her creative side. Patience told us that she went out into her front garden once a day, and kept busy with housework, secure in the knowledge that Keith and all of her children dropped by regularly to bring her shopping and help her. "It's pretty simple," Keith explained. "I change a light bulb, give her her prescription, we have a hug—all done." Linford, who, at the beginning, had revelled in the break from work, spent his time doing a twenty-eight-day exercise challenge and playing online games. They all seemed cheerful.

I wondered about their financial position. Patience lived off her pension. As a taxi driver, Keith's income had disappeared overnight— but he'd managed to recoup a quarter of his earnings by driving essential workers, organizing a bank loan and negotiating rent relief with their landlord. Angela, a nursery-school teacher, had been furloughed, as had Linford, from his job as a sous-chef at a high-end restaurant. We could have spent the whole session talking about the infuriating minutiae of the new normal, but I was keen to find out more about Keith's sibling relationships. I wanted to understand the root of their rupture, which I sensed, by the more open tone of his discourse, held the possibility of reconciliation.

Keith opened it up for me with a question: "We used to have so much fun with nothing. We had this unique bond. There was no money but everyone was together, no one left behind. Now we've gone our separate ways. How did we come from so much happiness with so little to so much sadness with so much?"

I felt my heart sting. I told Keith that, although we might not find an absolute answer, we might reach a point of understanding.

Through a number of sessions, we succeeded in piecing together that understanding. It was twofold, and connected. First, Keith's sister Grace had introduced Patience to the Jehovah's Witnesses. Second, Grace hadn't helped Keith at all during Amani's illness or afterwards—particularly financially. For Keith, it was an ultimate betrayal and hypocritical: as devout Christians, how could they have left him to struggle alone?

This was how it unfolded in our sessions. Three months after Amani died, Patience was distraught, and prayed every night, but "God wasn't listening." A Roman Catholic, who had been to a strict Catholic school in Antigua, she had brought up all her children in the same faith, and, to respect her, they in turn had brought up their children as Catholics. Patience told me that one day, during this intense suffering, her daughter Grace had suggested she join her at the Kingdom Hall, the Jehovah's Witnesses' meeting place. "What I heard them say that Sunday made me stop and think. I knew then it was for me. From that day I became a Jehovah's Witness and I'm quite happy with it." She said this in a tone that brooked no further discussion.

I could see that Keith, who was by now pacing around, sometimes out of view, would not take this quietly. "We're happy for you, Mum, but imagine how it felt to us. You were our leader, and now that leader has gone and we are lost sheep. How come you are a Jehovah's Witness? Mum, you were the most Christmassy person in the world. [Jehovah's Witnesses do not celebrate Christmas.] You used to start preparations in November, and now we don't know what to do with Christmas and you sit with your arms crossed. Is it an unconscious need to suffer because your granddaughter died?"

As Patience was straightening her back and raising her chin to answer, Chandice, who had been singing quietly to herself, piped up: "When is Amani coming back? Is she going to come to my birthday party?"

There was complete silence from us all. Even I, the death expert, hadn't seen that coming. Clearly shaken, Angela replied, "She's in Heaven, darling. She can't come to your party," and took her into the garden. The others looked at me. Patience said very slowly, with tears in her eyes, "A few months ago she grabbed my hand and said, 'Nanny, Nanny, I'm scared. I don't want to die.' What shall we do?"

I explained they needed first to check Chandice's understanding about Amani. Heaven can mean many things to a child, all unrelated to the permanence of death. It could be a hamburger joint or the name of a doll. I told them that Chandice needs to know that Amani has died, using that word, as hard as it is to say, and that she isn't coming back. She needs to know the same truth as all the adults around her: what she doesn't know she will make up and what she makes up will be more frightening than the truth. They breathed heavily, relieved to have guidance. We agreed we would continue the conversation about Patience becoming a Jehovah's Witness the next time we met.

It had been an intense session and I could feel the tightness in my body when the call ended. One of the myriad thoughts circling in my head was: How often does that happen? The enormity and shock of Amani's death, five years earlier, had cut through everything, silencing us all. It felt as if she had been given her place in that family system; in that silence was the acknowledgement that she had died, yes, but was always present in their hearts. I also wondered if Chandice's question was an example of what often happened in the family: painful issues were avoided by the need to care for children. So often the busyness of childcare or other tasks are used as an anaesthetic to grief, which, of course, blocks the grief from its natural adaptive process.

In our next session Patience explained that her mother had died when she was young and she was brought up by her devoutly Catholic grandmother. I took this to mean that, in some way, the Church was a key figure of attachment for a bereaved young child. "I was shown all the statues in the church by the priest and told to pray to Mary. When I was a child I didn't know any better. But I know different now. The only one who can help us is Jesus. I'm happier because the Bible has been explained to me. People say I'm silly but it has helped me." I commented that perhaps having faith in something bigger than human life was the only thing that could have helped her.

"I have been through quite a traumatic time, with the death of my husband and my daughter, and then Amani. I prayed and I prayed. Once, at three in the morning, I believed I could see a man. I didn't see his face, only his back. He was tall and he said to me, 'Patience, you have to change your ways.' I would say it was a visitation from Jesus, and since then I have changed a lot. I would never want to be a Roman Catholic again. This religion is what I want."

In Patience's voice I could hear her unswerving belief in this religion; her belief was so rooted in her it was like solid stakes in the ground, and she refused to discuss it. But Keith wanted her to acknowledge how difficult it had been for the whole family when she had abandoned their faith. In the years since she had converted, he told us, his relationship with all of his siblings had fragmented. He hadn't seen Grace for five years, or spoken to the others. But Patience simply repeated: "I've just said everyone has got their own opinion. It's up to you what you want to commit yourself to—no one is pushing you. All I want is my children to support me being a Jehovah's Witness."

Keith retorted with an anger I hadn't seen before: "My mum puts bad things in a box and prays when she goes to bed it will be better in the morning. All I want is for her to see how she's affected us." I looked at Keith, acknowledged his anger, and told him that, from what I had witnessed, Patience had no capacity to hold in her mind the conflict of her decision and Keith's difficulty with it.

Afterwards I reflected on how differently the generations deal with difficulty. Patience's generation tend to bury it, to forget and move on. It wasn't as if they had many other options: psychoeducation and counselling barely existed. For Keith and Angela, it was much more normal to voice how they felt and, of course, Gen Zs, like Linford, are more likely to report their mental-health concerns. Is one way better than the others? I'm a therapist, I'm biased, so, yes, I believe emotions are signals of information that we need to acknowledge and allow to flow through us. It is often the things we do to block those feelings that perpetuate the harm: unblocked, they allow us to adapt and change.

Patience wanted her feelings to be validated, but couldn't quite do the same for Keith, which made him angry. She couldn't recognize that her other children might have valid feelings of jealousy about her favouritism.

I believe there is something we can learn here: we need to be able to name and express what we feel to the significant people in our lives, as well as have the mettle to keep going, whatever life might throw at us.

It was Linford who began to build a bridge across the chasm. He said he knew everyone was shocked when Patience had become a Jehovah's Witness, but that he understood her perspective because he had converted to Islam when he was younger. He suggested that coming together for the Christmas meal was the linchpin connecting them all. It wasn't their different faiths that had caused the problem: it was that they no longer sat around a table together. There had been a spirit at the Christmas meal that welcomed everyone, gave them a sense of belonging which endured through the year. Since his grandmother could no longer do it, perhaps it was Keith's turn to be Mr Christmas.

Keith was nodding when Angela wondered aloud if Patience recognized that she was the leader in the family. Patience smiled. She knew, and she loved them as much as ever, and nothing had changed in that respect. Angela piped up, "I think they miss Christmas, Mum."

Again, Linford made the pivotal suggestion: "I feel we should make a day, any day, because everyone has a problem if it's called Christmas when so many of us have a different religion. What we need is it to be all together, catching up with each other. We can call it Togetherness Day—or Browne Day." Everyone laughed. Their familial signal of relief and agreement.

But Keith couldn't leave it there. He pushed Patience one more time to take responsibility for the hurt she had caused. Keith was distressed because the chasm with his sister Grace had not been mended, and his mother had not validated his anger that she'd changed religion. He also felt church was a sham: he had gone every week and it had not helped him at all when Amani died. Keith let rip his fury, repeating many times over: "When I needed Grace, where was she then? Where was the help? Where was the help? It was nowhere. What's religion doing if you can't help your brother? Where's the God?"

Again, Linford jumped in, suggesting they go to Grace's house and sort it out. It was becoming clear that Linford was an emotional connector and facilitator in the family. It is a vital role. A family needs only one but they can make such a difference.

Angela and Patience echoed the importance of their need to talk. Keith's rage shook us all. Yet it was important he expressed it, because holding on to it would block his ability to heal the rift with Grace.

I was glad we had all witnessed his pain, and that he'd released it enough to speak to Grace from a calmer perspective. Writing in retrospect, I can see now I missed the fact that Patience temporarily became part of the problem in not allowing Keith's perspective, which might have led the family towards reconciliation. Perhaps I, too, had been in thrall to her quiet power.

Therapy does not happen in a vacuum. Political and societal events affect people personally, and therefore in therapy. Racism has a direct impact on mental health. One of our sessions took place a week after Derek Chauvin, a white police officer in Minneapolis, murdered George Floyd, a Black man, while arresting him. I asked them all what they thought of the resurgence of the Black Lives Matter movement: did they see it as a real momentum for change in active anti-racism? Patience said she wasn't following it, yet commented, "But I don't like the violence." Patience had a clear sense of right and wrong. She continued, "I don't know the reason why people discriminate against Black people. We are not a problem to anyone. Everything bad that happens, it's Black people who get the blame. When I was working I had quite a bit of experience with patients who said, 'I don't want you to touch me.' I would say, 'Who's going to look after you then?' I would treat them with respect. After that they would calm down and say, 'Hello, how are you?'" In a more reflective tone, as she looked out of her window, she said, "It has changed. A Black child can go to a White child's home and vice versa. In my day they'd bang the door in your face." There was silence, as we took in the brutality of her words. I felt that sticky sense of shame in my gut. She didn't seem to notice. Looking out of the window again, a memory sparked brightness in her eyes: "Keith's best friend was a White Irish boy."

Keith put in: "Yes, my best friend was from an Irish family. It was the 1970s and you'd still see the odd sign that said, 'No Blacks, No Irish, No Dogs.'" Keith laughed. "We'd walk our dog, and giggle."

I wanted to ask why he wasn't angry, recalling that huge insult, but Patience intervened: "One of my very good friends was White. I went to her funeral and I was really welcomed. No one looked at me, 'Who is she?' Everyone came over to my table."

Keith interrupted his mum. "I think we didn't really appreciate how difficult it was for my mum and dad. They saw the sharp end of it and my sisters as well. My elder sister, Mary, told me name-calling was common, but her teachers didn't take any action to stop it or protect her. My sisters, strangely enough, were also discriminated against by darker children for not being dark enough. My mum never talked about race—nothing in the house made us feel 'Black'. The message was 'Get your head down, be respectful to others, get on with life, get your school-work done.' We all had the same problems regardless of ethnicity. Mum never let us think we should be against White people. My mum and dad carried so much respect—when my friends saw them coming quarter of a mile down the road they'd say, 'The Brownes are coming, no messing around.'"

For Angela it was different: she had been in the minority. "When I went to primary school, there was me and one other Black girl and two mixed-race girls, and that was it. Secondary school, there were about thirty people who were Black. We hung out together. But when Linford went to school, seventy-five percent of them were Black. It was, like, wow, where did they come from?"

I wondered whether she experienced racism at school. She told me, "A little bit—just one or two people in primary school." I was surprised she treated it lightly, like Keith and Patience, and wondered why it didn't hurt her deeply. Angela was clear in her response: "I had a big sister who would protect me. I never fell out with anyone at school. But I think BLM is good to raise awareness. We need change. I don't agree with the way they've done it. Now people look at me differently, as if I'm going to kick off. Now people look at me because I'm Black. And I'm thinking I'm just me."

Keith added, "It's a really interesting time. I forget about it and then I watch the soccer and I'm so excited. Everyone's shirt says 'BLM'. But I don't support people who pull down statues. The message gets lost in the violence. We can recognize the horror that happened in the past, but you can't tear down the past. We've all benefited in some way from those bad things. But people like Marcus Rashford make a positive difference. Maybe people didn't realize before the things we had to go through on a daily basis."

I wished I'd been in the room with them all. This was such a complex subject, which brought up powerful feelings, and I knew that the screen filtered out some of it. But I grasped their general alignment with each other. A kaleidoscope of thoughts circled in my mind. As a White person, who has never had to overcome the prejudicial barrier of my skin colour, I felt guilt for the wrongs of the society that I was a part of, ashamed of my own unconscious bias. This family seemed to have confidence in their racial identity and little overt anger over the racism they had experienced. Had they assimilated, been "colour-blind" (not acknowledged their Blackness), kept their heads down to avoid racism? And how had that seeped into who they were and how they dealt with strife and loss?

I thought Linford might bring contemporary views that reflected those we had heard in the demonstrations. He started, "I'm not the biggest activist." He'd had lots of discussions with his friends who were excited by it, but when they asked him to join them, he didn't go. When I wondered why, he dropped his head. There was a weighted silence. When I pushed, he swallowed his words, saying, "I will tell you another time." I made a mental note to return to the subject at a later date. Linford went on to say that he had experienced racism: "When I was thirteen I was walking down the street with a friend and a cheeseburger was thrown at me with yells of abuse. It hit the back of my neck." He put his hand to his neck. I shuddered with disgust. Linford nodded. "Yeah, it was bad." But I felt the thing he hadn't wanted to talk about blocked his full engagement with his experience of racism.

A few weeks later I asked Linford whether he was ready to talk. Faltering between words, and not looking his mother in the eye, he told me, "I had a drunken night and hit this guy in the eye. I was arrested. I was booked for ABH [actual bodily harm]. It was a terrible time. It took eighteen months with lots of court appearances. I was terrified I was going to jail and I got pretty depressed. In the end I got a suspended sentence and had to do community service."

I was clenching my teeth as he talked, looking at the fear in his eyes, aware of his quickened breath. Patience sighed a lot; Keith and Angela kept their affectionate gaze directly on Linford. I let him know how much I felt for him, recognizing how one drunken action had had such devastating consequences. Linford lifted his eyes and looked at his mother, acknowledging that she had motivated him to get into a good routine, and the structure gave him safety. His manager at work had stood by him throughout the whole process, helping him to find his confidence again. A huge smile lit up his face. "I love that place. I'm going to smash it when I go back."

It showed me yet again that it isn't what happens to you that defines your outcome, but how you respond to it. In Linford's case, his fear shut him down. It was the active support of his family, and his manager's belief in him, that enabled him to pick himself up. People need people. We need them in the good times, but we particularly need them in the bad.

And, in this family, Linford was an important force. His suggestion, weeks earlier, that they start talking to heal the rift with the wider family was bearing fruit. Patience had spoken to all her children, telling them, "This has to stop. There was a closeness you all had. I don't know what happened, but it's not right you brothers and sisters being against each other." As she repeated what she'd said, she took a deep breath and gave me the beady look she reserved for important moments. "And things have changed. It's a lot better."

It was fascinating to witness the power Patience had to influence her grown-up children. They respected her words. Everyone had been in touch with each other and was slowly rebuilding a connection. I smiled. "There is certainly mystery and magic in families," I said. "Sometimes you have no idea why a family has still not spoken to each other for decades, fighting over their inherited vase, and at other times, families reconcile after deep rifts with just a prompt from their mother." Emotional systems don't function logically. There is no point in trying to make them do so. Yet those ever-present familial bonds can offer the possibility of hope.

Keith knew their relationship was changing because, for the first time in years, they'd all had dinner in his brother's garden. "I have received apologies since then. It's worked out in the way I would have hoped. Grace apologized and Trevor said things he's wanted to say for years. It was like the dinners we used to have in the past." Keith's face lit up. "It means a lot to me that we've found a way to bring us back together. The love is inside us."

I felt the thud of joy to witness in their faces the relief that their family bond was being rekindled. As I reflected about the speed of their reconnection, I saw that the foundations of their mutual trust and affection for each other had been laid down throughout their childhood. This wasn't a dysfunctional family with toxic relationships. The schism had been caused by the trauma of Amani's death, following Marianne's (Keith's sister), the siblings' inability to support Keith, the pre-existing rivalry for Patience's attention, then Patience's new religion, which had ended their annual Christmas gathering. It was the time and effort from everyone that enabled their reconciliation.

I was interested at how important that one meal was in keeping their family united. Patience's care and attention for the benefit of them all contrasted starkly with Angela's family: her father had said he wanted them to repair their differences but had done nothing. Families require our time and attention to keep them on track. Silence often builds roadblocks.

And it might have been that Linford's role as mediator had given him the strength and assurance to strike out on his own. One day, seemingly randomly—you could call it therapist's intuition—I asked why he was still living at home. He laughed and said he had moved out before, but when Amani died he'd come back to help his mother, and somehow he'd stayed. I saw Keith and Angela glance at each other and asked them what that look meant. They laughed. They always laughed. Angela said, with some force, that it was time Linford lived on his own, and Linford retorted, "You'd miss me!" To which Angela speedily said, "Only a tiny bit." Then more giggling, Linford repeating many times, "Only a tiny bit," Patience smiling but staying quiet. I could see something shifted in Linford, and an I'll-show-you look stole across his face.

The next time we met he had just moved into his new flat. Bursting with pride, he said he'd found it pretty quickly. He and his girlfriend had a room in a flat they shared with two others. It was fresh and clean. Moving the lens of his camera, he showed me his room with such excitement that I could feel his happiness. It was an important step.

★

At the end of the session before our summer break Keith mentioned lightly, "I was seven when Mum and Dad separated."

I didn't say anything: I was too surprised. Everything I'd heard up to that point had led me to believe that Raymond and Patience's marriage had been long and happy. I knew from experience that a client may often leave "a bombshell" at the end of a session. In the profession it's called the "door handle drop." They want the therapist to have the information, but can't face dealing with it at the point of disclosure.

Our delight in seeing each other after the summer holiday was almost palpable. I was touched that Chandice was often the first person to speak to me at the beginning of a session, treating me like a family friend, saying, "Hello, Julia," as she jumped up and down on the sofa next to her mother. She asked me when my birthday was, and reeled off a list of everyone's birthdays, of course giving her own special attention. I remember being told when I was training that you can't fool the under-fours. With Chandice this seemed particularly true. This energetic much-beloved child did not miss a beat. She not only picked up on everyone's mood but instinctively knew how to get her needs met and when to amuse herself.

I started the session with my confusion about Patience and Raymond's divorce. Patience's voice was thoughtful as she recalled, "In the beginning of our marriage, everything was beautiful. I don't know what changed it. Suddenly everything went downhill. He was off drinking, laughing when I challenged him, pretending everything was all fine when it wasn't. I said, 'You have to do your responsibility, the children are our priority.' I said that for years, gave him lots of chances. But he didn't. It was too much for me . . ."

Keith explained further that his father's job was on a street with a bookmaker on one side and a pub on the other. The drinking and the gambling derailed him. "He had a couple of small wins. He thought if he had another he'd make everything right."

The opposite was true. It was clear how tough it was for Patience as a single working mother: "I had to make sure the children were safe, got to school at the right time, home at the right time, food on the table . . . but it was better than the chaos of his disappearance and having him in my brain."

For Keith, the happy rhythm of his early childhood was shattered. They'd had to sell their house. He didn't see his father for five years—until, out of the blue, Raymond came to visit him at secondary school. "After that, I used to go and see him, and got to know him. By then he'd had a heart attack. He was half the man he'd been, broken-hearted. Mum meant the world to him, but he knew he'd messed up and never said a bad word about her. Mary and I kept an eye on him. Mum cooked Saturday soup for him every week. But she never saw him. He had another heart attack and lost his speech, but he was always funny."

Keith's tone shifted as if his whole being was immersed in the memory of when his father was very ill, and had decided he didn't want to die alone in his flat in the UK : he wanted to go home to Antigua. "Before he left, we all got together. Mum came, and they had this lovely dance. It was really beautiful to see them dancing."

Tears came to my eyes. I could feel their love for Raymond, how much his love and laughter had given them, the sadness and the waste that he'd "messed up."

Divorce can set in train many bad outcomes for children. It's normally not the divorce itself but its consequences: poverty, parental acrimony and alienation. Often the adult children of divorced parents talk about it as the end of their childhood. We know fathers are important for the development and well-being of their children; what is less known is that they fare better when they continue to parent their children. Raymond had suffered. This wasn't true for Keith, who showed no lasting hurt at his parents' divorce. I was reminded of how important communities are in raising a child. Keith had his community: his very present loving mother, his older siblings and their partners, who all parented him.

To avoid the racial stereotypes about absent Black fathers, I turned to psychologist Guilaine Kinouani's *Living While Black*, which cites a study showing that "Black fathers do in fact live with their children (2.5 million versus 1.7 million who don't). And that, regardless of living arrangements, Black fathers are among the most involved in the life of their children."

I asked if Patience had had any other partners. She'd had one, for a couple of years, she said, but it hadn't worked out because he was a womanizer. She spoke of him lightly, as if the relationship had made no mark on her. "I've been on my own ever since. Must be thirty years now." With sadness, I understood that her only love had been Raymond. I felt our mood lower, aware of the layers of loss that could never be recovered.

Usually I encourage my clients to express their hurt, as a way to heal, to grieve the living loss. But I instinctively felt that would have been wrong in this case. With regard to the men who had disappointed and left them, the family felt only a pragmatic acceptance. Patience set the tone: she was a woman of her time, whose underlying belief was to get on with life, and not make a fuss. And the early happiness of her marriage still sustained her.

I could also see that Raymond remained a significant influence on Keith—for his love, laughter and spark—as well as a model not to emulate. Keith said it most clearly: "I learnt from their mistakes, how hurtful it is when it doesn't work. I can see their strengths, too. I try to be more respectful . . ." He turned to Angela: "I'm committed." Both Keith and Angela recognized they could change the script they'd learnt in their childhood. We can all change those first scripts.

There was a final piece of the Browne family jigsaw that we hadn't discussed: Linford's relationship with his biological dad. No one ever mentioned him. I never learnt his name. I needed to check if he was dead. But, no, he was alive. When I raised it, Angela's body shifted. Normally she leant forward, open and expansive. The minute I raised the question she crossed her arms. Linford paced. Keith and Patience were more relaxed, even curious. Angela's voice slowed: her anger was contained but pervasive. It came across the screen into my body, like a thump. "He was a woman-izer, a drinker, not reliable. We talked about a partnership and I thought I knew who he was—then he just disappeared."

We all let that sink in. Linford spoke next. "I used to think about Dad a lot. Who is this guy? I used to try to imagine him. But once I got to know him . . . Well, I went to find out who he was and found I didn't want to know. He's a drunk. I am furious or sad when I see him. I can't change him so I have to let go. Keith is much more my dad than him. He influences me better."

There was decisiveness in his voice, which I hadn't heard before. This was a subject he had thought long and hard about. I asked him if there was something he wanted his dad to know. Linford laughed. He liked my question. His pent-up anger was released in his final words: "He shouldn't have left my sister's mum [referring to his father's previous partner and their daughter], and, second, he should STOP DRINKING!"

There was a pause and, with a smile, Linford turned to Angela. "Mum wants to murder me sometimes because I look like him and even sound like him."

This took us in a different direction, and opened up an experi-ence that is common in many families with divorced parents. Angela, smiling but adamant, said: "Linford thinks he can be Lin-ford and use his charm, which is like his dad. I want him to be more like me, not 'Do what you like when you like.' One minute I'm his friend, the next I'm his mum."

I found myself jumping to Linford's defence (more protective friend than unbiased therapist—or perhaps he'd reminded me of my son in that moment). "To be fair," I said, "what has he done wrong? He finished his degree, the first in his family to do so, got a job, kept his job, sorted himself through the court case. He's got a flat, he's not drinking, and isn't it great he has a lot of charm?"

Linford, grinning from ear to ear, and confident now that he had an ally in me, burst out, "Mum does exactly the same thing. She switches between playmate and mother. Sometimes I don't come for supper, you're like, 'Come when you're ready.' And the other times it's like I'm not being respectful."

Angela didn't argue, saying, "Fair enough, you're right, but it makes me think you've got to put us first."

Linford countered, "You know I put you first. *Muuum!* You know it. I agree, sometimes you need to correct me. But . . . I'm legendary. It's impossible for me to be like my dad. You brought me up. I have Keith as my dad. People like Keith don't come around very often."

Patience ended the discussion in her inimitable powerful way: "Linford has a bright future."

I believed in him too, a remarkable young man. Linford raised an important issue, the undervalued nurturing role of stepfathers. I believe far too little value and credit are given to them. Also, as our paths are by no means set in stone, the right intervention at the right time can turn a child with a potential poor outcome on to a positive, resilient path.

Our final session focused on what had come to represent the family nexus of conflict: Christmas dinner. Through millennia, families have marked important transitions or seasons. The ritual in each family is unique and influenced by their culture; the familiar pattern of coming together is both celebratory and comforting. Society has lost many of its rituals since it became more secular but Christmas largely remains. And Christmas for the Browne family had more power to hold them together than anyone understood. When Patience could no longer be "Mrs Christmas," the connection between the members began to fragment. Through our conversations, they had agreed to have a celebratory meal. Angela told me, "We were talking about it the other day. 'Mum, come over here, have some dinner, relax and enjoy.' Not call it Christmas."

Patience agreed, "Let's get the ball rolling and be one family. We want to be close to each other."

It was an important moment. An unblocking from the injury of the past. A step into their new way of being together as a family.

They were by no means forgetting the losses and difficulties of the past, but overcoming them to be together.

Families are dynamic living entities that need updating and revising as family members grow, die, change and evolve. I had the privilege of witnessing how the key members of this family reviewed, clarified and shifted their attitudes to enable them to reconcile and function lovingly together.

Our work was done. They all agreed that by talking they understood each other better. Patience said, "It has helped me—and we are close now."

Keith added, "It is so good to know things have improved. Grace rang me on my birthday. I can't tell you how it felt."

Angela said, "We can all see each other's perspective better."

For Linford, "It was madly good."

Having me with them as an outsider enabled them to have the conversations they couldn't have on their own. Their closeness had been blocked by the tragedy of Amani's death. They'd tried to stabilize themselves by suppressing uncomfortable thoughts and feelings, not knowing how to express them without being combative. But that had brought to the surface and intensified pre-existing resentments and rivalries. Crisis does that. The sessions allowed them to be honest about what was difficult, to be angry, vent and reconcile. I believe my role ensured there was equal space for each of the family voices, something that is often blocked by family dynamics and hijacked by the person who shouts the loudest. They were able to recognize each other's views and to let go of their anger. When everyone's voice was given equal merit, they could be more open to new ideas.

It isn't the argument that matters: it's important to air thoughts and feelings that, when suppressed or left to fester, build up to resentments and fixed positions. It's how the fight is conducted. Angela and her siblings, probably lacking the leadership of their father, had not reconciled. Angela had moved her love and attention to those she trusted. The Brownes, led by Patience, didn't attack each other to hurt, or bring up a laundry list of previous misdemeanours: they focused on the present issue. They had the goodwill to listen attentively, not insist on being right, and found a way to reconnect lovingly afterwards. Their fights eventually built closeness and connection.

This was a family that had experienced significant adversity on many levels: untimely deaths, divorce, sibling estrangement, an arrest, many racist attacks. And yet, and yet . . . they thrived. Why? For me, Patience set the pattern. She was the force that transmitted the power for the family to hold together and survive the bad times. Her reliable, predictable love was the bedrock of their lives. Her love seemed to me to protect them from the worst injuries of the racist attacks. Her other qualities—endurance, humour and hope—transmitted to each family member. What she modelled by how she behaved had as much influence as what she said. They trusted her, which enabled them to trust themselves and each other. It had also, paradoxically, caused estrangement in the crisis of Amani's death.

Faith was the source of much of Patience's strength during the tough times.

When we are in intense grief, we get stuck in the ruminating story we tell ourselves. Stretched to breaking point, we have little capacity to incorporate each other's narratives of loss. Each individual will be doing the best they can to cope with their own grief, but without cooperation, the family system can fragment into little islands of pain.

In our sessions, Linford forged the vital link between the family members and their competing points of view. He was the one who reframed their argument and helped them to heal.

When a family is stuck it takes only one person to shift the dynamic, and get it moving again. Often children are in the best position to do this. Without the scar tissue of accumulated losses, they have the elasticity to see things with a fresh pair of eyes, and come up with new solutions.

Wisdom does not only come from experience, but from being supple enough to gain a new perspective.

The wisdom of youth is a much underrated resource.

The Rossi Family

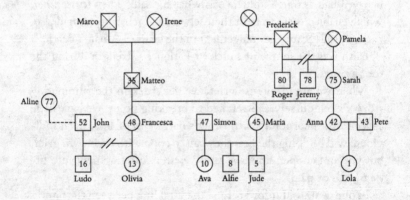

The Rossi Family

How to recover from the long tail of trauma

Case conceptualization

The Rossi family consists of Sarah, seventy-five, a retired physiotherapist, and her three daughters: Francesca, forty-eight, a single mother of two living in Italy and working as a curator in a museum; Maria, forty-five, married and a full-time mother of three; and Anna, forty-two, married and on maternity leave from her work as a nurse. They were practising Catholics, Sarah most particularly a regular churchgoer. Her husband, Matteo, an Italian policeman, died by suicide when the girls were young. Four years ago, when Francesca was in a treatment centre for alcoholism, it became apparent that there were unresolved family issues from his traumatic death, which impelled them to seek family therapy. We met over Zoom.

Suicide is like a cluster bomb. The shards pierce those closest to it, living inside them in the form of grief and trauma until such time as they are located and the injury addressed. Guilt and the repeated "what if" and "why" are but a few of the agonies survivors contend with. Matteo's three daughters had been living with the pain of their father's death for too long. Now, forty years on, they wanted to work through how it had affected them and their mother.

When I first met Sarah I was struck by the power of her voice, which was loud and gravelly. She looked at me through oval spectacles, her thick white hair neatly groomed and held back with a tortoiseshell clip. The message she wanted to convey was clear: "Don't mess with me. I'm strong." As a therapist, I make the assumption that harder defences mask greater vulnerability. I soon learnt that Sarah's carapace of protection was in place for good reason.

When I first meet a client I ask myself: how did she get to be this way? Sarah told me her story. Her early life had not been easy. She was the youngest and only daughter of three children in a middle-class family in York. Her father was a GP, and her mother had been a nurse until she gave up work when her children were born. But her father had strayed with her mother's best friend, resulting in a vicious divorce. Sarah was just seven. I was shocked to hear that, in the divorce settlement, the children were split between the two parents, as if they were chattels. One brother went to live permanently with their father, the other with their mother, while Sarah bounced between the two households, like a ball in a bitter game of ping-pong.

Her voice was uncharacteristically quiet, signifying a reluctance to remember, as she recalled that time: "It was all I knew from such a young age so I didn't question it. But I look back now and wonder what on earth they could have been thinking. The one bit of relief was that I only had to see my elder brother every other week. He intimidated me, treating me like I was this weak and idiotic girl . . . My relationship with him is better today," she added, "but I still get that whoosh of fear when he gives me a look, or speaks in a particular tone."

As Sarah talked, I thought about John Bowlby's attachment theory. At its simplest, it proposes that the primary relationships we have in our early years lay down the patterns that inform and predict how we behave in our future relationships, and how we manage our emotional selves—whether we are secure and robust, or insecure and more fragile. When a trauma happens to someone with insecure attachment, their ability to manage it is diminished as a result of the negative coping mechanisms they learnt early on. It is like an oak tree: one that has deep roots in good fertile ground is better placed to withstand the storms that blow. And it is not just our caregivers who shape us: our siblings influence our development for good and for ill. The contempt of Sarah's brother would have imprinted another layer of fear on her, quick to be ignited by traumatic events.

The divorce left a poisonous wound. Sarah told me, with some force, that divorce nearly seventy years ago held a terrible stigma—as a child she hadn't known anyone whose parents had divorced—which made her feel ostracized and different. This was compounded by the fractious feelings that swirled round her parents' split: the betrayal, the fury, and the price Sarah paid in never having a stable home. Inevitably, as was usual in that era, nothing was discussed. No one recognized the damage that silence was doing: they were expected to continue as if nothing untoward had happened.

Sarah turned to me with a smile that didn't match the hurt in her eyes. "So, for those reasons I always wanted a happy, stable marriage . . . I remember lying in my bed and picturing the lovely family I was going to have, literally that picket-fence-and-roses picture." She continued, with a bitter laugh: "That didn't exactly work out."

I took on board how destabilizing and unpredictable it must have been—ricocheting between her parents, living amid so much unvoiced tension. The overriding rule from both parents was "Don't make a fuss, just keep going," which Sarah did by being efficient and organized. Keeping going was a vital survival skill she needed, and it still worked for her. Looking now at the immaculate face she showed the world, I guessed that perfectionism and control would be among her coping strategies. Certainly, her experiences as a child would have been the unconscious influences that shaped her response to life events as they unfolded.

Unlike her brothers, Sarah didn't go to university: she was a young woman in the late 1960s. After working as a secretary for a number of years, she travelled to Palermo, Sicily, to learn Italian. "I hoped I'd discover the grown-up me," she related, "who felt more confident and happier. I'd been such a quiet, good child. I didn't have a clue as to what I liked or who I was."

In therapy-speak, she was "an adapted child," who only knows what she wants when she is meeting other people's wishes and needs. But you didn't have to scratch Sarah's outside deeply to find the vulnerable child hiding inside. I thought that, although she was in her mid-twenties when she left England, her emotional development was likely to have been interrupted at the time of her parents' divorce. I imagined the abandoned, scared, seven-year-old self could easily be triggered by the barest hint of abandonment.

Sarah blossomed under the Sicilian sun, bathing in her new Italian identity. Unsurprisingly, within six months, she had fallen in love—with Matteo, a young policeman. They had met in the burning air of a summer festival. He was handsome, funny and very attentive. They were engaged within a year. But it was only after they married that she discovered there were two versions of Matteo: the fun-loving charmer and the out-of-control alcoholic.

Within eight years they'd had three daughters, and Matteo's alcoholism had spiralled beyond reach. One afternoon, the female members of the family came home from lunch to no sign of Matteo. That night he shot himself. Sarah returned to England aged thirty-five, a widow, broke, with three traumatically bereaved children.

The focus of our therapy was the consequences of the suicide that had played out dramatically in each of them in the decades since his death. Suicide by no means ends at the death. The legacy of the trauma is wordless and terrifying. It lives in the body and interrupts every aspect of a person's life. It turns gold to lead.

I first spoke to the four women when they were on holiday together in Italy. They'd rented a house near where Matteo's parents had lived, and where they spent every summer. Sarah's three daughters looked across at me, golden-skinned, with smiling brown eyes. Although there was a familial likeness, each had carved out a look of her own. Francesca's hair was white-blonde, cut into a shapely bob; she wore layers of silver and turquoise necklaces and looked as if she worked hard at maintaining her fitness. Maria's long brown hair hung in waves to her shoulders; she gave off an air of precision through aviator spectacles, a white-collared shirt and her trademark damson lipstick. Anna was also a brunette, her hair held back in a scrunchy; she wore big hoop earrings, no make-up, and a linen caftan.

Even through the computer screen I could pick up the buzz of energy the sisters felt at being together. Sarah spoke first, clenching her fist. "I think the feeling was that this might be a good idea for Mother. Maybe she needs a little bit more help."

In speaking about herself as an object, rather than subjectively, I could hear how challenging it was for her to be in therapy with her three daughters. She knew we were meeting to talk about the event that had upended her life, that she'd tried and failed for decades to get over, and that it would be intensely painful. The expression "Time is a healer" is only true if people do the work that enables them to heal. Untouched grief lives on as vividly as it did on the day of the death if it has not been processed, however many years and even decades have passed.

Four years earlier, when Francesca had been admitted to a treatment centre for addiction, it had become clear to all of them, during a family group session, that there remained many unresolved issues arising from Matteo's death. I asked them what they remembered from the group, and Sarah, speaking quietly again, said to her daughters, "Come on, you know better than me. You've got good remembering brains. I do remember I got talked at."

When Francesca shot back, "You didn't get *talked at*," Sarah flinched.

I had the impression that, although Sarah wanted everything to be better, she didn't know how to go about it. What she showed was a kind of boredom with it—"Get on." Beneath the veneer of capability I sensed a tumult of troubling feelings. Above all she was terrified of revisiting the trauma—and it was that which kept her trapped.

They all told me, with a great deal of emotion, that once Matteo's funeral was over, they had not received any support from anyone, neither family nor friends. Sarah said, with understandable anger: "No one listened to me. I didn't get to voice anything." When she'd gone to her doctor for help and advice, he'd merely said, "You're all doing fine. Just keep going and enjoy your children." Sarah took that as the only option available to her: to protect her children, get a roof over their heads, earn enough money to pay for them, and to survive. They all agreed how hard it had been for her, and how vital her fortitude was in creating a home for them. At the time, there had been a dearth of information about, support for or psychological understanding of the needs of bereaved children in general, and suicide in particular. Their family had been thrown on to this devastating alien planet entirely alone.

Francesca, whose face was in shadow, making it hard for me to read, said, "We've never been this direct with Mummy before."

Sarah laughed, as if ambivalent. I sensed Francesca's frustration. The daughters felt they had put in the therapeutic work to deal with their father's death but their mother hadn't. They felt that while she was, as Anna put it, "this very competent, coping, get-on-with-it woman," she was also volatile. "You're angry or cross at one moment, when you're that dominant-parent voice, but the next you're very vulnerable and sort of struggling or weak. Then I feel that Mummy behaves like she's left out, or like we're ganging up on her—like there's an uneven power dynamic and she is the child."

Parents do not like being criticized by their adult children. I'd expected Sarah's response to be indignant and defensive. Instead, she said, "I totally agree and I'm ready now to do a bit more digging and delving. I think whatever's going on in the world at the moment, I feel it's good timing. I have actually had a few chats with Anna about finding a therapist . . . so, yeah, I'd love to be a bit more balanced with these three women. I know they've grown up better than I have . . . That sounds bad, doesn't it?"

Her daughters were pleased. Anna said, giving her a boost, "It's been wonderful to see you getting more confident with your friends."

Sarah smiled. But a few moments later she looked sad, tears in her eyes, and Maria, her middle child, who seemed protective of her mother, said, "I can see you're struggling, and I can't bear it. What can we do?"

I stepped in and said it wasn't for her to do anything: that was my job. It was time for some psychological input. First, I wanted to acknowledge that they were a family who loved each other, and had the goodwill to want to improve their relationship. I added that this was by no means a given. Often the crisis of suicide causes terrible conflict within families, the pain acted out in anger against each other. But they had a level of trust and love that meant they were willing to bear the discomfort, knowing it would be painful and difficult.

Above all, they wanted the truth—all of their different truths. They had lived through the same story together but how it affected them, including their mother, was dependent on their age, their birth order, the roles they took, their genetics and personality type. I wanted them to know I felt huge admiration for their having the courage to face their past trauma. And I reiterated that we would try to connect with what they had felt in their bodies at the time, but maybe didn't have the words for. We succeed as human beings by having a narrative, a story we can tell ourselves about what has happened. None of them—Sarah in particular as the only adult—could have known how to behave, or what they needed.

In this case, it was the forbidden, unacceptable shame of suicide that stalked Matteo's death—particularly as they were Roman Catholics. It wasn't until the early 1970s in Italy that it was permitted for someone who had died by suicide to be buried in consecrated ground.

Sarah was nodding as she said, "I've got to take it a step further. As the girls said, I have had more confidence recently—with friends and even with my brothers, who I was terrified of. I'd become three years old again, but it's more balanced now."

Francesca agreed, but then went back to our previous conversation, pointing out: "I think there's still quite a lot of pain there and, Mum, I don't want to embarrass you, but your tantrums, like yesterday on the beach . . ."

The sisters had been on the beach with their children, hadn't seen their mother behind them and gone off in the opposite direction. She had been very upset, and had what they termed a tantrum.

Sarah responded forcefully that she had been misunderstood. Then she calmed down, explaining that it had triggered the memory of Matteo's abandonment. "I hadn't realized it was my wedding anniversary until later. I went to a terribly painful place. It was deeply, deeply abandonment. I had a cry, which was good—but, darling"—this was said in a cross voice—"I don't want to be flippant, it was enormous." She took a moment to reflect, then added, "I wish I could behave more like an adult—it's embarrassing. That's what you're saying, isn't it?"

I acknowledged that, as painful as it was, her allowing herself to recognize her sense of abandonment and cry for the loss seemed to me an important release. Sarah admitted that she hadn't thought of Matteo's death like that before—as him abandoning her: she'd always tried to defend his honour, telling the world he was "ill." She had not given herself that same protection. I was relieved that she was, at last, beginning to recognize the consequences of his suicide on her. While we hold fixed views, we stay emotionally stuck. Shifting our lens can open us up to new and liberating emotions.

Sarah had taken a first tentative step into the troubles of her past. But her daughters clearly wanted her to keep moving, to open her eyes so that she could see how it affected her behaviour towards them. Observing the four of them on the screen, I noticed telltale signs of their frustration with her: slight frowns and twitchy movements. Maria kept rubbing her nose.

Anna spoke first: "I agree it was much deeper, and it's good Mum expressed herself. But, Mum, we often end up feeling we've wounded you. We don't want to feel like we have to tiptoe around you—particularly when we never intentionally hurt you."

I was midway through saying the feedback Sarah was receiving wasn't critical, when Francesca interrupted: "I think I do mean it critically," she said. "I know that doesn't sound very kind. I just feel, as the eldest, that from such a young age I was managing Mum's feelings, which swung from hurt to anger without much warning. And, in my late forties, I'd love not to be doing that any more . . . I feel like a bad person saying it, but I also really want you to do the work and I want us to be really honest and finally talk about this stuff."

As she spoke I could see the fear in Anna's and Maria's eyes, as to whether their mother would cope. But Sarah said she really was pleased to hear this and, despite the tears in her own eyes, told them she wanted to change. Although she thought of herself as powerless, she had a greater effect on her daughters than she had previously realized. Because she was their parent, and had been unpredictable in the past, her raised eyebrow could send waves of fear through all three of them. Her understanding this felt profoundly important.

Sarah put on a brave face. Despite being shaky she was also feisty, admitting, "I need to be more aware of what I'm saying— but I might just shut up permanently if I have to do that."

I challenged all of them to recognize that this was not about good or bad, or being perfect: it was recalibrating the power between them as adults, being able to be honest with each other, and comfortable with the discomfort it sometimes raised, to trust they can repair their relationship after a fight. All three daughters rallied to her side, saying their own version of "Mum, let's just communicate more, acknowledge when things go wrong, and be OK with it."

Francesca, making the strongest bid to reach her mother, said, "I get to be my authentic self with my sisters, warts and all. Mum, know that you're loved and hilarious and quirky and weird and amazing, and we love you for all of that. The powerful takeaway from us as your children is: raise your eyebrow, be yourself and let's be able to talk about it. Then, hopefully, it will be less painful for all of us." Sarah smiled, flushed and simply said, "Thank you."

This was a good beginning. I was impressed by their courage and honesty, and felt proud that Sarah was up for it. Finding strength by owning her vulnerability was counter to all she knew. The three people she loved most in the world were confronting her with aspects of her behaviour they wanted her to change. They had all been traumatized, and people who have been traumatized see themselves in a different, scary world, and feel helpless. I knew I could help them by slowly building trust between us all, as well as encouraging them to find the things that balanced each of them: therapy, yoga, dance, nature. The cycle of trauma they were in as a family sapped their strength and replaced it with a queasy swill of shame. In voicing it together, some of the poisonous residue was at last being allowed to drain.

It felt like we were forging ahead, releasing all sorts of previously unvoiced thoughts about the family dynamics, particularly between Sarah and her daughters. But we needed to keep going, towards the root of their trauma. Our next session started with Sarah mentioning that a family friend had said something kind about Matteo. It had touched her because, for the first time she could remember, she was happy to hear it—rather than thinking: If only you knew. Francesca, the eldest sibling, responded: "It's lovely to hear someone say something good about Dad. But my memory is that people are always going on about how great he was. I've never heard a single person ask: 'Was it really tough your father was an alcoholic depressive who killed himself?'"

It is true that often those closest to us avoid asking difficult questions—usually because they don't know what to do with the answers, since we think we can't fix other people's pain. It is worth remembering, though, that being empathically alongside someone who is hurting is a gift in itself. A simple way into important and potentially painful conversations is to ask, "Do you have any worries?" Or "What is hurting you?"

Sarah agreed that others never talked about the reality of his death because they didn't want to hear it. She went on, addressing her daughters: "That's what I haven't dared ask. What was it like for you?"

I let her powerful acknowledgement sink in, then asked them, in a tender voice, to tell me what it had been like.

There was silence for a few moments. I could almost feel their shudders. Anna spoke first, saying she didn't really know because she'd been so young. We all cried when she said, "My first three years were his last three years . . . I've often thought, Wasn't I enough for him to want to live?" She went on: she was conscious that it was worst for Francesca, because she saw and remembered everything as "it all went downhill."

Maria added: "I'm desperate to talk about it now. I thought it was normal, that awkwardness talking about anything emotional. We all pretended we didn't mind. I know Dad was fun. I love the jolly stories, and I look at his photograph and he was so handsome— but there are so many gaps. I want the truth, all of it. I'm fed up with it being pushed back."

I was looking at Sarah as she took in her daughters' words. She said they were right to want to talk, and she wanted to, but that there was a lump of fear in her throat. I could see she was gritting her teeth, barely holding on. I asked whether I could help. She smiled and said, no, she just wanted to listen.

They reflected on their father's story: that, as a policeman, he'd been in many violent situations, including one in which he'd shot a man—it must have caused his own trauma. His parents were warm but traditional, and never talked about how they had been traumatized by the war, instead coping with life by drinking and eating vast quantities. Sarah and her daughters agreed that all those bottled-up feelings made them sad, and that they were angry with the other adults in their lives, none of whom had been there in their time of need. It was all about protection.

I was left with another poignant image—of how it had always "stabbed" them to see children with their fathers. I could imagine that dart of pain every time they saw a child holding their father's hand, listening and talking together, hugging. It would have been a constant reminder of the hundreds of missing interactions—the space where their father should have been.

Francesca was smiling as the session ended, looking at her mother, as she said, "It does feel special to be doing this." I thought so, too. They'd voiced feelings and thoughts that had been sitting in their bodies for decades. I knew it was hard for Sarah, and I thought she was learning the power of naming pain: it didn't kill them. Instead it led to healing.

★

Unpacking painful feelings is never a smooth process. Just before the beginning of our next appointment, I learnt that Sarah wasn't well and wouldn't join us. When her daughters came online I could see their different reactions: Francesca was angry—there was still so much she wanted to know from her mother; the other two were worried. Sarah had had a rough spell, during which she felt nauseous and couldn't speak or sleep. She had bad pains in her neck and terrible headaches. The doctor thought perhaps it was long Covid. Anna believed it was everything, including lockdown. Sarah had been completely alone for months, her longed-for winter holiday cancelled. I guessed that, by starting to process it, the long tail of trauma was playing out in her body.

They were relieved that she was now feeling better and, importantly, that she was seeing a therapist and had indicated that she would rejoin us when she had worked through some of her issues, one-to-one, and was feeling more resilient. I pointed out to them that she must be furious with Matteo. Here she was, forty years later, still dealing with the consequences of his suicide. She had stuck around, brought up their children alone, and now she was being challenged by her daughters that she hadn't done it right.

There were still so many questions they wanted answered. Maria wondered why Sarah "always tried to justify why he didn't mention us in the note."

I asked what the note had said. Francesca looked away, remembering, "The hardest thing I ever asked Mum was to see the note. She left it on my bed for me to find and we never discussed it." Anna said how furious she was that he hadn't left a note for them. "I know how profoundly different I'd feel if he'd simply told me he loved me. Perhaps I would have had decent relationships with men."

In a sense, Sarah's absence had unlocked a gate, allowing her daughters to examine the profound and lasting effects of Matteo's suicide. As we talked, they swung between rage and sorrow. I could hear the hurt in Francesca's voice as she said, "We've never discussed the night he died . . . We've got that we went out, we went to bed, Mum found him in the garage . . . I was eight. I didn't know what grief was supposed to look like. Ever since then I've tried to tap into my grief, but I couldn't. I've never had the feelings I'm supposed to have as a grieving child."

I could feel the weight of her sadness and ignorance in my body as she spoke.

Maria and Anna looked at Francesca with a kind of longing in their eyes, willing her to reveal more. But all she could tell them was, "When we got into the car to leave for lunch, Mum was sad and hurt as Dad wasn't coming. He came out to us in the car. He was a hundred percent sober for once. He said, 'I love you.' I thought, That's nice. I do remember it being directed at us all . . . I do remember it being intentional for us all. He was a softie . . ."

Maria lit up, saying she'd never recalled that before, but now she'd heard it from Francesca, "It's totally there and I remember it."

Maria continued, "I remember Mummy crying, and I went to see her, and she said to go to bed and we'd talk about it in the morning . . . But we've never talked about those individual stories together. We didn't talk about going to see his body. We didn't see his body, which we should have done."

Anna joined in: "I remember coming down the stairs and everyone crying, and everyone having lunch, and thinking, I'm going to have chips . . . I remember chocolate buttons . . . Now I feel a bit fluttery and sweaty."

Francesca smiled at her warmly, affirming their memories: "Darling, all that happened."

I encouraged them to pause, and breathe. I asked them to tell me what they were feeling in their bodies. They said they had lumps in their throats, tightness in their chests. Breathing allowed them to metabolize the story they were telling.

I could see Anna crying as she spoke. "This is such huge data to have. Thank God for you. All this is new to me."

Francesca looked at her gently, saying, "Sweetie, he loved you, he loved all of us, and it's really sad . . . I think we were given the narrative that he did it for us—to give us a better life."

Maria agreed, saying that was what she always said to people so they wouldn't feel sorry for her. But now she recognized that "Our life is better because he wasn't around—*and* our life has been shit because he wasn't around." Although it was painful, having a coherent story stopped them continually searching for answers and hitting brick walls of confusion and ignorance.

I told them that bereaved children learn to grieve from what the adults around them model—and in the 1970s the common model was to hide grief, to act like everything was fine, and to protect children from difficult truths. The research of American psychologists, like Professor William Worden, has shown that the reverse is true. Children need to be allowed to grieve. If they aren't told the truth they make up stories, and get stuck in the holes where the truth should have been. Maria said how released she already felt. I reflected that the legacy of suicide had lived so long in them that, by talking, they could be furious with their father for leaving them, and at the same time allow themselves to love him for his good aspects. Keeping silent had bound them to feelings of shame, fury and abandonment.

They ended the session, saying, "Thank God we've got each other," and "This is the silver lining." When they were children, Francesca had stepped into a mothering role—along with their mother—for which Maria and Anna were profoundly grateful. As adults, the dynamic had equalized: it meant they could help the one who was low, disagree with or tease each other, and be able to surf it emotionally. Anna could be feisty. Maria was more the peacemaker but sometimes she challenged Francesca when she would say she was all right. It was clear to me that their love for each other was the bedrock of their lives. Unlike their mother's experience with her brothers, their sibling relationship was deeply nourishing.

A distrust of men. Drinking too much. Hating school. Feeling inferior and different from other children. Terrible sexual encounters. Worrying about money. Feeling scared. These were just some of the difficulties they'd all had to face, which we discussed over the next sessions. They talked of their regrets—and what they had done in the search for love, which they had thought they would never find. Despite their obvious beauty, they felt ugly. They'd all had periods of depression and huge spikes of anxiety, what Anna described as "massive meltdowns."

Maria and Anna felt it was miraculous they had good relationships now, thanks in part to understanding husbands. Francesca described the terrible marriage she had with a "classic narcissist," who was abusive and controlling. She was now a single parent with two teenage children, a state she had never wanted. As she was describing her regret, Maria and Anna leant towards her, raging against her ex, and also their powerlessness to help her.

I suggested they let me support her. I asked her to close her eyes and tell me what she could see. She said, "A little girl, all alone."

"What does that little girl need?" I asked.

"A hug."

"Imagine giving her that hug," I said.

With tears running down her face, Francesca told me: "I feel really uncomfortable . . . I can see Maria, that she needed a hug."

That simple exercise showed she found it almost impossible to turn to herself with compassion: all her attention was focused on her sisters. There was a pause, and in that moment I felt a shift in her as she acknowledged that, saying, "I'm really sad. I've got myself so stuck here. I need to look after myself."

Her sisters burst out, as if they'd been holding their breath, "Yes, yes! You must."

Anna said that, for her part, the difficulty was in knowing the pain her sisters had been through. "When I think of you guys, I get this great wedge of sadness. I love you. I don't know my dad, so I feel more upset about what you went through."

Francesca started to protest, then caught herself, and said: "It didn't feel OK. It was shit."

I asked Francesca what she would say to her younger self. She looked up at the ceiling, speaking slowly and brushing her hair back, as if to reveal the thought. "The reason you're feeling uncertain as to who you are is because you had two adults who weren't emotionally healthy enough to look after you. You must remove the responsibility from yourself. You weren't the weird one . . ." She continued: "I want to say, 'You aren't the wrong one. You are fine as you are, just going through a mucky situation.'"

I could feel the tension release as Francesca began to recognize what had been cutting into her for decades. Maria, with flushed cheeks and tears in her eyes, looked lovingly at her sisters as she said, "Ava [her daughter] asked, 'What was it like when your daddy died?' and I told her: 'Home felt so confusing—full of love during the funeral and then so empty again.' I was hoping after he died that home would continue to feel the love, but it disappeared . . ."

Anna said: "I'm raging hearing all that. I feel so helpless and cross." The level of her rage matched the love she felt for her sisters. I was touched to see how they would turn towards each other, reassuring and connecting, meeting the tragedy with love, and relief that the truth was emerging.

The research about those bereaved by suicide is brutal. Multiple studies have shown that they have a greater likelihood of attempting suicide themselves than those bereaved by other causes, and are at increased risk of several physical and mental health conditions. Dr Alexandra Pitman, from University College London, analysed the causes: shame, the emotional contagion of suicide, the complex unresolved grief and trauma it leaves behind. However, with ongoing support at and after the time of the death, those outcomes are by no means set in stone. Tragically, the Rossi family had had no such support.

It is worth looking back at your family history. Have any past family members died by suicide? Has it meant there is more alcoholism, drug addiction and depression in your family? Addiction has a genetic component, but it is also shaped by our environment, and learning to block feelings by anaesthetizing them—whether by drink or drugs—is often passed down through the generations.

Sarah's continued absence from our sessions enabled her daughters to talk about her more freely, though still with pain. They described again how her mood could turn to fury in a nanosecond, particularly when she was stressed. As Francesca remembered,

"The worst was when I was fifteen and she whacked me across the face, blindsided me. It was the exception to the rule that she hit me. That rage, though . . . I remember thinking, You can't ruin every nice time we have. It's not OK."

Her sisters nodded. They had all tiptoed around their mother, though Francesca felt it the most. She continued: "I don't like her touching me, which I know she finds hard . . . I completely shut down, though I wish I didn't."

I explained to them that their mother's lack of impulse control was directly linked to trauma. The wordless and terrifying nature of trauma means it's hard to stay calm because the fight/flight/ freeze part of the brain is always switched on. It comes from the amygdala, the smoke detector of the brain. In the words of Bessel van der Kolk, one of the world's leading psychologists on trauma, "Thus, they [people who have suffered trauma] are prone to go immediately from stimulus to response without making the necessary psychological assessment of the meaning of what is going on. This makes them prone to freeze, or, alternatively, to overreact and intimidate others in response to minor provocations." In other words, people with post-traumatic stress disorder (PTSD) have high levels of distress stored in the unprocessed memory, and become caught in a toxic cycle of constantly feeling as if they are under threat, despite the innocuous nature of their present.

We agreed that their mother's undiagnosed trauma had caused them all considerable distress. We hoped that the therapy she was finally receiving would release her to live in the present, without the haunting fear of the past. They wanted her to be kinder to herself. All three daughters were optimistic, Francesca saying she'd recently had a better conversation with her mother than she'd had for years.

One of the surprising revelations for Maria was the clarity of a memory that had bothered her for decades: "I had this thing that came back to me that's always been at the back of my head. I remember someone sticking their finger up me as a young child. I didn't understand it. I shut it away. After the session I remembered

being on a doctor's bed. I was alone. I thought why would someone to do that to me? I got myself in a real mess. My husband has
been amazing. I got the doctor's notes, which stated 'rectal examination', but the amazing thing was," tears of relief were running
down her face, "that Francesca remembered. She said, 'Maria,
there was something about your backside. I remember Mummy
being so angry and protective of you that the doctor had done that
to you, and she was on the other side of the curtain without being
told or being with you.'"

Francesca reiterated what she'd remembered, and it was wonderful to see the release in Maria's face as she said, "I can picture it all. As
soon as she said 'backside', I knew I hadn't made it up. It switched
the memory fully on. I feel a million times better. Ooh-ah. Such a
relief." It was a small but powerful vignette of how distressing half-
formed troubling memories can be, and how healing when they are
clarified. It is what we don't know that ends up haunting us. However hard the truth is, it is better than a lie or not knowing.

Our sessions percolated through me between appointments, as the
stories of traumatized clients tend to. When we next met, I suggested that the trauma of their father's death was still in *them*, as
well as in their mother. They had all given me plenty of indica-
tions of how their alert system spun to Code Red at the slightest
provocation. They were hyper-vigilant to avoid threat, and each
had a history of depression, as well as addictive behaviours. I
believed each of them needed to commit to eye movement desensitization and reprocessing therapy. EMDR heals the traumatic
memories of the past by releasing the distress in them. It is physiologically based through the dual attention system: the therapist asks
the client to follow their hand from left to right while asking questions. This switches on our natural adaptive processing and links
our present understanding with the past trauma, which then allows
new information to come to mind and resolve the old problems.

Anna agreed immediately: "I owe myself a good dose of therapy." Maria and Francesca nodded rather more reluctantly—and

then Maria sat up with some force, as if something had clicked. She said: "Trauma and me. I have never put myself in that category." She looked at her hands as she cast her mind back to that six-year-old girl. "I think we play down everything, all the time. We say we're OK. But it's much bigger than we ever let on . . . I lose my voice, it goes shaky. We need to acknowledge we're traumatized."

Maria's sisters appeared to be letting her words land in them. I explained that the therapy we were doing was important and working, but that EMDR would be a game-changer in how they engaged with their lives. It would help them to heal the multiple dysfunctionally stored memories of their father's death and its repercussions, which were being triggered over and over again.

I believed we'd come a long way. They had a more coherent narrative and understanding of their devastating experience, which was curative in itself. The next step would be for them to create a different relationship with their father—and I wondered whether they were ready. My approach to death and grief is that when the person dies they are no longer physically present, and that new reality needs to be grieved while maintaining and sustaining love for the dead person—that love never dies. Grief expert Phyllis Silverman and her colleagues have termed it "continuing bonds."

I asked the Rossi sisters whether they would consider writing to their father, or creating a ritual to remember and connect to him. They could, for example, plant a tree, buy or make something significant that represented him, like a picture, a pot, or a piece of sculpture. They looked at me with open mouths. This was something they had never considered, and about which they were initially reluctant. With tears pouring down her face, Anna responded first: "Hearing you talk about it made me realize I don't feel like his daughter. I don't feel like I had a dad. I couldn't conjure up a sense of relationship with him. I was this non-thing in his life. I don't feel like I've got a claim on him. To think of it in those terms feels so alien to me."

Maria threw up her arms as she said: "What am I going to put on a mood board? We've got the same five photos. They're pretty much all we've got. I don't feel there's anything I have a relationship with. I don't know if I want the plant to live."

I picked up on her anger—relieved she was able to express it.

Francesca was calmer, clearly wanting to comfort her younger sisters. "I feel similarly," she said. "But he was your daddy. He did walk around and play with you, hold you and all of those things. He'd often talk about his three girls. I know he was very absent in his last few years." Then, when I prompted her to speak for herself, she bit her lip. "I felt deep discomfort. I haven't thought of myself as having a relationship with him now—only a pre-death relationship. It would be interesting to try an adult-to-adult relationship with him." Turning her face away from the screen, she continued, "For me, the relationship with him died when he died."

We all sighed. This had been intense. The only relationship she had with him was one of absence—a kind of angry absence. Francesca agreed and, putting her hand on her chin, she reflected more calmly: "I'd like an adult relationship with my father. To hold the distance and hold it separately without the drama, just to think that I have a father, and reframe that through my adult lens without the trauma."

Her sisters laughed slightly hysterically and said, "Yikes!" But I could see they were moved by the idea of continuing bonds, of reframing the relationship with him, even in death, and I was interested to see where it might lead.

If the daughters had found it easier to talk outside their mother's presence, the same was probably true for Sarah. I contacted her to see how she was doing. The sessions with her daughters had been too hard for her, she told me. The high levels of emotion had brought on a major physical response. I wanted to create a bridge with her into the work I was doing with them, and give her an opportunity to air her insights.

I learnt how horrendous those first years of bereavement had been from her perspective: her desolate grief, desperate loneliness, the shame of Matteo's suicide, as well as the huge levels of stress related to parenting alone, working full-time, worrying about money and trying to "put a lid on the past so I could get on." She'd even considered suicide. I was struck that, although what Sarah endured was, of course, unique, there were parallels with her daughters' experiences.

Sarah laughed, somewhat cynically, saying that until I'd told her daughters they were traumatized she'd been "blind to the bloomin' obvious." With a croak in her voice, she said, "I thought I'd dealt with it all, but, ah, maybe I haven't." She was doing good work with her therapist, she told me, slowly addressing her traumatic memories. Although she couldn't bear to hear from "my girls" the things she knew they'd criticized her for, she had many regrets. "I know what I got wrong and, oh, how I wish I'd done it differently! I hate it that I scared them, that I was angry. I wish I'd talked to them more, had birthdays, anniversaries, been more open. I'd like to be that super-calm, collected, fun parent and grandparent—but I'm not."

Her honesty was impressive. It is tough to recognize our failings as a parent, but also essential if the relationship with our adult children is to grow. All of them had paid a huge price for Matteo's death and, inevitably, those she loved most, she hurt most.

We all fail as parents—against the ideal version of ourselves. I reminded Sarah that her daughters were extraordinary, wonderful women, in no small part as a result of how she'd parented them. And that it was not too late to acknowledge past mistakes and change all of their futures. Her daughters didn't want to punish her, but they did want to be able to resolve difficulties without having to tiptoe around her.

She asked me how, saying, "I will always raise my eyebrow . . ." I explained that it's never the ruptures that matter—they're inevitable— but the capacity to repair them afterwards that changes everything. Sarah got it. With a gleam in her eyes, she recalled a moment the previous week with Anna when they'd been a little short with each other. Excitedly, she said, "When we sat and talked about it, I apologized, and she said she was sorry she'd come across as impatient. Then it was fine, straight away." Sarah heaved a sigh as if she had, at last, been given the map of the alien territory into which she'd been thrown all those decades ago. At last she could see the correct route, name what had gone wrong, explain what it meant, apologize if it caused distress, and come together with warmth. I reminded her that reconnection had its own timeframe: it couldn't be hurried.

As an important waymarker on their path to a new relationship with their dead father, I asked Matteo's three daughters to write a description of him. After working on it themselves, Anna introduced it: "These are the things we talked about together that feel important to capture, if possible, about our father. To us these are the events that explain what happened to him but also honour the person he was and why this happened."

They settled on this:

Daddy had a very lonely childhood, his father was constantly away for work.

His childhood was old-fashioned and hard, with high expectations placed on him as an only son—this was a weight he always carried heavily.

He became a police officer, excelling in his exams during training and with a bright future ahead of him. He had a brilliant mind, was quick-witted and was the friend who was always the life and soul of the party . . . while being quite romantic and a bit of a "softie" at heart.

Despite all of this, he carried demons which were compounded by experiences he lived through in the police force, with some significant events in service leading to PTSD. At a time when mental health and addiction were little understood, it all became too much for him, and with financial pressures and his drinking taking hold, he took his own life.

They read it aloud to me, tearful and proud. At last, they had a narrative they trusted and believed in. It included all the important elements: the roots of his psychological fragility, the events that exacerbated it, his brilliance, humour, fun, and how being a man in that era meant he didn't get the help he most urgently needed. It was an important touchstone in their growing and changing relationship with him. I felt a swelling of emotion for their courage.

A work colleague with whom I discussed it made a further point: that writing this letter had helped to shift their perspective of their father. My work with them had been focused on their own pain and suffering, their sense of not being enough to keep him alive. In crafting this narrative, they had a new position, which allowed them to see his suicide more clearly from his perspective, not just their childhood view. It allowed them to recognize the extent to which his suicide related to a longer history of life events, many of which had nothing to do with them, and helped them to see it—and him—with compassion. By writing it down collectively, they freed themselves from the hurt-child perspective in which their memories of him were rooted. When we tell ourselves a different story, we do feel differently about ourselves.

What I have written here, which I shared with all four Rossi women, has become the focus of our ongoing work together. I only do this with clients about whom I write publicly. I have found that reading about their own process can engender catharsis and healing, as they recognize how much they have been "seen" and understood. Digesting it had been tough for all of them, and they'd had to take time over it to integrate their process individually, and together.

Sarah joined us again. I could see immediately, from the way they greeted and smiled at each other, the warmth between them had grown. There seemed to be less tension. They'd met together to discuss what I'd written, and that had been useful. I acknowledged my respect for their courage in facing this.

Sarah spoke first: "For me, the worst thing was hitting Francesca. I have absolutely no memory of it, which is terrible in itself. I'm appalled. I've apologized to Francesca. I've no excuse whatsoever, and I'm horrified." Clearly distressed, she patted her hands together, as though she was clapping but without sound, and swallowed her tears, recalling other times when she hadn't supported her children. Ashamed of and angry with her inability to deal with difficult things, she bit into her thumb and ended by saying to them: "You three are the centre of my world, but I've failed. Your life has been extraordinarily tough and I'm sorry."

I reflected how hard that was for her. Her daughters were tearful and bathed her in warm words. She continued that she was "grateful for the opportunity to say it to you, because I love you."

They all replied that they'd never doubted it. Her energy shifted as she sat more upright in her chair. "It's also a great relief. But it would have been good decades earlier." She told us: "Francesca gave me a long cardigan and told me to think of it as a hug from her. I'm going to go and put it on and have it with a bar of chocolate."

I was pleased to see that she had started to support herself with compassion rather than self-loathing.

Then she talked about something she remembered with pride: just after Matteo's death she'd taken her three small girls to the florist. They'd chosen the flowers and she'd encouraged each of them to write their father a little note. Tapping her fingertips against each other with relief, she said: "And I still have them." Her daughters nodded warmly, agreeing that it was a great thing to have done. It had not been easy for them to criticize their mother, and now it was nice to be able to acknowledge her strengths.

Sarah continued, leading the conversation: "As a family, we want to be more open and honest with each other. It is another step forward to where we can be relaxed and comfortable together. I haven't dared use my voice. I didn't know what to say, or feared I was stupid. I didn't think anyone was listening. But having this is lovely. I now have a strong voice. It's powerful, isn't it?"

I asked her daughters where they were. There was a long silence as they took in these shifts and changes. They agreed that their mother was speaking about her feelings with more confidence, and that the dynamic between them was beginning to evolve. Anna concluded: "It's good to be able to talk about these things and identify the elephants in the room. It means more healthy organic conversations will happen in the future."

Maria added, "I feel completely different. I now feel our conversations can be less forced, more comfortable and relaxed, and that we will have more and more of them." She finished with a big grin.

Francesca, sitting in the dark, so tired from work and life she hadn't even turned the lights on, but still very loving, had the last words: "It's been amazing. Just so powerful. We've all got our own pile of jigsaw-puzzle pieces and, by speaking and creating a bigger picture, we have a shared view we can all see. That's really healing."

Our work was coming to its natural conclusion as they moved into another phase. They would do their individual trauma work with an EMDR therapist, and continue their process of healing and adaptation individually as they stepped into their changed relationships with each other, and with Matteo. There would inevitably be pain ahead, and bumps along the road. But their foundations were robust and I had confidence that they would grow stronger, individually and together. It had been a profound privilege for me to work with them.

All four of the Rossi women's lives had been dominated by the shadow of an unspoken trauma. While, thankfully, taboos around speaking about mental-health issues and suicide are less culturally normative than they were at the time Matteo took his own life, it is still not uncommon for families to remain silent, or at least not to talk enough about past traumas, hoping—mistakenly—that time will heal all.

But time, without the oxygen of communication, can create further damage. There are very real dangers to "looking the other way." Every emotion has an ambition to be heard, and repressed feelings ferment and become increasingly toxic over time. Fantasies and destructive coping mechanisms grow in the gaps. The legacy of this is different for each person, but certain patterns emerge across the board: addiction and anger issues; an inability to trust or form healthy relationships; brittleness and rigidity.

It is never too late to face pain in the past. Great courage is required. Silence forms its own prison. But gentle unlocking releases renewed energy for living.

The Berger Family

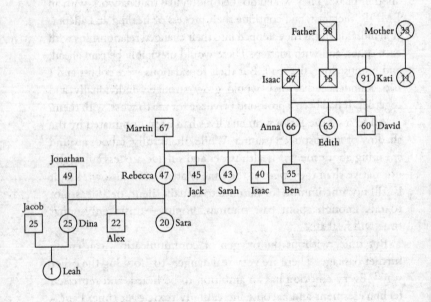

The Berger Family

*How to live with love and without fear in multiple generations,
despite suffering unimaginable trauma*

Case conceptualization

*The Bergers are ultra-Orthodox Jews living in Manchester. At the apex
of the family is Kati, ninety-one, a Holocaust survivor originally from
Hungary. Her husband, Isaac, who died thirty years ago, was also a Holocaust survivor. I worked with four generations of the Berger family: Kati,
her daughter Anna, sixty-six, Anna's daughter Rebecca, forty-seven, and
Rebecca's daughter Dina, who is twenty-five and has an infant daughter of
her own, Leah. It is rare and therefore valuable to have the opportunity to
work with so many generations of one family, and witness what is passed
down from generation to generation.*

Imagine looking at five generations of your own family. It's a
thrilling idea—yet almost impossible to conceive. That was how I
felt when I gazed at a photograph of the Berger women. At the
centre, small but smiling brightly, was Kati, mother, grandmother,
great-grandmother and, now, great-great-grandmother to Leah,
who was sleeping in the arms of Anna, her great-grandmother and
Kati's elder daughter. Anna, with her raven-black hair, brown eyes
and careful make-up, looked into the camera with an expression
of happiness. Standing behind them, also smiling proudly, was
Rebecca, slim, her long auburn hair tied back with a scarf. Her arm
was around her daughter—Kati's great-granddaughter—Dina,
who was taller than her mother, pale, with shy hazel eyes. To my
grandmotherly view, she looked about sixteen, by no means old
enough to be Leah's mother. They were all dressed modestly in

black, with white collars, or embroidered white shirts edged in black, and all wore pearl earrings. From the background, I could see from the photograph they were at a celebration: groups of men sat at tables, dressed smartly in suits, with yarmulkes on their heads. The women laughed in delight when, later, I told them I hadn't realized they were wearing wigs.

Individuals or families usually come to see me because a difficult event has precipitated a crisis in their life, and they need my support to help them come to terms with it. This was not the case with the Berger family. Instead, I had sought them: I had put up a notice on the website of a Jewish organization asking if an Orthodox Jewish family would be willing to contribute to this book. I hoped that working with them would give me a portal into another culture, a community like this one that seemed to live outside modern life.

I had a personal reason for my interest, too. I am married to a Jew, whose Jewish identity is a central part of who he is, and this has made me extra-interested in Jewish history, life, people and culture. I know too well that prejudice blooms in ignorance and difference can be used as a weapon of attack. Conversely, the more we know about each other, the more similarities we find, the greater empathy and understanding we feel. I trusted my relationship with the Berger family would be therapeutic and intimate, even if it was not on a contractual basis, and that it would show the healing power of simply being heard, of having one's story witnessed. I believed that opening up both our worlds would be meaningful for us all.

The dark shadow of genocide still hovers over the lives of many in the ultra-Orthodox Jewish community. For them, the Holocaust was by no means a finite event: it didn't end in 1945 but lives on, embedded in the collective memories of the families of survivors and, indeed, in the wider community of Jews. I was keen to discover how much of this was lived out in the Berger family and what was forgotten, what could be talked about easily and what was taboo. Known for their love of family, I hoped to learn the core elements that create stable and happy families within the Jewish community.

To my delight, Rebecca, a medical secretary who was interested in psychology, contacted me, curious to know more. She suggested this project to her family and, when they realized it wasn't therapy, they were happy to meet me. It's funny how the word "therapy" can be a barrier to many people, while "conversations" are less threatening. I think there is some mythical idea that therapists can get inside your head and somehow force you to face things you don't want to see. This, to me, couldn't be further from the truth: I want to facilitate a trusting, safe relationship in which my clients move at their own pace and find for themselves what they need to face—or not.

Kati was fourteen when her family was unloaded from the wagons at Auschwitz. Seventy-seven years later, she could recall every detail with chilling clarity. "As soon as we got off the wagons, my grandmother, carrying the only thing she'd brought from home, her burial shroud, was taken on a truck somewhere, with quite a few old people. I never saw her again."

She spoke softly, her Hungarian origins still alive in her accent, although she had lived in England for more than seventy years. "From the railway trucks the men and women were separated and we had to march towards Mengele [the Nazi doctor, known as the Angel of Death, who was largely responsible for selecting which of the arriving Jews would go directly to the gas chambers; he later became infamous for his gruesome experiments on human subjects]. I walked with my mother, my sister and brother towards him. Mengele said to them to go to the left and he said to me to go right. I was running after my mother. I wanted to go with them. He pushed me back to the right."

Her voice barely quavered as she recounted what had happened that day. "I remember when he selected us he looked at my ankles. Perhaps he wanted to see if I'm strong. I was fourteen years old, very tall—I didn't look so young. When we were with the people who were unloading us from the wagons they'd told me I should say I'm sixteen or seventeen. I kept saying, 'I'm sixteen.' But Mengele didn't ask my age . . ." She paused, and then, collecting her thoughts, continued, "I read a book, in which someone said the same thing: Mengele looked for strength in the people he selected. My ankles are not small or anything . . ."

There was another pause. "It's unbelievable, impossible to understand. As soon as we got to the barracks I said, 'My mother told me we will see each other in two weeks' time,' and a Polish girl said, 'Your mother is in the smoke.' She was right: my mother, sister and brother died within a short time. There were not many my age. We stayed together, shared everything."

Kati was only a teenager when her entire family was murdered. Before we met, I had assumed I would see expressions of that trauma being played out within the family. I was meeting them as an experienced listener who wanted to understand their story. I had hoped that telling their story would be useful to them. I didn't anticipate quite how devastating it would be to hear it.

A great deal of research shows that, although survivors of the Holocaust don't often talk about their experiences, their suffering is passed down through the generations—intergenerational trauma. The research documents two patterns of transmission from survivors to their children. The first is embodied in the mental illnesses the survivors suffer from as a result of their experiences, which include schizophrenia, depression, anxiety and paranoia. This is transmitted directly to their children in the ways that all parental mental-health disorders impact the next generation: being emotionally unavailable, not providing the secure, reliable love and affection that children need, and regular family discord or threat. The other pattern of secondary transmission comes from the enduring suffering of the parent, which renders them unable to function sufficiently effectively to be a "good enough" parent. For instance, they may be intolerant or unempathic in meeting their child's needs when they are distressed. When this is repeated over time, their child experiences it as neglect or deprivation.

Some research points towards the trauma being passed down epigenetically in the womb. Dr Rachel Yehuda has been a pioneer researcher in this field and said, in 2016, "The message of the study is that we respond to our environments in multiple ways that can have long-lasting, transformative effects. The implications are that what happens to our parents, or perhaps even to our grandparents or previous generations, may help shape who we are on a fundamental molecular level that contributes to our behaviours, beliefs, strengths and vulnerabilities." This is not a specifically "Jewish" study, or problem: it would be as true for the families of 9/11 survivors and veterans returning from conflict. It has far-reaching implications.

I had imagined that, although there was no presenting issue in the Berger family, I would see the many different forms in which the evil events of all those years ago were alive in them today. Before we met I had felt tense, worried that talking about her experiences in Auschwitz might reopen the wounds of trauma. Beneath my awkwardness was my own fear of the unbearable nature of what she would tell me.

But Kati reassured me, her sparkling smile dazzling on the screen: I could ask her anything. Some survivors, like Kati's husband, never talked about the Holocaust. Her composure was extraordinary and belied the horrors she described. As she talked, her daughter Anna and granddaughter Rebecca were crying, dabbing their eyes with tissues. Kati was smaller than them, but had a larger-than-life presence. The way she looked straight at me, unflinching, was powerful.

She continued, "My father worked in the crematorium. They always killed them after a time. He was very brave and he was part of a group that tried blowing up the crematorium with munitions. He was shot."

I had a clear picture of that young girl, whose entire family had been murdered, in a place whose sole mission was to eliminate her race. I didn't know how on earth she'd found the strength to live, and asked her. Kati replied simply: "It's a miracle. I was thinking, if I had been married and had children, it would have been impossible. If your children are murdered, there is no reason to live. If you're young you want to live."

I felt numb. Sitting in my warm office, never having experienced any life threat, I could hear her words but knew I could never understand what she had endured. Remarkably, not only had she survived Auschwitz but the unimaginable travails that followed its evacuation. "The Russians came near, bombing us. The Nazis were afraid the Russians would liberate us so they marched us for six weeks," she explained. "It's known as the Death March. So many of us died. We slept in barns. I was very weak. Sometimes we were given a little potato, a little water. In the factory where I worked filling grenades, there was a Czech girl, and she used to give me a little extra food. Then it was Christmas. The people who were in charge of us wore civilian clothes, not Nazi uniforms. Sometimes they would bring a little cake. I was very young, and every little thing that was extra helped you. I thought I must see the end. That kept me going to survive."

Anna interjected with her own insight: "I learnt on a trip through Poland visiting Jewish historical sites that prisoners were made to turn a heavy wheel, and they worked hard at it—until they were shown they were turning something for nothing. As soon as they saw that there was no purpose in what they were doing, they died. Having something to look for at the end of the road gives purpose, even in a concentration camp, but doing something for literally nothing is soul-destroying. Like my mother—even filling grenades was doing something."

Along with purpose, it seemed to me that having hope, however small, was key to Kati's survival. I also noticed that as Anna spoke she was coming to terms with her mother's suffering. Although she was now a great-grandmother herself, she would always be Kati's daughter at heart. She would want to protect her mother, and also to understand who she was.

Kati went on calmly, no angst—she was telling a tragically familiar story: "I was liberated from Bergen-Belsen by the British. I don't remember anything very much. They took my pulse. I remember them washing me and then I was unconscious. I woke up in white sheets. I don't know how long I was unconscious or how long I was in hospital. I do remember the salty milk they gave me—no solid food to begin with. [Cruelly, hundreds of people died after the liberation by eating on a stomach that was, literally, empty.] When I was well, I wanted to go home. I had an uncle who'd also survived. He came to find me and he took me back to Hungary. We went to my house in our village—but it was completely destroyed. Fortunately, another uncle, Harry, in England found my name on the Bergen-Belsen list of survivors, and contacted his brother, who found me. It was 1946, I was sixteen, and that uncle brought me to Manchester. I remember it like yesterday."

I wanted to know more about going home, but didn't ask: she had just told her whole devastating experience of Auschwitz. If she had wanted to say more, she would have. It was enough.

Anna and Rebecca were pink with emotion, blinking back their tears as they listened afresh to a story they already knew. They were in awe of Kati—as I was. I couldn't get my head around the sheer vitality of this ninety-one-year-old woman, who seemed able to look back at the terror of what had happened to her, to recognize its horror, yet not to be haunted by its ghost. I asked what was going on for them.

Anna, sitting beside her mother, was emphatic that, during her childhood, there was never any "backlog" of what her parents had been through: no anger or admonitions to be grateful for food and clothes. Her parents had come to this country as teenagers, speaking no English, "with nothing on their backs," and were happy. They'd made a good home, and suffused it with love. Rebecca, looking at Kati on the screen, speaking fast to get across all she felt, echoed her mother. She had an enduring image of the great love and care she had experienced staying with her grandparents. There was never any conflict, stress or tension. She hoped she could do the same for her grandchildren.

They looked at Kati with such warmth as they described the pride they felt in her survival. They smiled at each other, and then at Kati, as they agreed that, maybe, they didn't always deal with the day-to-day perfectly, but when the chips were down they had the strength to look for the positive and to keep going. While they were talking I saw Kati looking quietly pleased, and sensed she felt nurtured by their love and pride in her. I imagine very few households openly express their love and respect for their elders in the way I'd just had the privilege to witness. I also thought it was quite an act to follow. As the child or grandchild of someone so exceptional, wouldn't you feel inadequate? Although I hadn't sensed that this was the case, it was an area I hoped to explore further.

I asked Kati how she had bridged such horror and grown to trust and love. She replied that she believed it was the love of her husband, Isaac. Her face lit up as she remembered: "My husband was amazing, he had so much strength . . ."

She continued her story: "I stayed with my uncle Harry and went to school for a few months. Then I went to evening classes and worked embroidering clothes in the day. I always like to do something, and I'm good with my hands. At that time, I met my husband. I'd known him before the war. It was luck to see him." Kati looked me straight in the eye, speaking with such intensity as she remembered the feeling of meeting Isaac.

"My husband came to England two years later. I didn't think he'd marry me, but I hoped he would ask me. He did." This was accompanied by her megawatt smile. I was touched by the emphasis she put on "my husband," conveying the continued preciousness of her beloved partner. It was so tangible. She smiled more as she told us, "I was always happy once I was married. We made a home, had the children. Nothing was too hard for us—we would have done anything for them."

As if she was talking to herself, she said, "Yes, we had to have a purpose for living. I love my children and my grandchildren. My husband died very young—that was terrible, worse than anything—but I had a family already and they supported me a lot." This was the first time I'd seen sadness in her. No tears but a living sadness of missing the husband who had died thirty years ago. Anna joked that many people had wanted to marry Kati after Isaac's death, but she would only have married if she could have talked about Isaac all day. Kati's love for him was a vibrant force in her that had by no means dimmed since his death. I could understand that: since he had given her the strength to live at such a vulnerable time, she would never be able to love another man in addition to him.

Being loved and feeling safe, while having the purpose of raising her family, might have protected Kati from conscious thoughts. But I asked her if there were unconscious echoes of the camp. Kati told me that she slept with the light on and the door open, and when her children were small she'd dreamt that the Germans would come and take them away.

She talked about how much she still missed her mother and father, and often imagined that "I will open the door and my father will walk in, also my sister. My sister was three years younger than me, and if she'd still been alive, after liberation, I would have looked after her. I wouldn't have known how but I would."

I felt a stab of murderous fury at whoever had killed an eleven-year-old girl, and said as much. Anna stepped in again, putting her hand on her mother's, as if to say, "I've got this, Ma." She reiterated that her mother never had a bad word for anyone. If someone was annoying, she would always suggest there must be a good reason, or that they had had a bad day. Kati responded: "It's not in my nature to complain. I was so happy to have a home . . . you can't imagine."

That was the point. We couldn't know to what extent her experience had shaped her view of the world. Lived experience can't be replaced by theoretical insight. Anna and Rebecca said they would tell their children when they didn't eat their food: "Grandma would eat anything." And even the grandchildren had said that when they were cold they would think of their grandmother and try not to make a fuss.

While that cognitive view might help, telling ourselves not to worry doesn't work. Only having lived it does one have the emotional input and corresponding growth through adversity to reappraise what really matters in life.

Since I felt fury and had only just met the family, I couldn't help but think that some of their rage must have been sublimated in the next generations. I assumed it would play out through them wanting order and control in their lives.

In the weeks ahead I tried to access it. But I didn't succeed. Understandably, they had a strong desire to be as good as Kati, and if they had a darker side, which they might not, showing it to themselves, let alone me, was too big an ask.

It is well documented that, having been starved almost to death, many survivors' relationship with food was unsurprisingly changed for ever. It is a common Jewish trait to focus on food. It would be normal if this was manifested in anxiety when food isn't readily available, a propensity to store to excess, or an inability to throw food away. Not Kati. She told me, "Food doesn't affect me at all. When I came to this country I loved oranges. I kept buying oranges all the time, because we didn't have them at home. But no."

Anna interceded, telling her mother that what she had said was only partly correct: "Maybe the only big memories you have was the food that your mother made, the recipes, what you ate as a child." She turned to me: "My mother cooks recipes from home all the time. Food is important to her. She talks about what she is going to cook and discusses the food when we eat it."

Kati nodded vigorously. "I like cooking. I enjoy doing it and the children enjoy eating it . . . but a few months ago I fell off a chair when I climbed on it to find a recipe book!" She had broken her hip and gone quietly to bed without telling anyone, because she hadn't wanted to make a fuss.

There was a great deal here for me to think about. Food for all of us is complicated at best. We imbue it with emotions. We "eat our feelings" to comfort us, or to distract us from what we're feeling. In families, our relationship with food can be modelled by our parents, and tends to live on through our children. For Kati, although her trauma wasn't transmitted through food, her relationship with it was particularly powerful: it symbolized safety and survival.

Food is a touchstone to memory: the sight, smell, taste and touch of particular foods evoke body memories that take us directly to our past, with its associated feelings. In Kati's case, the food of her childhood conjured images of her beloved parents in their kitchen in Hungary, and the associated feelings of love.

Rebecca spoke slowly, her head down, as she remembered a painful time when she'd sought perfection; using food to control what she saw as her imperfections. Fortunately, she had been able to get professional help and had overcome it, although, her voice still low, she admitted, "I'm better, much better, but I can still overeat."

It seemed to me that Rebecca was open to feeling and expressing herself. When I asked her about this, she thought for a while, then nodded. Her face lit up as she had an idea: she wondered if she'd internalized the message that people in the camps were killed when they looked sick. She remembered being encouraged to "look good" by her mother—or "What might happen?" As she followed her thoughts further, she realized it had set up an internal battle in which she wanted control and perfection. She smiled as she looked at me: a little piece in the puzzle of herself had slotted into place.

I was surprised when Kati acknowledged that lockdown had been difficult for her. But, on reflection, I realized a vital coping mechanism for Kati was her sense of value from being with and helping others. She had always been connected to others, even in the camps. Cooking authentic Hungarian food, having her grandchildren appreciate it, gave her a sense of purpose. The pandemic had taken away her capacity to be generous and generative. Resilience is built not through waiting for something to happen, but by making it happen, being useful and helping others. We all laughed when Anna told us that her mother still went by bus to the shops, and that her neighbours were shocked that her "terrible children" didn't drive her. But she insisted on going on her own. She wanted to get out, see people, buy her own groceries, and feel the satisfaction of having completed a task. She said proudly, "I am quite capable of looking after myself."

Her determined positivity of setting tasks and completing them in order to give to others contributed to her extraordinary resilience.

After I'd got to know Kati and her family, I started looking for answers as to why she was, as Rebecca put it, "amazingly resilient when bad things happen to her. I've never seen her depressed, miserable or morose. I never remember her being ill."

What had enabled Kati to thrive despite the devastation of her past, and how did she continue to thrive in her nineties? Surely there was something we could all learn from her.

I spoke to a leading clinical psychologist, a professor of developmental neuroscience and psychopathology, who explained that the multiple pieces of this jigsaw fall into the three familiar categories: upbringing, genes and environment. Kati's sense of being loved, valued and cared for by her parents had provided rich foundations she was able to harness in her staunch response to the trauma. Her adaptive response was the result of the stable formative experience of her early years, before the war. It is the capacity to process and adapt to trauma that protects against it becoming locked into the brain's neural networks.

Genes play a much bigger part than I had realized. How an individual responds to threat, how adaptive they are, is partly written in their genes—we don't yet know to what extent, but we do know that different genetic variants are more prevalent in some populations. Kati, like all of us, was born with a genetic blueprint encoding her IQ, physical traits and her personality. But while her genes determined her potential, it was how they interacted with their environment that shaped Kati's outcome. The genes you are born with also influence the response you elicit from the world around you. Now a sparkly bright woman of ninety-one, Kati had almost certainly been a sparkly bright girl.

This iterative process shapes us: we are active agents in creating our social world, not merely passive recipients of it. So Kati, a positive, smiley, friendly and interested person, would have been able to build secure relationships with the people she met. That in itself would be psychologically protective. It might account for the Czech girl in the factory giving her a potato. Although Kati felt it was luck that she and Isaac fell in love, her outcome was shaped by the love she'd been given as a child, and how her genes interacted with the environment.

We can only play the cards we are dealt but how we play them makes the difference. In Kati's case, she chose the best card from that hand: Isaac. She was then in a virtuous cycle, with a new set of cards—her children—and so the cycle continued.

In addition to the three key components mentioned, the piece that completed the jigsaw of Kati's resilience was the meaning she made of her experience. We know trauma doesn't have an automatic outcome. Kati described her survival as "a miracle," which it was, but she could have experienced it differently, if, for example, she'd suffered from survivors' guilt. But when her children asked why she'd survived, she told them: "So you could have Mummy and she could have you." They gave her survival meaning. Without the purpose that building a family conferred, she might have not been as resilient.

As we were coming to the end of the session, Kati still shining brightly while Anna, Rebecca and I were emotionally spent, I asked how they dealt with conflict in their family. They told me they didn't fight. I sat bolt upright. I couldn't imagine being in a family that didn't fight. But Anna replied, while the others nodded, "Everyone cooperates. If someone has to give in, we always give in. Never ever do we let things cause a problem. It's not worth it, it's better to forget it. There have been many instances we could have fought, over possessions, all the usual everyday conflicts. But we don't say a word. We look away." Rebecca went on to describe how well she got on with her siblings, how they were brought up with a pack of cousins to whom they were still close; that, as a family, they would drop everything to help each other. They acknowledged how blessed they were, having acquired a heightened sense of gratitude from Kati.

They proved the work of Martin Seligman and others in positive psychology, which emphasizes how gratitude, focusing on what is good rather than what is bad or lacking, leads to greater feelings of happiness. As Rebecca proudly voiced it: "We all think about the people who are not here, how much we'd love to have them here. Of course there are irritations, there's plenty to fight about, our children have petty squabbles, but we never fall out."

Even families who never fall out can experience some friction. It became apparent that Anna wasn't close to her brother David. "We get on, but we're very different people. It's not that we fight exactly—" She stopped in her tracks when she saw her mother turn her face away. She rushed to reassure her: "We love each other, you know that, and you know I'm very close to my sister Edith."

But Kati was now emotional, saying: "I don't talk about it, but this upsets me. This is not good for me. I have to look away. My husband would be very upset. I try not to mix in between them. What can we do? This upsets me . . ." Anna and Rebecca jumped in to soothe her, telling her there was nothing to worry about.

Recognizing differences between siblings—who didn't even fight—didn't seem to me to be a big deal, particularly when set against research by the psychologist Karl Pillemer of Cornell University, who found that 5 percent of siblings are completely estranged and 23 percent barely speak. But what caught my attention with the Bergers was how powerful the moment was when Kati turned her face away, unable to tolerate even a hint of discord, and Anna and Rebecca rushed to reassure and protect her.

There are different ways of looking at such family dynamics. In the Berger family's case, it wasn't that there were no tensions or conflicts—but rather that those conflicts were not allowed or openly discussed. This kind of familial blocking (and its connection to individual blocking) is interesting. In every family there are rules—overt or hidden—concerning what can be spoken about, what can be expressed or denied. That in itself is not a bad thing, but it is worth examining what rules there are, and the psychological costs of having them, in the light that they could be changed.

My initial curiosity in this dynamic grew as I learnt that this pattern of protecting Kati from any kind of worry happened regularly. She found worry hard to manage and her family wanted everything to be perfect for her. This, of course, was an impossible bar to clear. Anna said, "We do express our own views but try not to be judgemental and rarely would it become a family dispute." I could see that the Bergers created harmony and trust within their family because they didn't fear being attacked. But I wondered about the cost of being unable to stand up for your own view: suppressing anger could move sideways into control, being locked into a fixed position, or lead to co-dependency.

There are spectrums and different forms of co-dependency. Put simply, co-dependency is when your self-worth is dependent on the approval of others—and you lose connection with having your own needs met. You are not able to say no, or to have different opinions—for fear of conflict. It can mean difficult feelings are buried, which can be stifling. Often the difficult feelings come out in other ways. I couldn't judge if the Bergers were co-dependent yet—but it is always useful for families to take a look at how they operate together.

Through a number of sessions it became clear that this was a family that worried—a lot. Kati admitted it: "I worry about them all, all the time. It's terrible. I worry they should be well, and I worry they shouldn't suffer." Anna, speaking more hesitantly than usual, hands crossed in front of her to keep her steady, described how she grappled with it: "I've learnt to say to myself that worry doesn't help. I really can't be in control of it . . . and I try not to worry . . . I try not to show it . . ." But she acknowledged that when Ben was upset or Rebecca was unhappy, "I was a wreck inside. I was physically sick. I couldn't eat or sleep." She felt as if she had persistent rolling anxiety.

Rebecca, who was sitting upright, hand on her chin, clearly very interested in this discussion, thought for a moment, then said she recognized that her response was similar. She managed her anxiety by making lists, which her mother teased her about. But she was also working on changing herself: "I want to be a useful person. I need to detach. If I didn't have a job I'd be all over the place. I want to meet their needs, but not to be overly consumed by them . . . It's not an easy thing."

Their worry played out in different ways: they wouldn't tell each other things because the level of worry they received in response was intense; or they wouldn't ask for help because they didn't want to be "a trouble." It was an unwritten law for each generation to protect their parents, behave well, and follow their religious path. There seemed to be a pull-and-push: they needed to be open with each other, receiving loving support, while recognizing that there is a limit to what each person can bear.

I wanted to understand this in a wider context. Research by family gerontologist Dr Amber Seidel, of Penn State York, indicates that we all worry more than previous generations, and particularly about our adult children. This is probably because most of us are closer to our children than our parents' generation were, and more involved in their lives: thanks to smartphones, we can be continually updated about every small kink, which can feed a loop of anxiety. There is truth to out of sight, out of mind. Worrying is often focused on future events in which we picture bad outcomes, ramping up our fear by imagining worst-case scenarios. It can be based on our beliefs about worry: that it may protect us from bad things or, perversely, that it will make us ill.

The psychologist Paul Gilbert has an interesting view on worry from an evolutionary perspective. He describes how the function of worry in the brain is to deal with threat and prepare for future events (in evolutionary terms this would be running out of food or being eaten by a predator). Our brain's worry system malfunctions because it has not yet evolved sufficiently to cope with the nature of contemporary threats and fears: we may end up with our brains permanently switched to a state of worry.

Many of us recognize this state of high alert. But developing good habits can help to stabilize it. Dr Sarah Vohra, author of *The Mind Medic*, says that, as well as de-stressing practices like yoga or meditation, we can manage our worries by categorizing them. We can ask ourselves: "Is this a worry I can turn into a problem to solve?" For example, I can deal with a worry such as whether there is a meeting tomorrow by checking with a colleague.

Or, is it a might-not-happen worry, which may never come to fruition but may utterly consume you and your day, such as is your child safe? In those cases, she advises us to write it down and move it to your "worry-curfew" list. She proposes you set aside a worry curfew of thirty minutes a day, at a set time, to look at the list and worry all you like. But when a worry pops into your head outside curfew time, distract yourself with positive activities, like chatting to a friend or doing a specific task. Finally, when you're in the worry-curfew slot, cross out what is no longer a worry, tear up the old list, and throw it away, then jot down on a fresh sheet what continues to worry you for the next day's session. It sounds complicated but the practice is simple, and since we're habit-forming beings, we soon find we switch automatically out of worry mode, freeing us to engage more fully in our day. I hoped to give Rebecca this helpful tool.

For the Berger second and third generations, worry came with the belief that they had "nothing to worry about" in comparison to Kati, so shouldn't do it. It seemed to me that this family circulated worry between them in a way that was difficult for all. At its root was the fear from Kati's past, which had alchemized into worry, and a constant need to seek safety. It was a consequence of the trauma. Although far less damaging, it was still bothersome.

Rebecca was curious as to how to balance worrying with authentic connection: telling her mother what was going on, getting her advice and holding boundaries of separateness. Anna didn't feel Rebecca needed to change it, that it was under control. But her daughter was in an ongoing process of awareness-raising in order to adapt and stop bad habits that no longer worked for her. Talking to me was a small part of taking herself in hand. It seemed useful to talk openly about it with a third person.

Rebecca had, for example, been a hoarder of food—a common trait in many families but particularly in survivors of the Holocaust. Recently, she'd realized that she catastrophized when small things went wrong, and it helped her to fact-check the scenario she was playing out in her head. For instance, when she ran out of eggs, she recognized that the sky didn't fall in and she could get some from a neighbour. She'd learnt a useful adage from the academic and broadcaster Brené Brown: "Strive for excellence but don't try to achieve perfection."

Anna teased Rebecca that sometimes it was as if "You are the survivor." The significance of what she said only hit me after the session—that perhaps Rebecca had internalized unexpressed trauma from her grandmother, but couldn't give herself permission to express it since Kati "never complained."

Looking at this from a psychological perspective called on my knowledge about mother–daughter relationships. This isn't denying the importance of fathers but the matrilineal line was where I focused my attention. We know from neuroscience that the part of the brain that mediates emotion is similar between mothers and daughters. The mother–daughter bond is the building block in how to make secure relationships, and develops self-esteem for the child.

A daughter learns most from what her mother models for her in her behaviour, more than what she says. The diktat "Do as I say not as I do" could not be more misguided. In the Berger family, secure love was passed down from mother to daughter. They witnessed in Kati and Isaac the importance of their romantic relationships and of having their own families. Kati had processed her trauma, but I felt that Anna and Rebecca were carrying traits of it while believing they shouldn't.

It became clear it had taken them many years to learn to be interdependent of each other—meaning they were close yet allowed space between them—and I saw they were still working on it. They knew that when this doesn't happen it can block the ability to form a bond with a partner.

I learnt that Rebecca had married very young, which meant she had leant too much on her parents, even texting her daily plans to her mother every morning. Over time, she'd been in touch less. Anna knew that was healthy, but admitted, with some sadness in her voice, "I might feel a little shut out when I don't know the small things and wonder why didn't she tell me." But then she looked at Rebecca and, with a proud smile, said, "Don't change." This was a lovely moment of acknowledgement of how difficult the dance of close and separate is between mother and daughter. And the key, as ever, is having open and truthful conversations.

Dina, whom I saw with her mother, Rebecca, was at the very beginning of this adaptive process. They sat side by side, Dina wearing a big black band to keep her hair in place, looking young and bright-eyed. She fizzed with energy. She saw her mother every day, and told her everything. But Rebecca, who was softer and gentler in the presence of her daughter, didn't want her to repeat her pattern, and asked her, "Do you feel pressured by me?" She explained that she was determined not to stifle her children.

Dina laughed, and brushed off her mother's worry. "I can talk to you properly . . . If you do, I will tell you." They leant in and hugged each other.

All the Berger women carried within them embodied trauma: fragments of suffering alive in them each and every day. They could never wear stripes, which were reminiscent of the camps, and when they walked past a smoking chimney they immediately thought of the gas chambers. Dogs spiked fear in them. Only Dina, from the fourth generation, was lighter. She spoke in a deep voice, laughed a lot, and teased her mother, sometimes disagreeing with her but always moving towards her affectionately. She seemed free of the burden of rumination. Kati's positive looking for happiness was imbued strongly in successive generations. Dina was the product of two generations who had lived in peace. The terror of the past was less intense in her. My assessment was that as each generation felt the security in their safety increase, trust also grew.

It was while talking to Dina that I was particularly aware that she lived in a bubble, which appeared almost untouched by time. At twenty-five, she was in an environment that her contemporaries, who maybe lived only a few miles away, would find hard to contemplate.

She spoke cheerfully, describing her way of life—"It's all I've known"—with total acceptance. She dressed modestly, never wearing trousers, and, like most young women in the community, was educated until the age of eighteen. Few went to university because, as Dina told me, "Getting married at twenty-two I was already old, the average is nineteen to twenty. I had a baby at twenty-four, and that's late."

The girls go to seminary in Israel for a year after school and then their marriage is arranged by a matchmaker. The couple date four or five times and, if they like each other, they become engaged. There was certainly a choice as to who they could marry, but not to be single for too long. And there was pressure to appear eligible in every respect: being attractive, pious and coming from a good family. Behaving badly, rebelling would be anathema to these families. As time passes, their options of suitable husbands run out so the pressure grows. Once married, being a mother (hopefully) is their primary role, and although some women work it is usually in the jobs that are expected of women: midwife, nurse, dental assistant. Few women in the ultra-Orthodox community have high-powered jobs.

As Dina spoke she was not railing against her way of life. I had been keen to discover from the inside what may seem restricting from the outside. I'd assumed, with their history, they were prepared to give up a great deal of freedom to have safety. But Dina didn't see it in those terms. She, like everyone in her family, felt grateful to be Jewish, living in the way that they did; I even sensed she felt a little sorry for me because I did not have the benefits of their way of life.

The Bergers had been courageous and generous in letting me into their world and allowing me such an intimate view of their family life. This was a community that stepped into contemporary society when they needed to for work, but did not invite people like me to rummage around in their family psyche. To be fair, that is true of most people—but it felt even truer for them. Their lives were boundaried by the geography and customs of their community: none of the Bergers had ever eaten in a non-kosher restaurant.

So, it was quite something for them to speak to me, a total stranger from a different culture. I knew that I must respect their boundaries—but still found it hard not to try to sort them out. They didn't need it and I spent many reflective hours, often on my bicycle, urging myself to be at peace with that. I found it difficult not to use my skills—which gave me agency and purpose—to connect to people and support them in shifting to new viewpoints or releasing old fears. I realized that these were my issues of control that I needed to deal with.

Where I couldn't stop myself stepping over the line was to do with work. I found myself saying to Anna that I felt she was missing having her own individual identity—a work identity. She could volunteer or mentor—it didn't matter what it was, but I wanted her to get out of the house and be a different version of herself. I was surprised at her lack of defence as she told me, with warmth in her smile: "I do feel there is a link missing. I need to find the right balance, but I need to find something for me."

I liked the acknowledgement that she needed something for herself. Dina, similarly, although a full-time mum for now, agreed she wouldn't rule out working in the future.

I know work is not an optional nice-to-have extra for many. For the Bergers, though, it was a choice. I spoke out because I'm biased: work has saved me many times. I accept that there are stages in life where work may need to be on hold or on the backburner, and that there is a crucial value in being a partner and mother—but I believe profoundly that women have much more to contribute to the world, and that it is healthy for families and for women to find additional purpose, meaning structure and self-esteem through work. The Bergers, on the other hand, had their own potent power: their faith.

Kati's parents had been pious Jews. The uncle who had taken her in was part of the ultra-Orthodox community. Kati reflected that she understood why others had renounced their faith after "seeing people burning" but for her it was a way of continuing her relationship with her family. The traditions of her religion were "tremendous": they lived on and kept her grounded when so much had been destroyed. She had been through hell on earth, but her faith gave her courage, embodying the belief that there was something greater and bigger than her. The women members of her synagogue went only on high days and holidays but "I just pray a little bit whenever I need to," she said. I smiled: Kati was not one to overdo it.

Anna explained that there was a difference between their faith, which was the practice of their religion, and their religion, which was more about belonging: "Our religion is so encompassing; for us it's basically a living-and-breathing entity. It's every Friday night singing the same songs, the same tunes, the same prayers. It gives me a feeling of being part of a community, a larger-scale family, so that I never feel alone. Anywhere in the world I can join a community."

The idea of Judaism being a living entity was fascinating. I like the ritual of church and synagogue but see them as fixed, objective buildings I visit, not as a being. It made me think of the levels of loneliness in the world today. A Harvard report suggests that over a third of all Americans feel "serious loneliness." In Canada, a survey found one in ten people fifteen years and older always or often felt lonely. The power of that sense of total belonging and absolute confidence of being able to connect with fellow Jews was very compelling. Anna continued, her voice strong, eyes bright— talking about this was her happy place: "On the religious side, when the chips are down, I would turn to my psalms. Anytime anyone is not well, I immediately go to our psalms. We all said prayers as a community with Covid. That is the truth of our faith. I may not feel it every moment, but it's there."

Rebecca spoke even more passionately. "God is there, a presence, a spirit. I wonder when there are tragedies or even sad things, difficult things, how on earth can anybody continue without faith?

"God knows what is going to happen and what is right for us. So even though, whatever point we are at, it may seem very bleak or dark or frightening, there is a bigger plan above us. There is God who runs the world, and we don't know it all. When tragedy strikes, we have the ability to surrender to God and to say, 'Over to you.'"

I could see Anna looking at her daughter with pride and love, witnessing all that she had brought her up to believe being voiced with such conviction. Rebecca continued, "I hope I will never be really tested to tap into what I'm saying, but it's what I try to hold on to. What my mother is saying about religion: we have an order, we have a predictability about the year. We know when it comes to particular months, the festivals. It gives structure to our year. Each different festival has its requisite places, songs and food. Throughout the world that is universal. Wherever you go in the world you are part of something and you belong."

Dina echoed her mother's words. She prayed every morning and at other times—when the baby allowed. She believed that family was an integral part of being a Jew and the continuation of the Jewish people, so the family was intertwined with their religion. They all had a deep sense of gratitude for being Jewish.

Interestingly, multiple research studies show there is a high correlation between those with faith and higher levels of well-being. For young adults, like Dina, being brought up in faith-based households adds a protective factor for their mental health. I don't think it's possible to put an exact value on spiritual practice and faith: that is uniquely individual. But as I thought about the Bergers, it was evident that their faith fills many difficult holes.

I needed to take on board how the presence of death was the backdrop to their life. Anna explained that on the Sabbath they couldn't use any electricity or transport. The Sabbath was always quiet. As a child, she would sit in the afternoon with her siblings and go through boxes of family photographs. These were not happy snaps of family holidays but of family members who had died, and included images of wheelbarrows filled with dead bodies from the camps. She described that they would look at those first, put them aside and then look at other family photos.

Discussion of death was not taboo for them, as it is in so many families. Anna had sat and listened to her father and his siblings talk about their burial plot in Israel, planning who would be beside whom as if they were discussing the seating plan at a dinner. Kati felt safe in Israel, and it comforted her to know she would be buried there, next to Isaac and his family. This had a particular poignancy when so many of their family members had never been buried, or had headstones to mark their lives. Isaac had put the names of close family members on his to give them a place. I was fascinated when I realized this was not depressing, as many of us would imagine, but the reverse. Feeling gratitude for being alive while acknowledging and openly discussing the inevitability of death gave them life and vitality.

*

I was happy that the Bergers had found our conversations helpful. Having me witness their views and ways of being allowed them to shine a light and see aspects of their life more clearly, even in different ways. Hearing my honest appraisal that they were a family that worried but were not a family that embodied secondary trauma brought a smile of relief to their faces. They had already known it, but it is always heartening to hear it from someone else. The words that remain in me from their reflections are Anna's: "I loved our sessions and enjoyed meeting you, and sharing thoughts and feelings. My recollection of our conversations leaves me with memories of a very cathartic experience, bringing my family together, and giving me a deeper understanding of my own children."

Isn't it interesting that we can get to know our own children better by thinking and talking about them, not just being with them?

And from Rebecca: "The conversations we had together were insightful and provoking in both thought and feeling . . . exploring family history and dynamics, which always felt familiar and known and still do. At the same time they enabled reflection on a deeper level, challenging territory as yet unexplored, simultaneously enhancing appreciation for what I have always known but perhaps taken for granted."

For me, this aspect of using our time to explore unknown territory in ourselves and in our families, as a way to better appreciate and know differently what we've always known was revelatory. Often we don't see what is right in front of us until we turn our attention towards it in a different way.

Kati, the ultimate matriarch, powerful in her quiet, deep capacity to love and her courage to survive was a tough act to follow. Her ability to love was her real legacy, passed down from generation to generation. That, and her faith. As Rabbi Jonathan Sacks said, "If you look at the Bible our story of happiness is not the first thing that comes to mind. We do degrees in misery, postgraduate angst, and when all of that is at an end, we celebrate . . . The definition of being a Jew is one who wrestles with God and humanity and prevails . . . When something bad happens I will not let go of that bad thing until I find the blessing within it."

That seems to sum up for me an attitude to life that can be profoundly meaningful. Not without suffering, not without angst and messiness, but letting God prevail and ultimately finding ways to feel blessed is a positive way of living.

Months after we'd finished our sessions, when I was thinking about identity and family, my mind turned to the Bergers. They came and took up residence in my brain in a way that was unfamiliar. I was trying to work out how different it makes us, belonging to such a strong faith. In the end I concluded that, although our lives looked different on the outside, our concerns and difficulties were ultimately the universal ones: love, family, belonging, survival, safety and purpose.

After I'd heard Kati's story I had found myself looking for evidence of intergenerational trauma, for the ways in which the horrors of the past might have been embedded in her family. In fact, I found something else. The forces most powerfully at play in the Berger family were of a different kind: Kati's extraordinary resilience, forgiveness and her capacity to be loving in the face of evil meant that she was revered by her children and grandchildren. It provided them with a touchstone for female strength, love, gratitude, faith and endurance.

But it also raised the possibility of difficulties. Remarkable family members present a particular challenge to the generations that follow them, who may find themselves wanting. They may judge their very normal human vulnerabilities against impossibly high standards. The experience of being Kati's offspring can be translated to the child of anyone who is well known or successful: a politician, businessman, rock star or writer. You are always someone's child first: the son of X, or the daughter of Y. The veneration of family legends can lead to suppressed emotions, perfectionism, co-dependency and a struggle to find an identity as meaningful as the ones that the family reveres.

By understanding this dynamic, learning to view themselves in their own context and time, and seeing themselves with greater compassion, family members can quieten their inner critic while still drawing strength from the fabled figures in their family: they can allow their stories to be connected, yet separate.

The Craig and Butowski Family

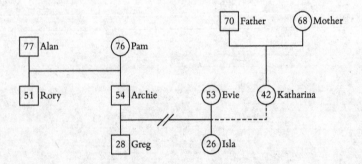

The Craig and Butowski Family

How to live in the face of death

Case conceptualization

Archie Craig was a fifty-four-year-old Scot living in the Highlands with his Polish fiancée, Katharina, and his twenty-eight-year-old son Greg. Isla, his twenty-six-year-old daughter, lived in the Borders. He was divorced from the mother of his children. Archie's first cancer diagnosis had been twelve years ago when he'd had a kidney removed. All had gone well for four years, but then his routine scan showed he had secondary cancer in his lungs and chest. Four months before I saw him, he had received the devastating news that he had a tumour in the brain. He was given a life expectancy of one year. Our work was to support him and his family through his illness. As time went on it became apparent that multiple aspects required our attention: that he had had to cut off his relationship with his parents to preserve his mental and physical health; the terrible side-effects of his radiotherapy, chemotherapy and steroids. All of the family was faced with the challenge of how he could live life in the best way possible, within the restrictions imposed by the pandemic, while he was facing his death.

I went to Cancer Research UK for the statistical context for Archie's medical condition, and also include some North American statistics here for further context. Statistics can be useful to gain perspective on a particular diagnosis, but they often ignite fear or fury when we're at the wrong end. The understanding I took from the numbers was that Archie was much too young to have a rare and terminal cancer. As he and all the members of his family reiterated, while they knew life was not fair, this unfairness was particularly cruel.

- There were more than 690,000 cancer deaths in North America in 2018.
- In males in Canada, kidney cancer was projected to be the seventh most common cause of cancer death, leading to around 1,250 deaths in 2021.
- Each year nearly half (43 percent) of all cancer deaths in the US are in people aged 75 and over (2015–19).
- Half (50 percent) of people diagnosed with cancer in England and Wales survive their disease for ten years or more (2010–11).

Reviewing my client caseload over the decades, at any moment in time, there is always one client whose situation calls on my deepest levels of compassion and at times concern. At this moment Archie Craig is that client.

I was looking at Archie on the screen; he was luminously pale, bald on his head and his eyebrows. He wore heavy-framed glasses that looked a little too large for him. It took me a few minutes to notice that Archie didn't move. He sat upright in his bed, dressed in a smart collared shirt; his words were not accompanied by any hand movements, or visual gesticulation. It was as if he had to conserve every molecule of energy to speak. Archie's opening words to me were "Cancer turns things on its head, turns white to black. Cancer is a thief. It steals bits of your body."

It does.

Archie was fifty-four, and had been diagnosed with kidney cancer in his early forties. He'd had successful surgery to remove the kidney and for four years he had lived cancer-free. The milestone five-year green light of it being less likely to come back seemed in sight. But then, cruelly, he learnt he had secondary cancer, and most recently after having headaches, a scan gave him the devastating news that he had a tumour in the brain. The consultant informed him there was no cure. They might be able to prolong his life with treatments, but his life expectancy was twelve months. Of course, Archie was the person most affected, but it would inevitably negatively impact everyone in his family.

I knew from a 2013 National Center for Biotechnology Information study Golics et al. (2013) that, in a family with a chronic illness, 92 percent of the family members interviewed were affected emotionally by the patient's illness, mentioning worry (35 percent), frustration (27 percent), anger (25 percent), and guilt (14 percent). That is a big cocktail of emotions swirling beneath their outward appearance. They are the emotions of grief, and a natural response to illness. I knew I couldn't reduce or release any of them from the intensity of this, but I sincerely hoped that I could support them in it. This wasn't a relationship where huge shifts of understanding were likely, more about stabilizing the family members to manage the ongoing onslaught of difficulties they were facing. If necessary, I could make suggestions of the things to do and say to protect them against potential regret.

I was a presence from outside their family, with whom they could be completely open, whom they didn't need to protect or worry about, and I trusted that would be of benefit. Even if this was only small, it was worth it. I never underestimate the value of being fully heard: good-quality listening was a valuable resource I wanted to offer.

Additionally, Archie valued the opportunity of participating in my book, telling me, "My experience has got to be worth something for somebody." Perhaps knowing his story would be out in the world was a small solace.

Archie was to be the main focus of our therapy, often joined by his fiancée Katharina. Greg was a biologist, who lived with Archie. Isla, an essential medical worker, lived a few hours away. I would see Greg and Isla separately. We decided it might be overwhelming for Archie to witness their collective distress. He would have access to what they thought and felt in the case study, which he could read at his own pace.

*

As I heard the words, "The cancer returned in my lungs and chest," I felt the anxiety spike in my body. Due to my own family's history of cancer this is not a neutral zone for me. I live in a place where I choose to be in denial. I don't believe a useful purpose would be served by dropping my defences in this, but the alarm bell of cancer coming back is never far away. Two years had passed since the person in my family had cancer and I felt resilient enough to work with cancer patients again.

It is an area of my work that I find rewarding and meaningful, but intense. I hoped I would have increased insight into this family's experience. I was aware of the other side of that: I would require extra supervision to ensure I upheld the focus on meeting their needs: this relationship was for them, and my job was to remain psychologically robust to support them. This was not about me.

I include this because I think it is important to mention that all of us therapists have our own history of losses, injuries, errors, faults and likely triggers. I am often told, "For a therapist you are very upset . . ." as if being a therapist means I should have magical powers to manage life with equanimity, love and peace. If only. No. I have my own ongoing work to do to stay loving, connected, curious and open, and that will include failing, falling and not coping.

In the crisis of Archie's terminal diagnosis, having his family as a resource of support, love and connection was for him, and anyone in his situation, the key component in his being able to bear the pain of his illness. The complexity is that each person in a family will have their own unique responses and ways of dealing with the difficulty, which will, in turn, impact the others.

Grief starts at the point of diagnosis. Every new diagnosis brings an additional wave of all the emotions of grief: shock, sadness, anxiety, anger, fear or even hopelessness. When every member of a family is experiencing those feelings, it can be overwhelming. Bad news activates our threat system to high alert. We inevitably and viscerally affect each other because our emotions are contagious. Being able to have honest and open communication between everyone, naming and expressing their feelings, discussing their fears and even hopes is the route to maintaining as much stability as possible in such a turbulent time.

It also means that every individual within the family system has to take responsibility for their behaviours: being sensitive to the needs of others, pulling together, recognizing and adapting their own responses when they are having a negative impact on those around them. Archie's parents were unable to do this.

In our first session I learnt from Archie that "My parents are alive but I am not speaking to them . . . It is painful but my mother says extraordinarily strange things, not just to me but to my fiancée and my children. The thing that did it was when she heard the devastating news that my cancer had gone to my brain and said to Katharina, 'Archie has always been a difficult child. He gave me a hard time growing up . . .' She went on for about twenty minutes, and finished by saying, 'Cancer patients love going into hospices.'"

Clenching his fists as he spoke, I imagined if he'd had more energy he would have expressed his fury with more than that clench. I felt a stab of shock in my stomach at the insensitivity of his mother's words.

Archie continued, "When I first heard that, I was outraged. I have a significant brain injury. I mustn't get upset or angry. I have a high risk of stroke or seizure. I couldn't expose myself to that danger. I had to stop seeing them."

Katharina later told me it had taken Archie two months to recover from the wounding of his mother's statement. I could still see the hurt in his eyes, as he nodded sadly. "Yes, it took me a long time to sort it. I got stuck in the pain. It took me a while to realize I had a choice. I could be the hurt teenager at the mercy of Mum's whims, or I could be me as a fifty-four-year-old who doesn't need my mother any more. Her words still cut into him but they aren't so raw now. I have to accept the way it is."

I told him that there was a profound difference between him and his mother. He had the insight, empathy and self-compassion to shift his perspective. But it was not without cost: memories of his mother regularly emerged along the lines of "She could have said something more compassionate . . . The need for compassion or the need for vindictiveness, and she went with vindictiveness." Despite his parents' inadequacies and even cruelty, it weighed heavily on Archie that he couldn't see them. They were still his parents and he loved and missed them, but he knew he had to hold the boundary. That was a burden I wished he hadn't had to carry.

As I grew to know Archie over several weeks, the significance of the dysfunction of his birth family became increasingly apparent. There was not a single session when he didn't talk about his mother in particular, and often his father. He had learnt ways to cope with it, but it didn't mean he could forget it. Like all of us, our wounds from our parents go deep: we may learn to manage them, but sadly we cannot erase them. When he spoke about his mother he often put on her voice, which was hectoring at best and threatening at worst.

He understood the roots of it. His mother had been molested as a child by her father and had never dealt with the trauma. Her unprocessed heightened emotions of trauma played out in her life every day. She constantly demanded attention, usually through exaggerating illness—her bad back, her diabetes or her mini strokes. Archie said, "All the sympathy has to be fed into her. She's a proper drama queen." She would indiscriminately hijack the suffering of others by elevating her own—even her son's terminal diagnosis. As for his father, although Archie's parents had "furious fights," basically his mother controlled him. When Archie spoke, I could see in his eyes, and hear in his tone of voice, the clarity of his understanding and the injury he carried.

He summed up the environment he grew up in: "There was no nurturing, no parental care. I think there was love but not tenderness."

To add another layer of complication his parents had been brought up as Jehovah's Witnesses, which Archie believed was a cult. It meant they lived in a household that was extremely dogmatic with fixed rules. No one was permitted to question or in any way be their own person. For Archie—and, I'd argue, any child being brought up under such a strict regime—their sense of being valued conditional on being good would be highly likely to produce anxiety and lack of confidence at the very least. It affected Archie in every aspect of his life until he had therapy. Until then, his understanding of himself and his world was that either he or someone else was to blame—a rigid and punishing approach to daily experiences, with the constant undercurrent of fear. A resultant sadness was that it had influenced Archie's parenting of his children; they were now dealing with the consequences.

A kind colleague of mine, Mary Russell, had sent me her paper titled "Totalist Recruitment Warning Signs" about the red flags to look for in identifying a cult. All chimed with what Archie described in the world of Jehovah's Witnesses. It highlights how a member is isolated from other close friendships, how no one can question the status quo, and that their imposed rules and community are viewed as the sole answer to all problems.

One of my learnings over the years has been recognizing that very little in life is black or white, good or bad. The need for control is fear-based and often the source of the most bitter disputes between individuals and families. When a person or an organization believes in their absolute rightness, my first question is, what do they fear? What is the risk for them of allowing multiple views or more freedom? The answers are the basis of how to move forward.

Archie had stopped being a Jehovah's Witness when he was twenty-eight, but the messaging and his reflexive response to life was still coded by it. It wasn't until his marriage ended, his business went bust and he had a breakdown in his forties that therapy taught him what he described as "a new operating system. I made better decisions."

Archie referred to his therapist Nigel G by his full name, with pride, in many of my sessions, which led me to think that effective therapy lives on long after the therapy is done. Nigel's voice would regularly come to Archie's mind in any challenging situation and informed him. Archie said, "He taught me my emotional system works faster than my thoughts, and that I was living by reacting. I learnt the signals in myself and how to identify them. Like, I'm feeling this, I'm feeling it, but coming from that response might not be helpful. What's the right response? Stop. Think about my reaction before engaging my brain. I used to get very angry. I slow down now. I'm more patient . . . I make much, much better decisions . . . like meeting Katharina. If it had happened a few years before I wouldn't have taken a chance on what turned out to be a very, very, very, very [grinning as he repeated "very"] good decision and dialled her number."

As he spoke I wanted to shout, "Yes! It's never too late to change your life. Bad patterns are not set in stone. We can change." But Archie was in the flow of warmth and connection to his fiancée: it was not the time for me to grandstand the value of therapy.

Katharina had joined Archie, as she often did, lying beside him on his bed, stroking his arm. She was also pale, with glossy blonde hair and chestnut eyes. She was tall, smartly dressed for her work as a communications executive, in a tailored outfit, and had a powerful presence.

They lit up as they remembered their meeting and the beginning of their relationship, when Katharina had been visiting Scotland. I love hearing those stories. They interrupted each other, giggled, and were energized. Archie had been in a bad mood, she was late, but he took her number and even kissed her that first evening. Showy. They'd Skyped and messaged each other and quickly they were a couple, though living in two countries. They grew to know and love each other online, meeting when and as often as they could. Within two years she had moved to Scotland.

I noted again that good memories live on in us as powerfully as bad ones, and by choosing to focus on them we can influence and change our mood and our attitude to life. Archie was permanently in physical pain, knowing his life was limited, but when he connected with Katharina it was as if all of that receded, and he was revitalized. Love can't cure us, but it does a damned good job of enabling us to live fully, even as we suffer badly.

Archie turned to her. "I have never been as happy and content as I am now. Katharina is a special woman. I wonder why she stays."

Katharina laughed. "We really love each other. We are happy. It is the most challenging thing and I wouldn't miss it for the world. I don't have to be anyone, I can just be me, and have him look at me. He is as crazy as ever. He loves me. It is terrible to see him suffer and not be able to do anything about it."

As she spoke, I thought love lets us dare to reveal who we are beneath our masks and liberates us to give and receive love fully. Poignantly, where Katharina loved most, she was hurt most: the agony for her of being unable to alleviate his suffering.

Archie reminded her, "I have everything I need and more. I have joy and peace in the time I have left. I don't need hurt and spitefulness [referring to his mother]." Then, with resignation in his tone, "We need a miracle."

I saw that part of my focus with Katharina would be to help her recognize the value and importance of her love, not to dismiss it because it couldn't actually cure him.

That Archie had such a loving relationship with Katharina gave him the resource to bear the pain of his illness, and even an extra gleam as he did so. He said repeatedly that he'd never been happier, which affirmed the value and meaning of the life he had now. Archie had enjoyed his career, but he knew, in the face of his death, that his barometer of happiness was based on the love and well-being of those closest to him.

As with Victor Frankl's existential message, "Everything can be taken from a man but one thing: the last of human freedoms—to choose one's attitude in any given set of circumstances, to choose one's own way," Archie had given himself power in his own life even when he was suffering deeply. At the core of his resilience was the love he, Katharina and his children shared. I believe it is virtually impossible to manage these overwhelming experiences without the love of others.

As I was thinking about Archie and the necessity for him to protect himself from his parents' negative coping, I could hear his words on not seeing them echoing in my mind: "I kind of hate myself for it." The tragedy of Archie's mother's childhood abuse and his father's weakness from his own story was continuing down the generations. Archie articulated it perfectly: "I object that my mum and dad dumped their problems on us. They are entitled to have their feelings for what happened to them, but it is not OK to dump them on us."

Archie's illness tripped his parents into their embedded defences and habits of dealing with difficulty. His mother had turned the attention on to herself, and his father had shut down. Both defences blocked them from supporting their son . . . most probably their beloved son. The misery I have witnessed through such lack of awareness and acting out of family patterns is vast.

Archie, though, had done the work. He recognized that "With my first wife I basically repeated with my children what I'd had as a child. But when I'd seen Nigel [his therapist] I made the changes. I apologized to my kids. I told them, 'I didn't realize how bad I've been and I want to change that. I want you to know that if something is wrong it's probably not your fault, it's probably my fault. You were just a child. I was the one who was responsible.'" That conversation completely reset his relationship with his children. They were now extremely close and functioning well.

This is not a call for everyone to have therapy—though it might help! It is a call to recognize that functioning families are led by functioning parents to adult as well as young children. I'd like parents to examine themselves and recognize the impact of their behaviour, take responsibility for it and change it if necessary. An apology as sincere and heartfelt as Archie's can go a long way to heal injuries from the past.

Archie could name his feelings, consider his thinking, have insight into his own state of mind, while making the imaginative leap to think about how another person is feeling. This brought to my mind the important addition to theories on human development by the renowned psychoanalyst and psychologist Professor Peter Fonagy and his colleagues. It's called "mentalization."

Fonagy states that the ability to "interpret their own and others' behaviour by attributing mental states"—being able to name your and someone else's mood—is significant in building secure relationships. Once Archie had learnt how to do that he was able to respond in a calmer, more empathic and thoughtful way to others. As a result, his relationships flourished. It was somewhat miraculous for me to witness the impact of this. As Archie so poignantly said, "Knowing my family is at peace with each other, after my work with Nigel, we are a good unit. There's a lot of strength to be taken from that." I silently applauded Nigel: what a terrific piece of work they had done together. It had been literally life-changing.

Archie's capacity to focus on anything apart from the everyday was limited. I didn't hear about his work. He'd had to stop eighteen months before. I knew he'd loved golf, and football, and his car. He grieved not being able to drive: it represented his lack of freedom and his very real immobility.

The only other significant person he spoke about was his younger brother, Rory. He was clearly fond of him, but said, "He can be a bit odd. He did after all get the same parenting tools as me. Rory had said when I was diagnosed that he'd be there for me. I was touched and opened up to him how upset I was. Within minutes he said, 'Stop it, you're upsetting yourself.' That's my mother speaking. We both knew what he really meant was 'It doesn't matter what's going on, let's pretend everything's all right.' When he said he'd be there for me he actually didn't know how to be. When I was very ill in hospital from the brain tumour he'd said, 'You had a rough patch.' A rough patch! It was more than that. It means I have to do the mental adjustment. I have to translate the words he says into what he actually means, and I don't doubt he means well. I do make allowances but it's exhausting."

Archie mentioned his brother in similar tones in further sessions, and it became clear he wanted to keep their relationship going. Their bond was meaningful to him: he didn't want to cut off from him. But he had to calibrate how much he saw Rory because it required of him such mental strength to remain calm.

I reflected that sibling relationships can be both deeply supportive and sources of huge distress. Those early dynamics are intrinsically wired in us: they can cut through newly acquired stabilizing mechanisms and reopen early wounds. For Archie it was an echo of his mother's words, voiced in Rory, which reignited inside him his dysfunctional childhood, and sent him into a familiar, but old, state of fear. It took a lot of energy to access his more recent calmer way of being. That meant he could only manage bite-size interactions.

At the beginning of one session when I asked carelessly, "How are you?" Archie gently reminded me of my insensitivity. "That's a difficult question, to which I only have a complicated answer." I should have known better. The number of times friends and clients have told me people ask, "How are you?" and they want to scream, "How the hell do you think I am, given . . . ?"

I asked Archie if there was a better question, remembering the Sheryl Sandberg suggestion: "How are you today?"

He said, "I don't think people really want to hear the answer. They want to hear you're fine so they don't have to put a lot of effort in. I've noticed people tend to stay away now. My social network has shrunk. It isn't deliberate. They feel helpless . . . If they ask I tend to talk around the edges."

I was moved by the truth of his words, and how isolating suffering can be. I told him I really wanted to know.

He took a breath, stock still as ever. "I feel like I'm an old man. Like an eighty-year-old. I want to scream every day. When I'm walking down the stairs the pain is unbelievable. I don't want to focus on it. It's caused by the treatments. The chemo, steroids and radiotherapy. The doctors told me the side effects would last a short time, but it never ends . . . Even with Katharina it's a bit lonely . . ." He finished by dropping his head, in tears and his cheeks flushed.

I told him I could see the heartbreak in his face. He cried some more, blew his nose, and replied, "We're meant to have a holiday. It'll be August and that's too far ahead to think. I'm ticking down my own clock and that's not a nice feeling—nobody wants to hear you talk about that. Even when I don't talk about it, it's in the back of my head the whole time . . . I'm angry at the situation, I'm angry I've got cancer. I know I'm not the only one, there are other people suffering more, but I'm still angry."

I was touched by his openness with me and felt at least he could voice his scream: he didn't have to protect me. I knew this was healthy coping, which is very different from simplistic positive thinking. It gives the person the freedom to express their worries, fears and pain while still having hope.

In every session we had, Archie would spend a fairly short but important amount of time, in his usual down-to-earth voice, on his symptoms: the pain in his head, the terrible difficulty in eating, his nausea, diarrhea, the physical trial of getting up, his permanent debilitating exhaustion, his sore mouth, loss of taste. "I've been attacked by every evil conceivable treatment known to mankind." The only welcome release was that he slept well in "the comfiest bed on the planet." Thank goodness for that.

Typically, he would then choose to turn away his attention: "I don't have closure, I have acceptance. I know what the situation is, and I live with it. Despite it all we're happy, I'm happy. It's a lot of hard work keeping it happy but it's worth it now. Even if I don't have long to go, there's something in me that makes me fine. I'll do what needs to be done. I accept the illness will come but I'm not ready to let it roll over me." He said emphatically, fairly often through our work together: "I'm not dead yet." He was very much alive.

Archie was managing the almost impossibly difficult negoti-ation between living with the terminal nature of his cancer while having hope. Hope, as well as the love of his family, was a vital factor for him to live as good a day as he could every day. I could only be in awe of his courage. He was an inspiration of how to live a good life in the shadow of his death.

Hope is a fascinating concept. It is the alchemy that turns a life around and is vital to see us through the darkest times. Yet false hope is harmful. The psychologist Dr Charles Snyder's theory on hope clarifies it for me. He says hope isn't just a feeling, although that helps, it is also cognitive: setting out a realistic plan, a Plan A and a Plan B, with the self-belief to make it happen. The combination of feeling hope and translating it into a plan means the hope is more likely to be realized.

From my experience of working with other families facing death, I knew it was important to talk about the practical things as well as the spiritual. Archie's robust pragmatism balanced by emotional honesty meant this was not a difficult subject to raise. Smartly turned out as ever, sitting in his bed, he told me, "I don't have a recognized belief system, I have mine. I don't think too far ahead. I have made all the plans for afterwards—my will, my life insurance, all the legalities. I don't mind what they do for my funeral . . ."

I took a moment to picture his funeral. I rather held my breath: these conversations are hard.

Archie continued, "They haven't asked me about it. I imagine they'll keep it small. I'm not going to come back and haunt them whatever they do."

I went with him, reflecting what I'd heard him say: there was no need for anything else from me. To manage the intensity of picturing his own funeral, he did his familiar self-regulating pivot: took a breath and turned his attention to something associated with it, not an about-face but something that gave him sustenance. His family. He told me the main thing was that there would be no falling out between his children and Katharina. They loved each other and got on incredibly well. He was, rightly, immensely proud of that.

Archie's face lit up as he remembered the previous weekend when he had seen his daughter Isla for the first time in months and months. The terrible cruelty of Covid had meant that the precious life he had left he couldn't spend with his beloved daughter or, when he felt well enough, go out and have positive experiences, create happy memories for them. He told me, "It was absolutely brilliant seeing her. I'd missed her so much, I hugged her so tight . . ." There were tears in his eyes from the release of pain, the relief of connecting viscerally, hugging with love. "I hadn't fully realized how much I missed her until I hugged her, she jumped on me. It was so special, we both cried." I joined him in tears.

From the important work of palliative-care consultant and author Kathryn Mannix, I was better informed about the psychological benefits of having knowledge of the process of dying well before we die: the changes in wakefulness, breathing and consciousness that occur. She advises that complicated issues such as these need careful thought and discussion. As with most things, what we don't know lets our imagination run riot and can be terrifying, but being well informed, based on facts, imbues us with less fear and more confidence, which can lead to a peaceful death.

Mannix suggests we talk about what matters most to the person who is dying, which can give guidance at the time and mean we use their precious energy mindfully. This can also protect against future regrets, a derailer of grief, as can awareness that we have had all of the important conversations, maybe even writing significant messages in a card or letter. Spending time together, perhaps listening to music (one of Archie's remaining sources of joy), recording their voice, writing a journal of times spent together are invaluable at the time and for ever. Turning to happy, loving memories is a key source of solace in grief.

I kept this in mind through our time together, waiting for the appropriate moment to bring it up. I saw my job was to be sensitive to the family's experience and their openness to these conversations, which went at their pace, not my predetermined certainty that we had to talk about it. I trusted the opportunity would arise with this emotionally literate group.

There are many families with whom this conversation would never happen. However much we may want to have it with someone we care about, we must respect their right to their denial. It is their only coping mechanism in the face of death, probably learnt young, and maybe their only protection. They have a right to hold on to it with force, and at this point more than ever.

Often, I saw Katharina with Archie and she would say openly how difficult she found their situation. I'd offered, in front of him, for her to have time alone with me if she needed it. She texted me. Interestingly she didn't ask to speak to me, the text just said: *This is Katharina, Archie's fiancée.* We agreed to speak.

Immediately I could see the distress on her face. "It's horrendous, seeing Archie waste away in the last six months." The problem was that he hadn't been able to eat, or only a few spoonfuls a day. He had this terrible taste in his mouth that made food either disgustingly sweet or metallic, and I'd seen the revulsion on his face as he'd described it. It was awful for them both. Archie loved food—it had been one of his remaining pleasures and now that was removed.

The difficulty for Katharina was that cooking for him had been a way of loving him, one of the few overt ways she felt she could help him and improve his day. But now that had been taken away. She told me, "I'm panicking. I'm petrified of losing him and now I'm punishing myself." She had got into a bad pattern of eating more when Archie ate less, and she was now morbidly obese. Hearing that was a shock: I hadn't noticed. She laughed. "I'm tall so I hide it well." We both recognized her unconscious response that somehow if she could eat for him she would keep him alive. There is also the magical thinking when we are facing our loved one's death that if we love them enough, are good to them in every possible way, it will keep death at bay. As well as the complex unconscious dynamics, Katharina recognized the more prosaic aspect of her behaviour: she was anaesthetizing her frustration, even fury, but mainly fear of Archie not eating. She absolutely didn't blame him. She knew this was hers to unravel.

I reflected that *in extremis* all of us have to find some kind of outlet. The fact that she didn't take it out on Archie was positive. She agreed, and she had insight: she knew this was also an old reflex hijacked by the pain. It came from an early message to be good, even perfect, having impossibly high expectations put on her as a child, and now she felt "helpless." She would resort to eating three packets of crisps or biscuits as a form of control. It released her to feel numb, a temporary relief, but in the end was a horrible cycle of self-attack. We discussed all the issues and explored possibilities that were realistic, tiny habits that might enable her to improve her behaviour slowly. Perhaps as she was drawn to the bowl or biscuit packet, she could take a breath, reach for a glass of water, take another breath, then walk around the house for a few minutes. Maybe the insistent urge would pass.

As the renowned American social scientist B. J. Fogg states in his book *Tiny Habits*, it isn't willpower that brings change but self-esteem and feeling good about oneself in the changes we make. Katharina and I needed to come up with a realistic small adaptation that might give additional support and leave her pleased with herself. We agreed on three walks a week, whatever length, with the reward of a big hug with Archie after each one.

When we spoke the following week I was glad to see her spirits had lifted. Katharina was smiling and walking around the room with some energy as she spoke. They'd had "a really fun day," an "I don't care day" at the weekend and she'd dialled down the eating. It had "started to settle." Talking had helped and Archie's energy had improved: he was doing more things. They had puttered in the garden together, which had felt life-affirming—the interdependence that is true for many of us: when the person we love is well, we feel better, and vice versa. As Katharina said "It's a really thin rope," between times of hope and enjoyment and the "harsh reality of seeing the man I love deteriorate before my eyes."

★

Katharina and Archie were side by side on the sofa in the sitting room. When Katharina had met Archie she had got to a point in her life when she had been struggling mentally. "I'd given up on meeting anyone. It's what I'd wanted but I never thought I'd get it." It transpired that before they met both had come to such a low point in their lives they'd contemplated suicide. Meeting each other transformed their well-being.

Katharina was saying they'd been together seven years and they'd never argued: they could disagree and respect each other's differences. Archie's face lit up, and they both beamed at me. Katharina continued, "I have a lovely relationship with his kids. I knew from the beginning if I didn't get along with them there is no point in our relationship." Being a step-parent is a difficult role to fulfil, so any additional pressures would make it even tougher. For Katharina there was the double whammy of her stepchildren's parent dying during a pandemic. I acknowledged what a feat it was that she and they got on so well together. Archie was nodding vigorously, so proud. It was just after Mother's Day and his children had sent Katharina a Stepmother's Day card. He spoke about it as if it was an Oscar. He asked her to fetch the card. It was huge, the size of her body—the pride and joy in their faces was almost palpable. Archie asked Katharina to read the message: *I'm so happy you came into our lives, especially Dad's. You make him happy every day, when he is at his lowest. We are so grateful. You are supportive and helpful to us, we need help too. Thank you so much for being here, we love you.*

Archie's pride in it was right. In terms of family awards, getting a card like that is the equivalent of an Oscar.

I noted the long-lasting value of written letters and cards in families. Texts tend to be ephemeral: we lose them in the digital ether. Tangible messages of love in families can be turned to time and again as a resource: they live on for years after they are sent.

In a following session they showed me photographs of the day, eighteen months ago, they'd become engaged. What a joyous time that had been. While happy memories are an ongoing source of sustenance and strength, Archie and Katharina were unable to create new ones because, infuriatingly, they'd had to cancel their wedding twice—Covid truly messing with their lives yet again.

It would be an incredibly important celebration and public acknowledgement of their love for each other. It was imbued with many layers of meaning; an honouring of their love, hard found, and their commitment to each other, also a celebration of them as a family. It was a different kind of family from any they'd known before, one based on honesty, trust and love. After all the trials of ill-health, they wanted to have fun with their friends, "have a great day." Archie knew it would be "a fantastic memory" to look back on, even feast on. There was the important consideration this was Katharina's first marriage and they both wanted the day to be as she'd always dreamt of: her wedding dress, the ceremony, the celebration with the people they loved most, in particular Katharina's parents. She was their only child, and close to them. They had been extremely supportive, in myriad ways, through all the pain of Archie's illness. She wanted her father to give her away, as she'd pictured it since she was a young girl.

There was also, of course, the underlying worry of Archie's health. He did not want to be weak or ill on his wedding day: "No deathbed wedding." Counter to that, the legal position of Katharina being his wife and the legal rights it gave her were no trivial matter. There was a very real time pressure. We ended the session with Archie saying, "Katharina takes care of the dates ahead of us. I know I can do today and tomorrow." The hope of getting married buoyed them, but its shadow, uncertainty, was always present. Keeping his horizons short was, in the end, the only way for them to cope with all they faced.

I talked to Archie's son, Greg, who was relieved that his work in a laboratory meant he wasn't at home every day. Prior to the pandemic he had been living alone but, given his underlying mental-health issues, they had all decided it would be better for him to stay with his father and Katharina. I'd imagined, though not actually heard, there were tensions between them. Adult children returning to a parent's home are likely to bring up issues around sharing domestic chores and space, both mental and physical.

Greg is by no means the only young person returning home. Young adults not leaving until they are older or returning after a number of years is a trend that has been growing in the last decade, reaching 25 million in the US in 2018, according to a Pew analysis of US Census Bureau data. The same data showed 52 percent of young people aged between eighteen and twenty-nine had boomeranged home since the outbreak of the pandemic for economic and mental-health reasons. What had originally been a temporary measure has become increasingly permanent. It has been stressful for the young person and their parents. The key to managing their difficulties is to recognize that what they are feeling is normal, given their circumstances, to create ground rules, like who does what, and to actively listen to each other.

Greg had a definite likeness to his dad. He looked strong, his muscular frame seen easily beneath his T-shirt. Red-haired, with a short beard, his darting hazel eyes showed he was appropriately anxious when talking to this total stranger about the most distressing thing in his life. We didn't start with his father's illness. I began on a gentler path to build a safe connection between us first. Greg spoke fast, gesticulating with his hands, his Scottish accent seeming to heighten for me the intensity he felt and his love for his father.

Greg told me how Archie had taken him and Isla out for supper and apologized for all the errors he'd made in the past. That heartfelt apology was profoundly healing for Greg. Since that time, they'd become closer, and Greg saw Archie, with his vulnerability, in a new light. It was a paradigm shift: he learnt from his dad that he didn't have to carry everything on his own—"I can get help. It's OK not to be OK." In allowing his own frailty he could embrace all that was good and bad about himself as well as his father.

On hearing of Archie's most recent diagnosis, he said, "I was like a deer caught in the headlights. Then I went numb . . . I don't know how to process this." As he was talking, I was reminded of Okun and Nowinski's new grief theory of loss, appropriate for a cancer diagnosis. They describe the stages as: crisis, unity, upheaval, resolution and renewal. They do not see them as linear but as a process over time when the ill person or family member can move between several stages simultaneously.

I could see that Greg was moving between crisis, unity and upheaval. He told me, "I'm not sure my dad will be here next year and that's a thought no one wants . . . Thinking of my dad's death is hard. I want to do everything I can to help, spend time with him . . . I can only hope that time is as far away as possible." With his head down, tears in his eyes, he went on, "When he loses a drastic amount of weight, walks like an old man, the fact that he's not going to meet his grandchildren, that's so, so sad. It isn't fair . . . He's endured so much and he's still enduring . . . The cancer is going to take away my dad and there's nothing I can do to stop it. All I can do is make the very best of the time we have."

I was aware that the psychological toll of those feelings can lead to depression, anxiety and guilt. I had an eye open for those symptoms, given Greg's history. Although he had said he went numb, that wasn't what I saw. While he was speaking, he was adjusting to the unbearable reality he and his family were facing. In saying the words, he faced it, not to make him feel all right about it, but to know all the intensity of his experience and find a way to allow it.

The fundamental protective factor for Greg against the sideswipe of depression and anxiety was the relationship he had with his dad. There was between them a dynamic we therapists call collaborative effective coping and adaptation. It means that, alongside each other, the movement of their feelings between the poles of loss and hope was perpetual, in varying intensity at varying times. And it was in the movement that they incrementally adapted to their new circumstances.

Most importantly, the love they shared enabled them to endure it. Looking into the distance, he told me, "I want to make special the time we've got . . . I can't prepare for the future and that's where the powerlessness comes from, separating what I feel from what I know. Today matters, tomorrow matters." I told him he'd said almost verbatim what his father had said, and he laughed. "I don't know whether to be proud or what." He brushed his hair off his face, his smile bringing softness to his voice. "It shows how alike we are. I like to think I got some intelligence from him. He's the smartest man I know, witty and loving. If I can be half the person he is I'd be proud."

He continued speaking slowly, turning his attention inwards to connect with his most direct truth. "I want to be a decent person, not a perfect person. He taught me that you can make mistakes and take responsibility for them." We both agreed warmly how much his father influences and connects in him now and will do so all his life.

As I ended the session, I told him what a wonderful son he was, and he took a few moments to register it, then shook his head, smiled like a young boy and said, "Yeah."

A few weeks later I met Isla, Archie's daughter. She had jet-black hair held in a high ponytail, and when she flicked her fringe, which she did regularly, I saw her two-tone orange-and-black painted nails with rings on every finger. They contrasted with her voice, which was quiet, her brown eyes turned away from mine when she spoke. I intuited she was shy, or perhaps she'd heard from Greg that it would be an emotional conversation, and she was trying to balance herself. Yet she opened up immediately. "I love my dad, I hate this happening to him. It's so sad. It's been tough as I've hardly been able to see him. When I saw him the other weekend we both cried. I tried not to. I wanted to be brave. I don't want him to worry about me—he's got enough on his plate." Her words came with a rush of emotion: conflicting feelings of worry and care for him, which don't sit comfortably together. I reminded her that she couldn't protect her father from her sadness, and if she tried, she might perhaps create an unwelcome distance between them. Honesty was more straightforward and allowed proper connection.

Isla had desperately wanted to spend more time with him, but she was a medical support worker, interacting with hundreds of people every day: even if she'd wanted to break the rules, "I was terrified I'd give him Covid. I couldn't live with myself if I'd given it to him . . ." Finally she said, with some force, "I didn't want to kill my dad, but also I don't want to regret anything . . ."

She spoke some more about their relationship and how it had changed since that dinner when he'd made amends, how close she felt to him now. "I will always be there for my dad. I'd drop everything for him . . ." Her head turned away and tears were running down her face as she said, "I'm worried something would happen to him and I'm not there . . ." Her voice shook, and I could see the fear in her body, her eyes darting. There was a few minutes' silence as she settled herself. I gently acknowledged how painful this was.

She continued: it was important to get all her concerns out. They had been sitting in her, untouched, for months. "At Christmas we had the conversation. It was hard. I told my dad how much I loved him. We agreed we need to be open, that we'll get through this as a family . . . It went through my mind," her voice was rising as she spoke, "that I found it difficult! I can't imagine how it was for my dad. He's got courage. We all cried. He's amazing, he's fought for so long."

Then she, following her father's role modelling, took a breath, and remembered the happiness of that Christmas. "It was fun, Christmas. I bought him a pocket watch, saying, 'I will always be your little girl, I will always love you' . . . I didn't want to make him cry but I'm also happy I made him cry. I bought him a funny mug, Del Boy. Then Dad got me back! He told me I'm a good person, and he got me crying. He won that one. I do love him." She was laughing as she remembered the love and the humour they shared. She described the completely delicious beef Wellington Katharina had made, the joy they'd all felt sitting around the table together. They'd laughed and loved. She would revisit those memories as an important resource of love and connection to her father for ever.

Recognizing anew the years they had been battling with his health, with pockets of remission, gave me renewed admiration for their courage, the extraordinary human spirit not only to keep going but to keep it together. I was not sure I would have been able to. Isla was confident she wouldn't have any regrets for things left unsaid, but she was worried about the future. Her narrow shoulders lifted and dropped with her sighs, and there was so much sadness in her voice. "I just want it to stop . . . I try to be prepared. But I know I will never be prepared . . . I will always be distraught, as I have been every time he's had hope and then the treatment hasn't worked."

The truth was she would not be able to control her feelings when she got bad news. It would hit her deeply. She said, "I'm over-emotional."

I vehemently disagreed. I thought that that expression should be banned: no one is over-emotional. Perhaps others don't like the extent of what the "over-emotional" person feels and criticize them for it. I told her, "Your feelings represent how much you love your dad. You are a sentient emotional being, thank goodness."

She smiled shyly. "I always think I cry too much, but maybe it's OK."

In another session Isla turned her attention to her father's medical results. "I want confirmation that the radiotherapy has kinda helped. He said it felt like it had been ironed out . . . I feel anxious waiting . . . He said in his little joke, if it didn't work he'd need some plumbing done . . . Typical Dad!" Her thoughts followed a familiar track that took her to the scary unknown future, without her father. "I don't know if I've said this to Dad, but I've said it to Katharina. What will I do if he's not there?"—her head in her hands—"I always turn to him." A big sob. Then she looked up at me through her tears. "Katharina said, 'I will be there for you. You can talk to me,'"—gulping her tears, those brown eyes both sad and more open—"and that made me feel happy . . . Knowing my dad will be dead is a reality, it will happen. He told me he dreamt that the doctor told him he didn't have cancer any more." I remained

quiet, gave her space to process. That is how we update our understanding, by allowing information from different channels to be
accessed: it can be visual, emotional, auditory, movement-based
or relational. In her case it was allowing her feelings, her relationship with her father and her cognitive understanding to align. A
few minutes passed. Breathing more lightly and with some energy,
Isla spoke up: "I want to make a day to forget all that stuff, a day
to forget cancer and have just one day a happy day." I could feel
the waves of emotion running through me as she spoke. It was
beautiful and intense. I agreed and very much hope that, with the
Covid restrictions lifting, they could make it happen.

I wanted to let Isla know that Archie felt lucky to have her as a
daughter. She was a wonderful daughter. Hearing it from an outsider can sometimes reach someone without the usual reflex
defences. I could see by the quietly pleased look in Isla's eyes, she'd
taken in my words. We concluded that she can't control what happens. "I want to show him how much I do love him. I want him to
know that." I reiterated I didn't think there was any doubt he
knew how she felt. Loving him in the way she did made his life
worth living every day he had.

I was happy to see Archie on a day when he felt better. "I feel good
today, less everything." He'd told me before that he would always
make a point of telling everyone when he was more energetic and
in less pain. It was a significant difference from his mother, who
did the reverse.

We discussed his gorgeous children and he welled up with
pride, which led him to tell me, "I worry about them. I want them
to be OK. What can I do to make them OK?" Tears followed as
his powerlessness and sadness washed through him. He wanted to
buy them something they could have on their wedding day, or
another special day. A watch for Greg, a pair of earrings for Isla.
"I can be with them in some sort of way." Then he really sobbed.
I wished I could have reached through the screen to put an arm
round his shoulders, no words, the simple support of touch. As

it was, I could only voice how terrible it was in as warm a tone as possible.

He took some time to settle, swearing under his breath, saying how awful it was, and then, being Archie, consciously turned his attention in another direction, saying, "Enough. It's too painful when I project too far forward. I have to come back to today. I like to have a plan."

For the rest of the session we talked about the gratitude he felt for the help he got from the Maggie Centre (a charity providing support and information for people suffering from cancer), his wedding, his brother, all in a lighter tone. By the end Archie was making jokes and cheery. When I thought about it afterwards, and his deep sadness stayed with me for some time, I marvelled at the human capacity to find resilience by facing the fear, feeling it, letting the emotions be expressed and then, knowing it was enough, look to hope. I had witnessed Archie go through that difficult but empowering cycle in a matter of minutes.

It meant we ended with his profound reflection: "I have positivity and hope. If the outcome is bad, I did everything in my power to stop it. There's a bit of peace in that and a huge amount of sadness."

The time pressure of my book going to print meant that I had to stop writing about this family. But I am very happy to let you know that Archie and Katharina did succeed in having the most beautiful wedding. It was a joyous celebration, full of the people they cared about. Archie spoke with humour, heart and love. He told me it gave them all a wonderful memory, which they all shared and participated in.

I sent them these words, their story as they have shared it with me. I told them reading it comes with a government health warning. It is one thing talking about your most intensely painful and difficult experience, another reading about it in black and white. Seeing each other's feelings, thoughts and worries could be overwhelming. I suggested Katharina read it first, to check if it's too much for Archie. Archie, with his usual steadfastness, said he would read it too. I hope that, as well as it being a very emotional read, they have all seen how they found the impossible path between living and dying while looking both in the eye.

Since the wedding Archie has been very seriously ill, but he has, yet again, recovered. He sent me a message to say "Congratulations! I am enjoying your book. It has been really helpful in the last few weeks. Thank you for all you did for us, you helped me and my family so much. I know it will help others."

I hold out for the belief that where certainty ends hope begins: hope and possibility walk hand in hand. While acknowledging his limited life, Archie will certainly be turning to the light of hope and leading his family in that direction.

I am deeply touched to be included in this family's journey up to now. I felt I had learnt some important lessons from them that will stay with me and for which I am extremely grateful.

It showed me that even when we are adults, our parents matter enormously, something I believe is often unrecognized. Having a conflicted relationship with them costs us dearly. They are a part of us. We don't need them to survive as we did as a child, but there is always the child in our adult selves who wants to be loved and close to our parents, and in some way feels we need them to thrive, not just survive.

We all hope for happy resolutions. But sometimes we need to cut bonds to heal. It would never be what one would choose, yet knowing when to walk away from family members requires courage, strength, and self-awareness, prioritizing those who are reciprocal and positive.

Archie's capacity to transform his life by changing what he calls "his tools" when he was in his forties, find love, repair his relationship with his children, then face both the physical and psychological pain of his terminal diagnosis with honesty and love is truly remarkable. It means that Katharina, Greg and Isla are able to be with him, loving, connected, suffering and tearful, too—not needing to protect each other from the terrible pain they all feel and, through their honesty, having the capacity to face together what each day brings.

Love is not a soft skill. In a family, nothing is more important, and nothing is as hard.

Conclusion

Humans learn best through stories.

My hope is that while you read, or were reading, the eight case studies, you will see aspects of yourself, and your family, in them and glean some insights and methods for changing dynamics and giving yourselves more space to grow.

Perhaps most of all I wanted to show, through the universality of these experiences, that we are not alone, that through the multiple layers of these families' lives you will see you are not the only one, that we all struggle with different versions of similar issues. There are no straightforward answers and wrestling with difficulties doesn't mean there is something wrong with you. It is the stuff of life, as well as, of course, the joy and beauty. My hope is that it will encourage you to befriend your challenges, discover new aspects of yourself and your family, and find ways to celebrate your strengths and joys, as well as naming hard truths, to make space through that process for love and connection to flourish. In doing so, you surround yourself with kindness, love and new potential. Discovering those truths will allow you to give new meaning to those relationships, which will shape how you behave in them.

Most of what goes on in families is hidden below the waterline. As individuals and in our families we all inevitably suffer, in multiple ways and intensities. I absolutely believe we always want to do the best we can. The terrible paradox is that in the fear and pain of injury, we often shut down or attack and end up stuck and hurting—in the full range of that spectrum from managing but brittle to utterly desperate. The difficult truth is that we can only fix what we face.

In every one of these stories, my clients discovered, as they voiced their distress, that through being heard and met with compassion, something changed, and that change was reparative. When they could turn to themselves, and others, with honesty, empathy and healing followed. Their innate bonds of love were reconnected.

The business of suffering is complex. In families it is doubly so when we recognize we carry the unprocessed trauma of previous generations as well as the pulls and pushes of normal human interactions: the need to be loved, to be seen, to be fully known; the fear of being abandoned, or loved "less," the agony of hurting alone and the swathe of confusion, blame, guilt and anger that ensues. Sometimes we are forced to bump into versions of ourselves we didn't know existed and certainly don't like or want. At others we discover our absolute best selves as we navigate the everyday of family life.

As I worked with these families, I saw how many layers of misunderstanding needed to be revealed. In every family, there were competing narratives that had to be heard. Keith and Patience's conflict wasn't about her becoming a Jehovah's Witness but about each of them being given space for the truth of their experience to be acknowledged. Likewise, Ashley's desire for a pizza with his father, Paul, was really about his need to feel special, given the contested territory for his father's attention and love.

Everyone's life in each family was influenced by their personality and their back story—how they carried wounds from the events that happened to them. Then there was their deeper intergenerational history, which was invisibly shaping their responses. What is surprising in this tangle of layers was the speed of their repair once their narratives were heard in full. The window of therapy allowed space for all of their emotions—more than are usually expressed in a family dynamic when hardworn patterns repeat and voices get lost.

In some cases, a painful-but-necessary decision has to be made to cut ties. Repair is not possible for all. For others we discovered that their ability to fully love and be loving was hidden underground, beneath the weight of their untold stories of pain. Once it surfaced, it liberated them to reconnect.

Anyone looking at their own family would benefit by examining their inherited family patterns and behaviours, looking with openness to see what may need adapting. For example, we know we eat a particular brand of food because it is what we ate in childhood, or we don't eat it for the same reason. We support football clubs or hate particular sports because our mother or father took us to see them or forced us to take part in them, as their parents had before them. Our experiences are embedded in us, and they remain, shaping our decisions and choices.

My expanded view from doing this work is that we may go into one-to-one therapy because we have a problem with a member of our family, and perhaps we will find ways of better coping with it. But if we really want deep systemic change that is not just tinkering on the edges, we need more information. If it is possible to get everyone on board, family therapy is the answer. For a therapist who is not trained in family systems this is a bold statement, but one I truly believe in.

When I reflect on the families in these chapters, fundamentally it is their sense of safety, love and belonging that allows them to thrive. This is a prerequisite for us: we need to feel safe before we connect. Emotional connection is a basic human need. We need to connect in order to adapt and grow. We need to feel at home in our relationships, be truly ourselves with the team of people we call family. Each individual needs to feel safe in their home, around their kitchen table and in their body, not fighting it or poisoning it to numb the pain; instead, uncovering new ways to be in tune with themselves and each other. That will ensure each individual in the family system feels heard, valued, respected, allowed to be different and, of course, to be loved.

Which brings us to that perennial question: when does parenting end? I hope this book has brought you closer to my answer: it never does. It changes and reconfigures, but those ties remain and need regular, mindful updating.

★

While writing these case studies, my relationship with my own family has evolved. Learning about other people's families has helped me process my relationship with my own—those stacked behind and ahead of me. I have a more expansive view. I see my grandparents and parents with more compassion. It hasn't removed my sense of responsibility when I think of the errors I made with my own children, but perhaps it has softened my guilt. It has meant I have had important conversations, and learnt surprising truths, good and bad. Despite significant unknowns that have emerged, I stand on firmer ground and feel more confident as to who I am. Which is strangely paradoxical. The exploration and openness matter just as much as the results.

The proverb "It takes a village to raise a child" was a recurring theme in these stories. Its importance as a foundation for the well-being of families and society as a whole has been magnified in my understanding for many reasons. Collaboration and cooperation within our families become a superpower when they are extended to our communities: the level of our resilience to adversity and crisis is significantly connected to those networks and neighbourhoods.

Reciprocity in our relationships builds our confidence. It is protective of our mental health to have good social interaction; it literally grows our brain networks. As humans we evolved to hug and touch, to be held, to flirt, to have sex, to chatter, debate, fight, laugh, cry and dance together. Interacting in groups is central to building a healthy life. As children, and even as adults, our brain is plastic, and when we have more social interactions it is a protective force: we become active agents in creating our social world as opposed to what the neuroscientist Professor Eamon McCrory terms "social thinning," which detrimentally affects our well-being. The suggestion is that a child used to have at least nine people who were directly involved and interested in their lives. It has now dropped to two.

With the concept of creating our own village in mind, I was drawn to the Singh/Kelly idea of creating a team of eight people (obviously the number is a subjective choice) to whom they turned for advice and support on all aspects of their child's and family life. The most important aspect was that the family never felt judged, and always felt valued. This seems to me an excellent repurposed version of godparents. People need people, and the path to healthy families should be paved with the help of others.

Governments state how important families are but their policies do not match their rhetoric. Those who need the most support are the least likely to be able to access it, often for economic reasons, availability or a cultural bias. But these problems will, in turn, become society's. We all need to prioritize family: our government, our community and ourselves.

We are fortunate to have a great store of research, knowledge and information to help guide us personally and collectively in our families. In this book I have aimed to extract the nuggets of wisdom that can help us build confident, resilient families. The questions I and many of us will often ask ourselves are: Am I normal? Am I failing? From my research and work with these families, I believe these are the wrong questions. The better questions are: Where have we come from? What are our family values, beliefs and ways of being with each other? What aspects within myself am I denying? Living in what you may deem blissful ignorance may be the contaminating force in your life. We grow wise by discovering, sometimes rediscovering, what has been forgotten.

For this to happen, I want to shout out to those who feel stuck and are hurting in themselves and their families, carrying those looping messages in their minds and bodies: *It didn't start with you or even your parents*. Look at the untold stories, unprocessed injuries and losses that have been handed to you by ghosts of the past, and find a way to deal with them now so that you don't hand them down to the next generation. Be intrepid and find the sources of those stories. Write them down or, for example, draw your own genogram.

Through exploration comes information, and new perspectives. When we shift our lens and view of what is going on internally, and has taken place externally, our behaviour changes. Outcomes change. Focusing on improving small things rather than gunning for a life-altering solution is the source of most growth. It could be as simple as agreeing to go for a regular walk-and-talk together, or infusing creativity and culture in family life by visiting galleries and concerts, in person or online. What may have blocked us is now a doorway to a new connection and a new way of being, a revitalized family, a family open to growth.

The power to change your family's story starts in your mind. To imagine the family you wish for is the first step in making it your new reality.

Twelve Touchstones for
the Well-being of Family

I vehemently disagree with Tolstoy: "All happy families resemble one another; each unhappy family is unhappy in its own way." Families operate on a spectrum of doing well and less so depending on what is going on: it is not possible to be doing well all the time. When families function effectively they are adaptive shifting systems that respond to individual feelings and external events more positively and supportively than dysfunctional families. For that reason, there can't be rules for families: we are all too different.

I thought it might be helpful to create a matrix of touchstones to reflect on and refer to when we feel stuck or troubled by our family. Each person's interpretation will necessarily be subjective, which is healthy. The touchstones are interconnected, as are all things relational. They shape and influence each other. It might be useful to look at them and see how one aspect is affecting another, then explore how they are impacting you and your relationship with your family.

Remember, they are touchstones, not rules. Allow flexibility and self-compassion: don't use them as a stick to beat yourself with. These are the ones I value. You might want to keep some, reject a few and add others. I encourage you to make your own matrix of touchstones for your family.

When reviewing them, remember that focusing on improving small things, rather than a huge transformative solution, leads to expansion.

It is important to acknowledge that families don't take place in a vacuum. How we think and act will be profoundly impacted by wider financial, cultural, ethnic, diverse identities, physical and mental health, and generational circumstances and expectations.

1. Be Self-Compassionate

Self-compassion is vital. Where we love most we care and feel hurt most, and we are at our most vulnerable. It can mean we criticize ourselves mercilessly when we make mistakes, which we will inevitably do. Recognize that in all the roles we play in our family—parent, partner, child, sibling—we can never be perfect. Being "good enough" really is good enough. Forgive yourself for the bad day.

It's helpful to try to be as compassionate to ourselves as we are to those we love. It also models to those we love that kindness to ourselves is important. It enables us to have the resilience to come back from our mistakes with an open heart. Being open to those close to us, revealing who we truly are beneath our masks, is what, in the end, enables us to feel more connected and trusted.

Self-compassion enables us to show up and take responsibility for our part in the difficulty, not, as is often misconstrued, let ourselves off the hook.

2. Have Effective and Open Communication

Connection runs through all of these touchstones. It is most obvious through communication. We communicate love and connection with each other through verbal and non-verbal cues. Our loving connection is key, as is acknowledgement, having it reflected back to us that we are enough. That we matter is a core need. It is helpful to recognize that connection and disconnection are part of a continuum: sometimes we are more connected, at others less so.

Open communication is where listening is as important as talking, where all feelings, ideas, views and opinions are allowed. Open communication is when there are no barred topics, hidden agendas or rules as to what can or cannot be conveyed and discussed.

There are no rules in a family on what you are allowed to be upset about. In parenting mode with children, it is important that they know they can report what is troubling them: they don't have to fix it.

Communication may at times be more directive to younger children, like telling them what to do and when, but the general tone works best when it is more discursive and collaborative. (See 7. Be Aware of Power Dynamics.) Adults have different brains and they can help their child.

The tone of your voice, your eyes, body language, attentiveness and empathy are all important factors in communication. Silence can allow space for someone to speak or be used as a manipulative tool. We read people's body language, but we often make up what we don't hear. It is cleaner and clearer if we voice our thoughts and feelings, with respect and sensitivity.

When hoping to find out collaboratively what is going on, open questions are helpful. There can also be hypothetical questions, like "What if you . . . ," which can reveal unvoiced hopes, fears and aspirations. Or mind-reading questions, like "What do you think Grandpa would say?" which show the extent of each other's thoughts.

Giving each other honest feedback helps keep relationships clean, and prevents resentment from growing. A way to give feedback is to own your feelings: start with "When you . . ." then describe the particular behaviour or habit you find annoying or difficult in your child, parent, sibling, partner. Then say, "I feel . . ." This is a way to communicate that isn't making judgements or assumptions but owns what you feel and why. It is thereby easier to hear, is less likely to be responded to defensively and maintains self-esteem for everyone.

Being able to reflect as a family, together and individually, through this kind of communication means big issues, difficulties and sources of joy can be discussed and negotiated, important decisions made, and big moments celebrated.

3. Learn to Fight Productively

Having those honest conversations where differences are aired can lead to conflict and even rupture.

It is not possible to have close relationships without disagreements. It is through developing the robustness to bear and manage differences and misunderstandings that we learn about ourselves and the other.

How you fight matters. It is important to avoid name-calling, denigrating or using words as weapons of destruction. Allow hostile, furious, jealous, difficult feelings to be expressed: when driven underground they grow and mutate into physical symptoms or emotional problems. Switch the light on in a room full of difficult feelings. Insisting on good feelings leads to bad. When bad is allowed, good comes. This is not at all easy. It may sound contrary, but it is possible to express powerful feelings without demonizing or abusing the other.

Once the heat of the disagreement has settled, it is often through the discussion after the fight that we feel closer, known in a different way, which engenders deep trust. Do this when you are ready. It does not work to have a fake reconciliation when you are still angry or resentful.

Create a model that includes an embedded habit of reconciliation and repair after a fight. That may well mean saying sorry. Also recognize that there may come a point when you agree to disagree and that's fine.

Proper repair means that the truths being told are not used as weapons against the person. It also means the repair is fully integrated so the disagreement is not brought up in the next conflict: the terrible pattern in families when age-old fights are pulled up again and again as an accusation—"When you . . ."

We need collectively to find ways to be soothed and comforted, to feel safe again after the distress of a fight, what the psychologist

Dr Dan Siegel calls PEACE: Presence, Engagement, Affection, Calm and Empathy.

4. Allow Difference

Multiple people will have multiple views. There is no single way to look at beliefs or issues, or to resolve a problem.

It can be emotionally lonely to feel you are different in your family: for example, in adulthood being the only one who is single, or the child who hates sport. Finding ways for that to be acknowledged, respected and valued, and for attempts to be made to connect, is important.

Be curious and create the time and space to know each other fully. You could spend time as a smaller unit—like parent and one of the children, or siblings together—as well as collectively.

In families that allow a broad input from family members, not one "right" way, there will be a deeper base from which to draw mutual support when there are bumps in the road, as there always are. Narrow views give shallow support.

It is also helpful to recognize that each member of a family may have a different subjective take on the shared experience. For example, the father telling a joke: one person might remember it as very funny, another that it was stupid, and a third that it was hurtful.

There can be fights in families recalling "truths" of the past when there is unlikely to be one truth. There can be one truth about the facts, where they were, the date, but not the lived experience of that memory. Every family member has their subjective truth.

Support and encourage every member of your family to be fully themselves, not shaped according to your preconceptions of how they should be or the conditions of success you set.

5. Have Five Times More Positive Interactions Than Negative

Aim to have five times more positive interactions than negative, in which each family member, including yourself, feels respected, valued and heard. This doesn't mean you keep a checklist and count to five, but it is a good guide: if you can see things spinning out negatively, check with yourself. Have you tended to be more critical than positive? Maybe one member of your family is getting the tough end of your criticism more than another. Find out for yourself what this is about. It may be that what you don't like about them is what you don't like about yourself. Knowledge is power.

6. Set Boundaries With Each Other

Boundaries are physical and emotional, and consequently important in families for mental and physical health.

Children and adults need boundaries to know what behaviour and what expectations are acceptable or not. These boundaries will adapt and change over the life of a family. Each member takes responsibility for and respects their part in keeping the family system safe and balanced. For example, not transgressing someone else's boundary, which could be their emotional space, by asking inappropriate questions. It may be a physical boundary: a common one is "Don't hit your brother/sister!" Or their physical space: not going into their bedroom. In setting boundaries, we need to be consistent and trustworthy.

Less is more. A few clear rules that you stick to are better than lots of confusing ones.

Boundaries can also set realistic expectations to protect against disappointment and resentment—being on time, or returning "borrowed" clothes.

As the well-known proverb states, "Good fences make good neighbours." This can be used on myriad aspects of family life, such as chores, privacy and our possessions.

7. Be Aware of Power Dynamics

All families have power dynamics. Power in families shifts at different times and over time. Those holding the power make or block decisions.

Each family has its own way of managing power and the decision-making process. It is what enables a family to function, for the family unit to make important decisions about their lives, relating to money, housing, schools, holidays and more.

For a family to function successfully, each member, whatever their age, needs to feel they have agency in their life, that their feelings and thoughts are considered and have value in those decisions.

Collaborative power, which is shared equal power between family members, is often referred to as the functional model in families. Patterns of who holds the power can move between collaborative to chaotic or symmetrical (top down), which can cause difficulties in families if they become fixed in them. Power that is fear-based or coercive leads to dysfunctional families.

Power is complex: even young children need to have their voice heard, but they also need to know that their parents hold the responsibility for their lives and decisions. Too much power, too young, can be overwhelming for the child and can lead to dysfunction. This is also linked to boundaries. For parents, aim to be "bigger, stronger, wiser and kind." That means you are not giving your child an overwhelming or scary amount of power, but you are respecting how they feel and what they say.

8. Time for Fun

Carve out time to have fun. Putting chores and tasks aside, being together and playing together are important in families. It can be very simple, like watching a family movie together, playing a game or making a cake. It allows for spontaneous creativity, fantasy, stretches boundaries, reveals aspects of ourselves that can be hidden in the daily grind.

It can release tension and allow joy to bubble up from simple playful pleasures.

Holidays often completely reset a family when everyone can at last relax and focus on being together rather than doing together. Holidays like Christmas can be fun but may also bring huge tensions when the expectation of "fun" is so high. The underlying pulls and pushes of family being together at Christmas may prove explosive, when its members have many unresolved issues and many fault lines are exposed.

9. Elevate Habits to Rituals

Human beings are habitual: we like habits because they remove a lot of the decision-making that takes up our headspace and enables families to function.

It is helpful to develop family habits into meaningful rituals in our family's life: it gives them soul. Calling on our curiosity and creativity, like making a music playlist for a particular celebration, forges stronger bonds and imbues powerful feelings in families that can be curative as well as a source of joy.

Rituals when celebrating family life—birthdays, naming ceremonies, weddings and funerals—ease the passage of transition, acknowledging the new phase. They can unlock the process that may have been stuck, resisting the reality of this new phase of life, like having a married adult child or the death of a family member.

Marking important events and transitions with rituals can also make what is invisible visible and significant. They can be celebrated in myriad ways—for example, special candles with prayers or walks with meaning and purpose, which enrich family life.

Each time we carry out a ritual we come to it with new meaning. We are different every time we meet it, enlivened or deadened with what is happening in our life in the new present. It helps us reset and regroup, coming together even when we may not want to.

Rituals create a source of memories and stories we can tell ourselves about our family and recall with pleasure, as well as, of course, being something to look forward to. They also imbue us with the body memory that we matter, that we belong in a physi-ological as well as psychological sense.

10. Allow Change Within the Family

Perhaps not too much ongoing shifting chaotic change, but change that gradually evolves in response to new circumstances supports individuals and families to flourish. As we change, as difficult as it is, we need to step out of our comfort zone and allow the change to change us. It is then that we thrive.

Rigidity can lead to brittle families, which leads to fracture. There will naturally be roles that each family member takes, but let these roles change and adapt as the people do. For instance, a younger sibling who has always been "the little brother" may be able to help his older sibling with his expertise in a particular area of life. This might also mean "paying it forward"—there are peri-ods in families when one member will be taking more than giving, and vice versa.

This will be particularly important as children become adults, and parents grow older.

11. Reflect on Yourself and Family Patterns

Every member of a family having the insight to look inwards and outwards reflectively, to think about their thinking, is a significant component for healthy families.

Handle your feelings before they handle you. Remember, emo-tional systems don't function logically: find ways to process the strong emotions you may be feeling, to centre yourself before you communicate what is important to you. Know your strengths and vulnerabilities. Know your own *Jaws* music, which sends you into overdrive quicker than you can say, "Pause." This is not easy and is a lifelong process.

You can begin by being aware of the chatter in your mind, what I call your "shitty committee." Write down what you are saying to yourself. Begin to notice the triggers that send you into high alert. Is it a particular look, a sound or a feeling? Name them. Perhaps you can find a way to express them.

If it is not the right time or place, and you haven't enough control to choose your response, stop. Breathe. Self-control at the appropriate time matters. Taking time out for yourself is a much better mechanism than expecting your child, sibling, partner or parent to do so. If you slow yourself down and understand what is going on inside you, you are much more likely to be able to support your family member to calm down.

12. Model the Behaviour You Wish for from Others

It is through what we model as individuals, partners, parents and grandparents in our actions, our communication, our choices and our ways of living that everyone in our family learns. Those around us learn from what we do, not from what we say. We may often say to our family members, "All I want is for you to be happy," but if we don't model how to be happy, we are not living happily in ourselves, and those around us cannot learn it.

We may say, "I love you," but behave in a contradictory way. Love in families is shown in action as well as being.

Take responsibility for yourself as the adult, which means acknowledging the consequences of your actions. Recognize as an adult, whatever your past, that you are now responsible for how you behave and what you believe. You may be thrown into a childlike state but manage your emotions (see 11. Reflect on Yourself and Family Patterns) to come back as a mature parent or partner.

Often, we want others to show qualities and behaviours that we do not demonstrate ourselves, or we dislike them because we have them too. This is connected to the other touchstones of knowing yourself and adaptability. If we recognize that what we are modelling is negative, we should acknowledge it and strive to change it. Then the family is more likely to thrive.

A Brief History of Family

Families, like the people in them, are shaped and changed by the context within which they exist. There is always, has always been, a cyclical relationship between families, politics and culture. Families function as a microcosm within the macrocosm of the larger society. Traditionally when we have spoken of "families" there is an image of a father, mother and two children, widely recognized as "the nuclear family." Structurally that stereotype has the mother as the caregiver of the family and home and the father as the breadwinner and head of the house. Yet this image is not accurate when you look at families over time.

For centuries, up to the industrial revolution, families existed in large units as a social bubble and a workforce. We often assume that it is in more recent times, with step and extended families, that multiple households are a new phenomenon. However, in the late eighteenth and nineteenth centuries there were often large households made up of extended family and employees. Marriage was not about love but an economic contract, often an arranged marriage of shared beliefs and property, or peasants agreed to work the land together. Rural life was hard: people needed to be self-sustaining and produce goods to earn enough money to survive, so families lived and worked together in their home and on their land. Children were born to be part of the contribution to the working family life and take over once the parents died. Love in these families would have been demonstrated through acts of service to the family—remembering the definition of "family" comes from "servant in the household," thus "being of service to our family." It meant that the practicality of family life took precedence over emotional development and care.

There was always a clear hierarchical order within families, supported by the Church, which was hugely influential. Families were shaped by the views expressed in the Bible on marriage and reproduction; rules and laws governed households and were based on those religious teachings, like those against adultery or having a child out of wedlock. This area marks one of the biggest shifts in families: the role of religion in governing what people must look like, how they must act and the values to live by. While it still impacts the lives of some today, its grip is infinitely lighter and many of those fixed obligations and rules no longer hold sway.

Industrialization brought about an upheaval in rural family life. The eighteenth and nineteenth centuries were a time of immense change, which impacted family formation and lifestyle: essentially the industrial revolution in North America is often thought of in terms of the separation of home from work. It brought about big social and family shifts. Then two world wars changed the landscape of family life in the short and long term. After the First World War many women were widows and there was a scarcity of men to marry. In the Second World War women had to take the place of men in the workforce. This brought about the key transition of women from homemakers to the labour market. Now almost as many women as men are in work, although more women work part-time.

How time was spent as a family changed enormously. After the Second World War, North America enjoyed an economic boom. The US became a global influence and the economy expanded at an annual rate of 3.5 percent. Within a generation the average family income had increased, lifting millions into a growing middle class. In Canada, with continued Liberal governments, services that had once been the responsibility of the family moved to the state, such as universal healthcare, social welfare and pensions. The gradual introduction of and developments in technology in and outside the home had a major influence on family life. Dishwashers, washing-machines and modern cookers meant mothers had more time. Radios and record players brought with them new life, new sounds and new ideas. Televisions brought contemporary visions of families into homes, and advertising sold ideal lifestyles. Families moved from focusing solely on getting tasks done for survival to being a connected, caring group of people who sought closeness and had more opportunities for leisure together. Youth had the freedom to go out and have fun.

There was a slow but significant transition from the man of the family being in charge and holding the power to more equality between the sexes. As women got jobs outside the home, they were less reliant on men for financial security, which gave them much more choice in the relationships they established or left. Families still spent quite a long time living together: often couples would live in one of the family homes until they were financially able to afford a place of their own.

Today we are in the midst of enormous change, but it is worth noting that it consists of further steps on a path set by previous generations. Families have become more fluid, and while the traditional view of family still persists as the "norm," we can see the waters shifting. New families include single-parent families, stepfamilies, polyamorous families, extended families, and blended families made up of the couple, the children they have had together and those from their previous relationships. While family formation is lengthening, meaning there are more extant generations as people live longer, it is also widening. We are once again more frequently starting to see large, combined, multi-generational families coming together. Over the past decade the number of Americans living in multi-generational households has nearly quadrupled, according to a report by Generations United 2021, with an increase of 271 percent from 2011 to 2021. Multi-household families may be made up of elderly parents living with their children and grandchildren, or even groups of friends living together in shared accommodation. Just as in pre-industrial times, families can be made up of those not biologically related to us—the aunts and uncles in name but not blood, the urban family born out of mutual life stages, the childhood friend who feels more like a sibling. These special, chosen, socially constructed family ties can also make up a modern family.

The term "beanpole families" is often used to reflect how a family comes together today. With couples having fewer children (approximately 50 percent of lone parents and cohabiting couples have one child), combined with a higher life expectancy, we are seeing grandparents and great-grandparents involved in the lives of their grandchildren and great-grandchildren. Adults today will spend more years as an adult child than they will parenting their own children. This is a stark difference when compared to the 1960s when fewer than one in five adults still had a live parent. This brings with it an interesting tipping in family dynamics when the adult child is still being parented: as time passes, the balance of power between them reverses—often with the older generation angry and stubborn because they don't like being told what to do but are vulnerable in old age.

Families are overall becoming less hierarchical than they previously were, more emotionally open and less didactic. Some argue that this change has been influenced by the mother having equal power to the father. Families certainly have more psychological information available to them and are beginning to recognize the importance of teaching children about autonomy to build self-confidence within the contained setting of the family home.

We cannot know how the digital era will influence the formation and values of family, but it is likely to be significant. It could be as powerful as the political decisions and the industrial revolution of the past in reshaping future families. Perhaps it will contribute to the atomization of family: the decrease in communal family experiences, like watching a TV drama together, as each child and adult has a separate digital interaction in their bedroom, with ongoing debates and battles for a child's main relationship not to be with their phone. The big shift will most probably be in the flexibility of working from home rather than having to go daily to an office, a trend that was already in evidence, accelerated by the pandemic.

Choice has been an important aspect of the progress in the lives of women and men and so in the shape of families. This includes the freedom to divorce or leave a marriage. The statistics show divorce rates in North America peaked in the 1980s and have dropped in the last decade. However, that statistic runs alongside a decline in marriage as couples choose to live together instead. Recent statistics show 45 percent of married couples divorce, with one in two cohabiting-parent families splitting before their child's fifth birthday. Today children may have grown up in shifting family formats, with potentially changing sibling formations, different dynamics, varied home locations, different rules and values. They may also be living across multiple locations (mothers', fathers' and grandparents' homes). The outcome might be increased resilience or vulnerability. Either way it is one of the stand-out differences for families, and particularly children, from the past to the present.

The unifying connector throughout the centuries is the multi-faceted role women have taken in the family dynamic, that of caregiver, cleaner, cook, manager, while also taking on the workplace. The work of feminist sociologists Christine Delphy and Diana Leonard looked at how women's roles in families maintained patriarchal systems and oppression. It seems to me that in practice the roles of men and women are not changing as fast as we imagine. Women still do most of the unpaid labour in family households. Hopefully these gender-based tasks will be shared more equally going forward: at least they are being discussed. Additionally, new partnerships of non-heteronormative families may shine a light on new ways of being.

The traditional view of heteronormative families is being remodelled, which brings with it greater fluidity. The numbers in North America highlight the transition, with sharp growth in the numbers of same-sex couples adopting a child since it was made legal across both the US (2016) and Canada (2015). The US Census Bureau states that "same-sex couples are four times more likely than opposite-sex couples to have adopted children or stepchildren. 43.3 percent of children of same-sex couples were adopted or stepchildren in 2019." In 2020 one in five adoptions were placed in LGBTQ+ families—there were 212,000 same-sex families in the UK, having increased by 40 percent since 2015.

Contemporary families reflect social *and* emotional changes: there is a parallel between gender and sexual fluidity in how to form family units and the expansion of other elements of our emotional lives. It is almost as if our ability to see diverse ways of being has grown in tandem with our understanding of our emotional worlds. The binary views of gender, sexuality, single and married are being challenged.

An aspect of family research that has to be addressed, which I am aware of in my framing of this topic, is the White Western lens with which, until recently, families have been researched in the UK. This creates a self-fulfilling prophecy of what a family "should look like" and what their values "should be." It is important that we expand our view of families to include broader, more inclusive values and beliefs informed by cultural, racial and ethnic diversity.

We embody so much of our family in ourselves: our personalities, ways of being, values, beliefs and, crucially, our sense of safety and belonging. Importantly, family shapes our future relationships and our future families, whatever they look like and however they function. We can play our part individually by understanding our own family's origins and how they affect us in the present.

Appendix

Adverse Childhood Experiences Questionnaire

I am including this because it may enlighten your understanding of yourself and how you function psychologically.

The Adverse Childhood Experiences study found that people who had experienced difficult or adverse events in childhood had a greater risk of developing physical and mental-health problems during adulthood.

The risk increases significantly for people with larger numbers of adverse experiences in their childhood. Adverse experiences include not only trauma and abuse, but also non-traumatic stressors like parental divorce and household dysfunction.

Adverse Childhood Experiences Study Instructions: There are ten questions, each answered by selecting yes or no. If yes enter
1 _____

These questions are in English and have been designed for adults (age 18 and older). Warning: These questions may cause distress. Some questions ask directly about experiences of child abuse.

Check that you have a support person or helpline number available before beginning.

Finding Your ACE Score

While you were growing up, during your first eighteen years of life:

1. Did a parent or other adult in the household often or very often swear at you, insult you, put you down, or humiliate you?

   or

   Act in a way that made you afraid that you might be physically hurt?

   Yes/No If yes enter 1 _____

2. Did a parent or other adult in the household often or very often push, grab, slap or throw something at you?

   or

   Ever hit you so hard that you had marks or were injured?

   Yes/No If yes enter 1 _____

3. Did an adult or person at least five years older than you ever touch or fondle you or have you touch their body in a sexual way?

   or

   Attempt to or actually have oral, anal, or vaginal intercourse with you?

   Yes/No If yes enter 1 _____

4. Did you often or very often feel that no one in your family loved you or thought you were important or special?

   or

Your family didn't look out for each other, feel close to each other, or support each other?

Yes/No If yes enter 1 _____

5. Did you often or very often feel that you didn't have enough to eat, had to wear dirty clothes, and had no one to protect you?

   or

   Your parents were too drunk or high to take care of you or take you to the doctor if you needed it?

   Yes/No If yes enter 1 _____

6. Were your parents ever separated or divorced?

   Yes/No If yes enter 1 _____

7. Was your mother or stepmother often or very often pushed, grabbed, slapped, or had something thrown at her?

   Yes/No If yes enter 1 _____

   or

   Sometimes, often, or very often kicked, bitten, hit with a fist, or hit with something hard?

   or

   Ever repeatedly hit for at least a few minutes or threatened with a gun or knife?

   Yes/No If yes enter 1 _____

8. Did you live with anyone who was a problem drinker or alcoholic or who used street drugs?

   Yes/No If yes enter 1 _____

9. Was a household member depressed or mentally ill, or did a household member attempt suicide?

Yes/No If yes enter 1 _____

10. Did a household member go to prison?

Yes/No If yes enter 1 _____

Now add up your Yes answers: _____ This is your ACE Score.

Adapted from: http://www.acestudy.org/files/ACE_Score_Calculator.pdf, 092406RA4CR

The Do You Know Scale

Dr Marshall Duke and Dr Robyn Fivush created the "Do You Know?" scale in 2001 to ask children questions about their family to test the hypothesis that children who know more about their families are more resilient and can handle challenges better than children who have limited knowledge about their families. The questions, designed to ask children things they would not know directly, are:

1. Do you know how your parents met?
2. Do you know where your mother grew up?
3. Do you know where your father grew up?
4. Do you know where some of your grandparents grew up?
5. Do you know where some of your grandparents met?
6. Do you know where your parents were married?
7. Do you know what went on when you were being born?
8. Do you know the source of your name?
9. Do you know some things about what happened when your brothers or sisters were being born?
10. Do you know which person in your family you look most like?

11. Do you know which person in the family you act most like?
12. Do you know some of the illnesses and injuries that your parents experienced when they were younger?
13. Do you know some of the lessons that your parents learnt from good or bad experiences?
14. Do you know some things that happened to your mum or dad when they were in school?
15. Do you know the national background of your family (such as English, German, Russian, etc.)?
16. Do you know some of the jobs that your parents had when they were young?
17. Do you know some awards that your parents received when they were young?
18. Do you know the names of the schools your mum went to?
19. Do you know the names of the schools your dad went to?
20. Do you know about a relative whose face "froze" in a grumpy position because he or she did not smile enough?

Ten Critical Questions (to ask if you are planning to be in a committed long-term relationship)

This comes from the research of Professor Anne Barlow at Exeter University

Are my partner and I a "good fit"?
Do we have a strong basis of friendship?
Do we want the same things in our relationship and out of life?
Are our expectations realistic?
Do we generally see the best in each other?
Do we both work at keeping our relationship vibrant?
Do we both feel we can discuss things freely and raise issues with each other?

Are we both committed to working through hard times?
When we face stressful circumstances do we pull together to get through it?
Do we each have supportive others around us?

EMDR

Eye movement desensitization and reprocessing (EMDR) is a powerful therapy designed to help people recover from traumatic events in their lives. It is recognized by the World Health Organization (WHO) and the American Psychiatric Association (APA). I often mention this form of psychotherapy. If you want to know more go to https://www.emdria.org/

Bibliography

Introduction

Abel, J., et al. (2018), "Reducing Emergency Hospital Admissions: A Population Health Complex Intervention of an Enhanced Model of Primary Care and Compassionate Communities," *British Journal of General Practice*, 68(676), e803–e810

Allen, K. R., et al. (1999), "Older Adults and Their Children: Family Patterns of Structural Diversity," *Family Relations*, 48(2), 151–7

Birkjaer, M., et al. (2019), "The Good Home Report 2019: What Makes a Happy Home?" Happiness Research Institute/Kingfisher Plc

Bowlby, J. (2005), *The Making and Breaking of Affectional Bonds*, 1st edn, (London: Routledge)

British Association for Psychotherapy and Counselling (2014), "Men and Counselling: The Changing Relationship Between Men in the UK and Therapy," www.bacp.co.uk/news/news-from-bacp/archive/28-april-2014-men-and-counselling/

Britton, R. (1989), "The Missing Link: Parental Sexuality in the Oedipus Complex," in J. Steiner (ed.), *The Oedipus Complex Today* (London: Routledge), 83–91

Burnham, J. (1986), *Family Therapy: First Steps Towards a Systematic Approach* (London: Routledge)

Cagen, S. (2006), *Quirkyalone: A Manifesto for Uncompromising Romantics* (New York: HarperCollins)

Carter, E. A., and McGoldrick, M. (eds.) (1988), *The Changing Family Life Cycle: A Framework for Family Therapy*, 2nd edn (London: Psychology Press)

Copeland, W. (2014), "Longitudinal Patterns of Anxiety from Childhood to Adulthood: The Great Smoky Mountains Study," *Journal of the American Academy of Child and Adolescent Psychiatry*, 53(1), 1527–48

Cryle, P., and Stephens, E. (2018), *Normality: A Critical Genealogy* (Chicago: University of Chicago Press)

Donath, O. (2017), *Regretting Motherhood: A Study* (California: North Atlantic Books US)

Dunning, A. (2006), "Grandparents—An Intergenerational Resource for Families: A UK Perspective," *Journal of Intergenerational Relationships*, 4(1), 127–35

Fingerman, K., et al. (2012), "In-Law Relationships Before and After Marriage: Husbands, Wives and Their Mothers-In-Law," *Research in Human Development*, 9(2), 106–25

Fivush, R. (2011), "The Development of Autobiographical Memory," *Annual Review of Psychology*, 62(1), 559–82

Fuentes, A. (2020), "This Species Moment," interviewed by Krista Tippett for On Being, onbeing.org

Galindo, I., Boomer, E., and Reagan, D. (2006), *A Family Genogram Workbook* (Virginia: Educational Consultants)

Golombok, S. (2020), *We Are Family: The Modern Transformation of Parents and Children* (New York: PublicAffairs Books)

Lippa, R. A. (2005), *Gender, Nature and Nurture* (Philadelphia: Routledge)

Mayes, L., Fonagy, P., and Target, M. (2007), *Development Science and Psychoanalysis: Integration and Innovation* (London: Routledge)

McCrory, E., et al. (2019), "Neurocognitive Adaptation and Mental Health Vulnerability Following Maltreatment: The Role of Social Functioning," *Child Maltreatment*, 24(4), 1–17

McGoldrick, M. (2006), "Monica McGoldrick on Family Therapy," interviewed by Randall C. Wyatt and Victor Yalom, psychotherapy.net

Messinger, L., and Walker, K. N. (1981), "From Marriage Breakdown to Remarriage: Parental Tasks and Therapeutic Guidelines," *American Journal of Orthopsychiatry*, 51(3), 429–38

Patel, V. (2018), "Acting Early: The Key to Preventing Mental Health Problems," *Journal of the Royal Society of Medicine*, 111(5), 153–7

Siegel, D. J. (2013), *Parenting from the Inside Out* (New York: TarcherPerigee)

Singer, J. A., et al. (2012), "Self-Defining Memories, Scripts, and the Life Story: Narrative Identity in Personality and Psychotherapy," *Journal of Psychotherapy*, 81(6), 569–82

Waldinger, R. (2016), "What Makes a Good Life? Lessons from the Longest Study on Happiness," TED Conferences

Watters, E. (2003), *Urban Tribes: A Generation Redefines Friendship, Family and Commitment* (New York: Bloomsbury)

Winnicott, D. (1960), "The Theory of the Parent–Infant Relationship," *International Journal of PsychoAnalysis* 41, 585–95

Wolynn, M. (2016), *It Didn't Start With You* (New York: Viking)

Yehuda, R. (2015), "How Trauma and Resilience Cross Generations," onbeing.org

The Wynne Family

Bradford, D., and Robin, C. (2021), *Connect: Building Exceptional Relationships with Family, Friends and Colleagues* (New York: Currency)

Duffell, N. (2000), *The Making of Them: The British Attitude to Children and the Boarding School System*, (London: Lone Arrow Press)

Feiler, B. (2013), "The Stories That Bind Us," *New York Times*, 17 May

Fry, R. (2017), "Richard Beckhard: The Formulator of Organizational Change," in Szabla, D. B. et al. (eds.), *The Palgrave Handbook of Organizational Change Thinkers* (Cham: Palgrave Macmillan), 91–105

genesinlife.org, *Genetics 101: Main Inheritance Patterns*

Hicks, B. M., Schalet, B. D., Malone, S. M., Iacono, W. G., and McGue, M. (2011), "Psychometric and Genetic Architecture of Substance Use Disorder and Behavioral Disinhibition Measures for Gene Association Studies," *Behavior Genetics*, 41, 459–75

Liu, M., Jiang, Y., Wedow, R., et al. (2019), "Association Studies of Up to 1.2 Million Individuals Yield New Insights Into the Genetic Etiology of Tobacco and Alcohol Use," *Nature Genetics*, 51, 237–44

Martin, A. J., et al. (2016), "Effects of Boarding School," *Psychologist*, 29, 412–19

McCrory, E., De Brito, S. A., Sebastian, C. L., Mechelli, A., Bird, G., Kelly, P., and Viding, E. (2011), "Heightened Neural Reactivity to Threat in Child Victims of Family Violence," *Current Biology*, 21, R947–8

McCrory, E. J., De Brito, S., Kelly, P.A., Bird, G., Sebastian, C., and Viding, E. (2013), "Amygdala Activation in Maltreated Children During Pre-Attentive Emotional Processing," *British Journal of Psychiatry*, 202 (4), 269–76

McCrory, E., et al. (2019), "Neurocognitive Adaptation and Mental Health Vulnerability Following Maltreatment: The Role of Social Functioning," *Child Maltreatment*, 24(4), 1–17

Plomin, R. (2018), *Blueprint: How DNA Makes Us Who We Are* (Cambridge, MA: MIT Press)

Prochaska, J., DiClemente, C., and Norcross, J. (1992), "In Search of How People Change: Applications to Addictive Behaviors," *American Psychologist*, 47(9), 1102–14

strategies-for-managing-change.com, "Beckhard Change Equation"

UK Trauma Council, "How Latent Vulnerability Plays Out Over a Child's Life," https://uktraumacouncil.org/resource/how-latent-vulnerability-plays-out-over-a-childs-life

The Singh and Kelly Family

adoptionUK.org, *It Takes a Village to Raise a Child*

Anon. (2012), "Overwhelming Majority Support Gay Marriage in Ireland," *Gay Community News*, https://web.archive.org/web/201203021 53735/http:/www.gcn.ie/Overwhelming_Majority_Support_Gay_Marriage_In_Ireland

Anon. (2015), "Ireland is Ninth Most Gay-friendly Nation in the World, Says New Poll," *Gay Community News*, 22 July

Anon. (2017), "Understanding the Difference Between Adoption and Mental Health Issues," Vertava Health Massachusetts, online article

Aryan, A. (2012), "Why Hinduism is the most Liberal Religion," *Apna Bhaarat*, https://apnabhaarat.wordpress.com/2012/03/10/why-hinduism-is-the-most-liberal-religion/

BBC Bitesize, *What Does Hinduism Say about Homosexuality?* www.bbc.co.uk/bitesize/guides/zw8qn39/revision/5

Beauman, N. (2016), "Do Different Generations of Immigrants Think Differently?" *Aljazeera America*, online article

Borba, M. (2021), *Thrivers: The Surprising Reasons Why Some Kids Struggle While Others Shine* (London: Putnam)

Children's Bureau (2021), "The AFCARS Report," U.S. Department of Health and Human Services, https://www.acf.hhs.gov/sites/default/files/documents/cb/afcarsreport28.pdf

Chopra, D. (2016), "Are You Where You Thought You Would Be?" https://chopra.com/articles/life-expectations-are-you-where-you-thought-you-would-be

Colage.org

Coramadoption.org.uk, "Five Facts about LGBT Fostering and Adoption" Gayparentmag.com

First 4 Adoption (2017), "The Great Behaviour Breakdown," training programme run by First 4 adoption, www.first4adoption.org.uk

Hakim, D., and Dalby, D. (2015), "Ireland Votes to Approve Gay Marriage, Putting Country in Vanguard," *New York Times*, 23 May, A(1), Section A, page 1

Herman, E. (2012), *The Adoption History Project*, https://pages.uoregon.edu/adoption/topics/adoptionstatistics.htm

Iqbal, H., and Golombok, S. (2018), "The Generation Game: Parenting and Child Outcomes in Second-Generation South Asian Immigrant Families in Britain," *Journal of Cross-Cultural Psychology*, 49(1), 25–43

Kendrick, J., Lindsey, C., and Tollemache, L. (2006), *Creating New Families*, 1st edn (London: Routledge)

Lifelongadoptions.com, *LGBT Adoption Statistics*

Maisal, E. (2011), "What Do We Mean by Normal?" *Psychology Today*, https://www.psychologytoday.com/ca/blog/rethinking-mental-health/201111/what-do-we-mean-normal

Rudd Adoption Research Program (1994), *Outcomes for Adoptive Parents*, https://www.umass.edu/ruddchair/research/mtarp/key-findings/outcomes-adoptive-parents

Sanders, S. (2019), "Families and Households in the UK: 2019," Office for National Statistics, online article

Solomon, A. (2014), *Far from the Tree* (London: Vintage)

Taylor, D. (2020), "Same-Sex Couples Are More Likely to Adopt or Foster Children," United States Census Bureau, https://www.census. gov/library/stories/2020/09/fifteen-percent-of-same-sex-couples-have-children-in-their-household.html

Walker, L., and Taylor, D. (2021), "Same-Sex Couple Households: 2019," United States Census Bureau, survey brief

Winterman, D. (2010), "When Adoption Breaks Down," www. 123helpme. com

Woolgar, M., and Simmonds, J. (2019), "The Impact of Neurobiological Sciences on Family Placement Policy and Practice," *Adoption and Fostering*, 43(3), 241–351

Ziai, R. (2017), "The Evolutionary Roots of Identity Politics," *Areo Magazine*, online article

The Thompson Family

Anon. (2018), "The Declining State of Student Mental Health in Universities and What Can Be Done," Mental Health Foundation, https:// www.mentalhealth.org.uk/blog/declining-state-student-mental-health-universities-and-what-can-be-done

Armstrong J. (2017), "Higher Stakes: Generational Differences in Mothers' and Daughters' Feelings about Combining Motherhood with a Career," *Studies in the Maternal*, 9(1)

Arnett, J. J. (2006), *Emerging Adulthood: The Winding Road From the Late Teens Through the Twenties* (New York: Oxford University Press)

Badiani, F., and Desousa, A. (2016), "The Empty Nest Syndrome: Critical Clinical Considerations," *Indian Journal of Mental Health*, 3(2), 135–42

Barber, C. E. (1989), "Transition to the Empty Nest," in S. J. Bahr and E. T. Peterson (eds.), *Aging and the Family* (Washington: Lexington Books), 15–32

Borelli, J. L., et al. (2017), "Gender Differences in Work-Family Guilt in Parents of Young Children," *Sex Roles*, 76 (5–6), 356–68

Bouchard, G. (2014), "How Do Parents React When Their Children Leave Home? An Integrative Review," *Journal of Adult Development*, 21(2), 69–79

Brown, S. L., and Lin, I. (2012), "The Gray Divorce Revolution: Rising Divorce among Middle Aged and Older Adults, 1990–2010," *Journal of Gerontology: Series B*, 67(6), 731–41

Bukodi, E., and Dex, S. (2010), "Bad Start: Is There a Way Up? Gender Differences in the Effect of Initial Occupation on Early Career Mobility in Britain," *European Sociological Review*, 26 (4), 431–46

Dunning, A. (2006), "Grandparents—An Intergenerational Resource for Families: A UK Perspective," *Journal of Intergenerational Relationships*, 4(1), 127–35

Gottman, J., and Gottman, J. (2017), "The Natural Principles of Love," *Journal of Family Theory and Review*, 9(1), 7–26

Gottman, J. M., and Levenson, R. W. (1999), "What Predicts Change in Marital Interaction Over Time? A Study of Alternative Models," *Family Process*, 38(2), 143–58

Harkins, E. B. (1978), "Effects of Empty Nest Transition on Self-Report of Psychological and Physical Wellbeing," *Journal of Marriage and the Family*, 40(3), 549–56

Hendrix, H., and LaKelly Hunt, H. (2021), *Doing Imago Relationship Therapy: In the Space-Between* (New York: W. W. Norton & Co.)

Hunt, J., and Eisenberg, D. (2010), "Mental Health Problems and Help-Seeking Behaviour among College Students," *Journal of Adolescent Health*, 46(1), 3–10

Joel, S., et al. (2020), "Machine Learning Uncovers the Most Robust Self-Report Predictors of Relationship Quality Across 43 Longitudinal Couples Studies," *Proceedings of the National Academy of Sciences of the United States of America*, 117(32), 19061–71

Jungmeen, E. K., and Moen, P. (2002), "Retirement Transitions, Gender, and Psychological Well-Being: A Life-Course, Ecological Model," *Journals of Gerontology: Series B*, 57(3), 212–22

Maté, G., and Neufeld, G. (2013), *Hold On to Your Kids: Why Parents Need to Matter More Than Peers* (London: Ebury Digital)

McKinlay, S. M., and Jefferys, M. (1974), "The Menopausal Syndrome," *British Journal of Preventive and Social Medicine*, 28(2), 108–15

Mitchell, B. A., and Lovegreen, L. D. (2009), "The Empty Nest Syndrome in Midlife Families: A Multimethod Exploration of Parental Gender Differences and Cultural Dynamics," *Journal of Family Issues*, 30(12), 1651–70

Mount, S. D., and Moas, S. (2015), "Re-Purposing the 'Empty Nest'," *Journal of Family Psychotherapy*, 26(3), 247–52

NUK.co.uk (2013), "Simply Not Being Good Enough," www.nuk.co.uk

Parker, J., Summerfeldt, L., Hogan, M., and Majeski, S. (2004), "Emotional Intelligence and Academic Success: Examining the Transition from High School to University," *Personality and Individual Differences*, 36(1), 163–72

Radloff, L. S. (1980), "Depression and the Empty Nest," *Sex Roles*, 6(6), 775–81

Rubin, L. B. (1979), *Women of a Certain Age: The Midlife Search for Self* (New York: HarperCollins)

Sartori, A. C., and Zilberman, M. L. (2009), "Revisiting the Empty Nest Syndrome Concept," *Revista de Psiquiatria Clinica*, 36(3), 112–22

The Taylor and Smith Family

Anon. (2021), *OJJDP Statistical Briefing Book*, https://www.ojjdp.gov/ojstatbb/population/qa01203.asp?qaDate=2020

Bray, J. H., and Hetherington, E. M. (1993), "Families in Transition: Introduction and Overview," *Journal of Family Psychology*, 7(1), 3–8

Bray, J. H., and Kelly, J. (1998), *Stepfamilies: Love, Marriage and Parenting in the First Decade* (New York: Broadway Books)

Fosha, D., Siegel, D. J., and Solomon, M. F. (2009), *The Healing Power of Emotion: Affective Neuroscience, Development and Clinical Practice* (New York: W. W. Norton & Co.)

gingerbread.org.uk

Gordon, D., et al. (2000), "Poverty and Social Exclusion in Britain," Joseph Rowntree Foundation

Gottman, J. M. (1993), "A Theory of Marital Dissolution and Stability," *Journal of Family Psychology*, 7(11), 57–75

gov.uk, "Financial Help if You Have Children," https://www.gov.uk/browse/childcare-parenting/financial-help-children

Guinart, M., and Grau, M. (2014), "Qualitative Analysis of the Short-Term and Long-Term Impact of Family Breakdown on Children: Case Study," *Journal of Divorce and Remarriage*, 55(5), 408–22

Guy, P. (2021), "Households by Type of Household and Family, Regions of England and UK Constituent Countries," Office for National Statistics

Hall, R., and Batty, D. (2020), "I Can't Get Motivated: The Students Struggling with Online Learning," *Guardian*, 4 May

Hetherington, E. M. (1987), "Family Relations Six Years After Divorce," in K. Pasley and M. Ihinger-Tallman (eds.), *Remarriage and Stepparenting: Current Research and Theory* (New York: Guilford), 185–205

Hetherington, E. M., and Arasteh, J. (1988), *The Impact of Divorce, Single Parenting and Stepparenting on Children* (New Jersey: Lawrence Erlbaum), 279–98

Inman, P. (2020), "Number of People in Poverty in Working Families Hits Record High," *Guardian*, 6 February

Joel, S., et al. (2020), "Machine Learning Uncovers the Most Robust Self-Report Predictors of Relationship Quality across 43 Longitudinal Couples Studies," *Proceedings of the National Academy of Sciences of the United States of America*, 117(32), 19061–71

Joseph Rowntree Foundation, Impact of Poverty on Relationships, https://www.jrf.org.uk/data/impact-poverty-relationships

mother.ly (2019), *Motherly's 2019 State of Motherhood Survey Report*

O'Neill, O. (2015), "How Students and Young Entrepreneurs Can Start Their Own Business While at University," *Independent*, 27 November

Papernow, P. (2006), "Stepfamilies Clinical Update," *Family Therapy Magazine*, 5(3), 34–42

Papernow, P. (2012), "A Clinician's View on 'Stepfamily Architecture'," in J. Pryor (ed.), *The International Handbook of Stepfamilies: Policy and Practice in Legal, Research, and Clinical Environments* (Hoboken, NJ: Wiley), 422–54 phys.org (2019), "Female Mammals Kill the Offspring of Their Competitors When Resources Are Scarce"

Pill, C. (1990), "Stepfamilies: Redefining The Family," *Family Relations*, 39(2), 186–93

Poverty and Social Exclusion UK (2011), "A Single Parent," www.poverty.ac.uk

Reis, S. (2018), "The Female Face of Poverty," Women's Budget Group, www.wbg.org.uk

Richter, D., and Lemola, S. (2017), "Growing Up with a Single Mother and Life Satisfaction in Adulthood: A Test of Mediating and Moderating Factors," *PLOS One*, 12(6), 1–15

Rutter, V. (1994), "Lessons from Stepfamilies," *Psychology Today*, online article, May

Stock, L. et al. (2014), "Personal Relationships and Poverty: An Evidence and Policy Review," Tavistock Institute of Human Relations

Tominay, C. (2021), "Five Children in Every Class Likely to Need Mental Health Support as Lockdown Bites," *Daily Telegraph*, 30 January

Vaillant, G. E. (2000), "Adaptive Mental Mechanisms: Their Role in Positive Psychology," *American Psychologist*, 55(1), 89–98

Verity, A. (2020), "Coronavirus: One Million Under-25s Face Unemployment, Study Warns," BBC News, 6 May

Wittman, J. P. (2001), *Custody Chaos, Personal Peace: Sharing Custody with an Ex Who Drives You Crazy* (New York: Penguin)

Woodall, K. (2020), "Parental Alienation and the Domestic Abuse Bill UK," https://karenwoodall.blog

The Browne and Francis Family

Adler-Baeder, F., et al. (2010), "Thriving in Stepfamilies: Exploring Competence and Well-Being among African American Youth," *Journal of Adolescent Health*, 46(4), 396–8

Bethune, S. (2019), "Gen Z More Likely to Report Mental Health Concerns," *American Psychological Association*, 50(1), 19–20

British Medical Journal (2020), "It's Time to Act on Racism in the NHS," February

Faust, K., and Manning, S. (2020), "To Truly Reduce Racial Disparities, We Must Acknowledge Black Fathers Matter," *The Federalist*, 12 June

Gonzalez, M., et al. (2014), "Coparenting Experiences in African American Families: An Examination of Single Mothers and Their Non-Marital Coparents," *Family Process*, 53(1), 33–54

Heald, A. et al. (2018), "The LEAVE Vote and Racial Abuse Towards Black and Minority Ethnic Communities Across the UK: The Impact on Mental Health," *Journal of the Royal Society of Medicine*, 111(5), 158–61

Kinouani, G. (2021), *Living While Black: The Essential Guide to Overcoming Racial Trauma* (London: Ebury)

Klass, D., Silverman, P. R., and Nickman, S. L. (1996), *Continuing Bonds: New Understandings of Grief* (London: Taylor & Francis)

Knight, M., et al. (2020), "Saving Lives, Improving Mothers' Care: Lessons Learned to Inform Maternity Care from the UK and Ireland; Confidential Enquiries into Maternal Deaths and Morbidity 2016–18," www.npeu.ox.ac.uk

Massiah, J. (1982), "Women Who Head Households," in *Women and the Family* (Barbados: Institute of Social and Economic Policy)

Plummer, K. (2021), "David Lammy Makes Another Powerful Point about Racism Following Viral Clip about 'Being English'," *Independent*, 31 March

Sharpe, J. (1997), "Mental Health Issues and Family Socialization in the Caribbean," in Roopnarine, J., et al., *Advances in Applied Developmental Psychology—Caribbean Families: Diversity among Ethnic Groups* (New York: Ablex Publishing)

The Rossi Family

Beck, A. and Steer, R. (1989), "Clinical Predictors of Eventual Suicide: A 5- to 10-year Prospective Study of Suicide Attempters," *Journal of Affective Disorders*, 17(3), 203–9

Borba, M. (2021), *Thrivers: The Surprising Reasons Why Some Kids Struggle and Others Shine* (New York: Putnam)

Bowlby, J. (1982), *Attachment* (New York: Basic Books)

Erlangsen, A., Runeson, J., et al. (2017) "Association Between Spousal Suicide and Mental, Physical, and Social Health Outcomes: A Longitudinal and Nationwide Register-based Study," *JAMA Psychiatry*, 74(5), 456–64

Ilgen, M., and Kleinberg, F. (2011), "The Link Between Substance Abuse, Violence and Suicide," *Psychiatric Times*, 28(1), 25–7

Klass, D., Silverman, P., and Nickman, S. L. (1996), *Continuing Bonds: New Understandings of Grief* (London: Routledge)

Pitman, A., Osborn, D., King, M., and Erlangsen, A. (2014), "Effects of Suicide Bereavement on Mental Health and Suicide Risk," *Lancet Psychiatry*, 1(1), 86–94

Ross, C. (2014), "Suicide: One of Addiction's Hidden Risks," *Psychology Today*, blog

Scutti, S. (2016), "Committing Suicide Increases Family, Friends' Risk of Attempting Suicide By 65%," *Medical Daily*, https://www.medical daily.com/suicide-bereaved-self-destruct-371022

Shapiro, F. (1995/2001), *Eye Movement Desensitization and Reprocessing: Basic Principles, Protocols and Procedures,* 1st/2nd edns (New York: Guilford Press)

Shapiro, F. (2002), "Paradigms, Processing, and Personality Development," in F. Shapiro (ed.), *EMDR as an Integrative Psychotherapy Approach: Experts of Diverse Orientations Explore the Paradigm Prism* (Washington, DC: American Psychological Association Books), 3–26

Shapiro, F. (2007), "EMDR, Adaptive Information Processing, and Case Conceptualization," *Journal of EMDR Practice and Research*, 1, 68–87

Shapiro, F., Kaslow, F., and Maxfield, L. (eds.) (2007), *Handbook of EMDR and Family Therapy Processes* (New York: Wiley)

Shellenberger, S. (2007), "Using the Genogram with Families for Assessment and Treatment," in Shapiro, F., Kaslow, F., and Maxfield, L. (eds.), *Handbook of EMDR and Family Therapy Processes* (New York: Wiley), 76–94

Van der Kolk, B. A. (2014), *The Body Keeps the Score: Brain, Mind, and Body in the Healing of Trauma* (New York: Viking)

Worden, J. W. (2009), *Grief Counselling and Grief Therapy: A Handbook for the Mental Health Practitioner* (New York: Springer)

The Berger Family

Behere, P. (2013), "Religion and Mental Health," *Indian Journal of Psychiatry*, 55(2), 187–94

Bierer, L. M., Schmeidler, J., Aferiat, D. H., Breslau, I., and Dolan, S. (2000) "Low Cortisol and Risk for PTSD in Adult Offspring of Holocaust Survivors," *American Journal of Psychiatry*, 157, 1252–9

Borkovec, T. D., et al. (1983), "Preliminary Exploration of Worry: Some Characteristics and Processes," *Behaviour Research and Therapy*, 21(1), 9–16

Campaigntoendloneliness.org, "The Facts on Loneliness"

Chen, Y., Kim, E. S., and Van der Weele, J. (2020), "Religious-Service Attendance and Subsequent Health and Well-Being Throughout Adulthood: Evidence from Three Prospective Cohorts," *International Journal of Epidemiology*, 49(6), 2030–40

Cooley, E., et al. (2008), "Maternal Effects on Daughters' Eating Pathology and Body Image," *Eating Behaviours*, 9(1), 52–61

Currin, L., et al. (2005), "Time Trends in Eating Disorder Incidence," *British Journal of Psychiatry*, 186(2), 132–5

Danieli, Y., Norris, F. H., and Engdahl, B. (2017), "A Question of Who, Not If: Psychological Disorders in Holocaust Survivors' Children," *Psychological Trauma*, 9(Suppl 1), 98–106

Eckel, S. (2015), "Why Siblings Sever Ties," *Psychology Today*, https://www.psychologytoday.com/gb/articles/201503/why-siblings-sever-ties

Epstein, H. (1988), *Children of the Holocaust* (New York: Penguin)

Gilbert, P. (2010), *The Compassionate Mind: A New Approach to Life's Challenges* (Oakland: New Harbinger Publications)

Grossman, D. (1986), *See Under: Love*, trans. Betsy Rosenberg (London: Vintage Classics)

Halik, V., Rosenthal, D. A., and Pattison, P. E. (1990), "Intergenerational Effects of the Holocaust: Patterns of Engagement in the Mother–Daughter Relationship," *Family Process*, 29(3), 325–39

helpguide.org, "How to Stop Worrying"

Hogman, F. (1998), "Trauma and Identity Through Two Generations of the Holocaust," *Psychoanalytic Review*, 85(4), 551–78

Kellermann, N. (1999), "Bibliography: Children of Holocaust Survivors," AMCHA, the National Israeli Centre for Psychosocial Support of Holocaust Survivors and the Second Generation

Kellermann, N. (2001a), "Psychopathology in Children of Holocaust Survivors: A Review of the Research Literature," *Israel Journal of Psychiatry and Related Sciences*, 38(1), 36–46

Kellermann, N. (2001b), "Transmission of Holocaust Trauma—an Integrative View," *Psychiatry Interpersonal and Biological Processes*, 64(3), 256–67

Kellermann, N. (2008), "Transmitted Holocaust Trauma: Curse or Legacy? The Aggravating and Mitigating Factors of Holocaust Transmission," *Israel Journal of Psychiatry and Related Sciences*, 45(4), 263–71

Lebrecht, N. (2019), *Genius and Anxiety: How Jews Changed the World* (London: Oneworld Publications)

Lorenzi, N. (2019), "What to Know about Older, Younger, and Middle Child Personalities," *Parents*, https://www.parents.com/baby/development/sibling-issues/how-birth-order-shapes-personality/

May, R. (1994), *The Discovery of Being: Writings in Existential Psychology* (New York: W. W. Norton & Co.)

Neo, P. (2018), "What Codependent Behaviour Looks Like These Days (and How to Change It)," interviewed by Angela Melero, *Perpetuaneo*

Nir, B. (2018), "Transgenerational Transmission of Holocaust Trauma and Its Expressions in Literature," *Genealogy*, 2(4), 1–18

Pillemer, K. (2020), *Fault Lines: Fractured Families and How to Mend Them* (London: Hodder & Stoughton)

Rakoff, V., Sigal, J., and Epstein, N. (1966), "Children and Families of Concentration Camp Survivors," *Canada's Mental Health*, 14(4), 24–6

Robichaud, M., Koerner, N., and Dugas, M. (2019), *Cognitive Behavioral Treatment for Generalized Anxiety Disorder* (New York: Routledge)

Rowland-Klein, D., and Dunlop, R. (1998), "The Transmission of Trauma Across Generations: Identification with Parental Trauma in Children of Holocaust Survivors," *Australian and New Zealand Journal of Psychiatry*, 32(3), 358–69

Sacks, J. (2010), podcast with Krista Tippett onbeing.org

Scharf, M. (2007), "Long-Term Effects of Trauma: Psychosocial Functioning of the Second and Third Generation of Holocaust Survivors," *Development and Psychopathology*, 19(2), 603–22

Seidel, A., Majeske, K., and Marshall, M. (2020), "Factors Associated with Support Provided by Middle-Aged Children to Their Parents," *Family Relations*, 69(2), 262–75

Seligman, M. (2011), *Flourish: A New Understanding of Happiness and Well-Being—and How to Achieve Them* (Boston: Nicholas Brealey)

Shrira, A. (2017), "Does the Holocaust Trauma Affect the Aging of the Second Generation?" paper presented at the Annual Seminar on Innovations and Challenges in the Fields of Gerontology and Geriatrics, Beer-Sheva, Israel

Statistics Canada (2021), "Canadian Social Survey: Loneliness in Canada," https://www150.statcan.gc.ca/n1/daily-quotidien/211124/dq211124e-eng.htm

Villani, D., et al. (2019), "The Role of Spirituality and Religiosity in Subjective Well-Being of Individuals with Different Religious Status," *Frontiers in Psychology*, 10(1525), https://www.frontiersin.org/articles/10.3389/fpsyg.2019.01525/full

Vohra, S. (2020), *The Mind Medic: Your 5 Senses Guide to Leading a Calmer, Happier Life* (London: Penguin Life)

Weissbourd, R., et al. (2021), "Loneliness in America: How the Pandemic Has Deepened an Epidemic of Loneliness and What We Can Do About It," Making Caring Common Project, https://mcc.gse.harvard.edu/reports/loneliness-in-america

Welch, A. (2017), "Parents Still Lose Sleep Worrying about Grown Children" www.pubmed.ncbi.nlm.nih.gov

Yamagata, B., et al. (2016), "Female-Specific Intergenerational Transmission Patterns of the Human Corticolimbic Circuitry," *Journal of Neuroscience*, 36(4), 1254–60

Yehuda, R., Daskalakis, N. P., Bierer, L. M., Bader, H. N., Klengel, T., Holsboer, F., and Binder, E. B. (2016), "Holocaust Exposure Induced Intergenerational Effects on FKBP5 Methylation," *Biological Psychiatry*, 80(5), 372–80

The Craig and Butowski Family

Abel, J., and Clarke, L. (2020), *The Compassion Project: A Case for Hope & Humankindness from the Town That Beat Loneliness* (London: Octopus)

Allen, J., Fonagy, P., and Bateman, A. (2008), *Mentalizing in Clinical Practice* (Washington, DC: American Psychiatric Press)

Berkman, L. F., Leo-Summers, L., and Horwitz, R. I. (1992), "Emotional Support and Survival After Myocardial Infarction," *Annals of Internal Medicine*, 117(2), 1003–9

Bloomer, A. (2020), "New Research into Biological Interplay Between Covid-19 and Cancer," *GM Journal*, 26 October

Canadian Cancer Statistics Advisory Committee, in collaboration with the Canadian Cancer Society, Statistics Canada and the Public Health Agency of Canada (2021), *Canadian Cancer Statistics 2021*, https://cdn.cancer.ca/-/media/files/research/cancer-statistics/2021-statistics/2021-pdf-en-final.pdf

Cancer.net, "How Cancer Affects Family Life"

Canceratlas.cancer.org, "The Burden: Northern America"

CancerresearchUK.org

Cole, M. A. (1978), "Sex and Marital Status Differences in Death Anxiety," *OMEGA: Journal of Death and Dying*, 9(2), 139–47

Cook Gotay, C. (1997), comment on C. G. Blanchard et al., "The Crisis of Cancer: Psychological Impact on Family Caregivers," *Oncology*, 11(2)

DePaulo, B. (2020), "More Than Half of Young Adults Are Now Living with Parents," *Psychology Today*, https://www.psychologytoday.com/ca/blog/living-single/202009/more-half-young-adults-are-now-living-parents?eml

Esnaashari, F., and Kargar, F. R. (2015), "The Relation Between Death Attitude and Distress: Tolerance, Aggression and Anger," *OMEGA: Journal of Death and Dying*, 77(2), 1–19

Evans, J. W., Walters, A. S., and Hatch-Woodruff, M. L. (1999), "Death-Bed Scene Narratives: A Construct and Linguistic Analysis," *Death Studies*, 23(8), 715–33

Florian, V., and Kravetz, S. (1983), "Fear of Personal Death: Attribution, Structure and Relation to Religious Belief," *Journal of Personality and Social Psychology*, 44(3), 600–607

Fogg, B. J. (2019), *Tiny Habits: The Small Changes That Change Everything* (Boston: Houghton Mifflin Harcourt)

Fonagy, P. et al. (1997), *Reflective-Functioning Manual, Version 4.1, For Application to Adult Attachment Interviews* (London: University College London)

Golics, C., et al. (2013), "The Impact of Patients' Chronic Disease on Family Quality of Life: An Experience from 26 Specialties," *International Journal of General Medicine*, 2013(6), 787–98

Maggies.org, "Advanced Cancer and Emotions"

Mannix, K. (2017), *With the End in Mind* (Glasgow: William Collins)

Medicalxpress.com (2015), "Emotional Health of Men with Cancer Often Unaddressed"

Mikulincer, M. (1997), "Fear of Personal Death in Adulthood: The Impact of Early and Recent Losses," *Death Studies*, 21(1), 1–24

Morasso, G. (1999), "Psychological and Symptom Distress in Terminal Cancer Patients with Met and Unmet Needs," *Journal of Pain and Symptom Management*, 17(6), 402–9

National Cancer Institute (2022), *Cancer Stat Facts: Cancer of Any Site*, https://seer.cancer.gov/statfacts/html/all.html

Okun, B., and Nowinski, J. (2011), *Saying Goodbye: How Families Can Find Renewal Through Loss* (New York: Berkley)

Pinkser, J. (2020), "The New Boomerang Kids Could Change American Views of Living at Home," *The Atlantic*, https://www.theatlantic.com/family/archive/2020/07/pandemic-young-adults-living-with-parents/613723/

Rabkin, J. G. et al. (1993), "Resilience in Adversity among Long-Term Survivors of Aids," *Hospital and Community Psychiatry*, 44(2), 162–7

Samuel, J. (2017), *Grief Works: Stories of Life, Death and Surviving* (London: Penguin Life)

Sandberg, S., and Grant. A. (eds.) (2017), *Option B: Facing Adversity, Building Resilience and Finding Joy* (London: W. H. Allen)

Smith, Y. (2019), "The Effects of Cancer on Family Life," *News Medical Life Sciences*, online publication, February

Snyder, C. R. (2002), *Hope Theory: Rainbows in the Mind* (Lawrence: University of Kansas Press), 249–75

Stein, A., and Russell, M. (2016), "Attachment Theory and Post-Cult Recovery," *Therapy Today*, 27(7), 18–21

Timmerman, C., and Uhrenfeldt, L. (2014), "Room for Caring: Patients' Experiences of Well-Being, Relief and Hope During Serious Illness," *Scandinavian Journal of Caring Sciences*, 29(3), 426–34

Tomer, A. (2000), *Death Attitudes and the Older Adult: Theories, Concepts and Applications* (New York: Brunner-Routledge)

Wall, D. P. (2013), "Responding to a Diagnosis of Localized Prostate Cancer: Men's Experiences of Normal Distress During the First 3 Postdiagnostic Months," *PubMed*, 36(6), E44–50, www.pubmed.ncbi.nlm.nih.gov

Conclusion

Goemans, A., Viding, E., and McCrory, E. (2021), "Child Maltreatment, Peer Victimization, and Mental Health: Neorocognitive Perspectives on the Cycle of Victimization," *PubMed*, DOI: 10.1177/15248380211036393

Yehuda, R., Daskalakis, N., and Lehrner, A. L. (2021), "Intergenerational Trauma is Associated with Expression Alterations in Glucocorticoid- and Immune-Related Genes," *Neuropsychopharmacology*, 46(4), 763–73

Twelve Touchstones for the Well-being of Family

Bettelheim, B. (1995), *A Good Enough Parent*, 2nd edn (London: Thames & Hudson)

Bowlby, J. (1982), *Attachment* (New York: Basic Books)

Bradford, D., and Robin, C. (2021), *Connect: Building Exceptional Relationships with Family, Friends and Colleagues* (New York: Penguin)

Faber, A., and Mazlish, E. (2012), *Siblings Without Rivalry: Help Your Children to Live Together So You Can Live Too* (London: Piccadilly Press)

Gendlin, E. T. (2003), *Focusing: How to Gain Direct Access to Your Body's Knowledge* (London: Rider)

Gibson, L. C. (2015) *Adult Children of Emotionally Immature Parents* (Oakland: New Harbinger)

Jory, B., and Yodanis, C. L., "Power: Family Relationships, Marital Relationships," *Marriage and Family Encyclopedia*, https://family.jrank.org

Neff, K. (2011), *Self Compassion: The Proven Power of Being Kind to Yourself* (New York: HarperCollins)

Neufeld, G., and Mate, G. (2019), *Hold On to Your Kids: Why Parents Need to Matter More Than Peers* (London: Vermilion)

Siegel, D. J., and Bryson, T. P. (2020), *The Power of Showing Up* (London: Scribe UK)

Siegel, D. J. and Bryson, T. P. (2012), *The Whole-Brain Child: 12 Proven Strategies to Nurture Your Child's Developing Mind* (London: Robinson)

UKEssays.com (2018), "The Role of Family Power Structure"

A Brief History of Family

Barker, H., and Hamlett, J. (2010), "Living Above the Shop: Home, Business, and Family in the English 'Industrial Revolution'," *Journal of Family History*, 35(4), 311–28

Bengtson, V. (2001), "The Burgess Award Lecture: Beyond the Nuclear Family: The Increasing Importance of Multigenerational Bonds," *Journal of Marriage and Family*, 63(1), 1–16

Berrington, A., Stone, J., and Falkingham, J. (2009), "The Changing Living Arrangements of Young Adults in the UK," *Popular Trends*, 138, 27–37

Burgess, E. (1930), "The New Community and Its Future' *Annals of the American Academy of Political and Social Science*, 149, 157–64

Burgess, E. W. (1931), "Family Tradition and Personality," in K. Young (ed.), *Social Attitudes* (New York: Henry Holt), 188–207

Chambers, D. (2012), *A Sociology of Family Life: Change and Diversity in Intimate Relations* (Cambridge: Polity Press), 1–25

Clarke, S. (1995), "Advance Report of Final Divorce Statistics, 1989 and 1990," *Monthly Vital Statistics Report*, 43(9), 1–2

Clulow, C. (1993), "New Families? Changes in Societies and Family Relationships," *Sexual and Marital Therapy*, 8(3), 269–73

Delphy, C., and Leonard, D. (1992), *Familiar Exploitation: A New Analysis of Marriage in Contemporary Western Societies* (Cambridge: Polity Press)

Dunlop Young, M., and Willmott, P. (1957), *Family and Kinship in East London* (London: Routledge)

Edgar, D. (2004), "Globalization and Western Bias in Family Sociology," in Treas, J., Scott, J., and Richards, M. (eds.), *The Wiley Blackwell Companion to the Sociology of Families* (Oxford: Blackwell), 1–16

Goyer, A. (2021), *Family Matters: Multigenerational Living Is Here to Stay*, Generations United report, https://www.gu.org/app/uploads/2021/04/21-MG-Family-Report-WEB.pdf

Hantrais, L., Brannen, J., and Bennett, F. (2020). "Family Change, Intergenerational Relations and Policy Implications," *Contemporary Social Science*, 15(3), 275–90

Howard, S. (2020), "Is It Ever Acceptable for a Feminist to Hire a Cleaner?" *Guardian*, 8 March

Ives, L. (2018), "Family Size Shrinks to Record Low of 1.89 Children," BBC Health, 22 November

Jenkins, S., Pereira, I., and Evans, N. (2009), *Families in Britain: The Impact of Changing Family Structures and What the Public Think*, Ipsos MORI Policy Exchange

Mabry, J. B., Giarrusso, R., and Bengtson, V. L. (2004), "Generations, the Life Course, and Family Change," in Treas, J., Scott, J., and Richards, M. (eds.), *The Wiley Blackwell Companion to the Sociology of Families* (Oxford: Blackwell Publishing), 85–108

McCartan, C., Bunting, L., Bywaters, P., Davidson, G., Elliott, M., and Hooper, J. (2018), "A Four-Nation Comparison of Kinship Care in the UK: The Relationship between Formal Kinship Care and Deprivation," *Social Policy and Society*, 17(4), 619–35

Schwartz Cowan, R. (1976), "The 'Industrial Revolution' in the Home: Household Technology and Social Change in the 20th Century," *Technology and Culture*, 17(1), 1–23

Smart, C. (2004), "Retheorizing Families," *Sociology*, 38(5), 1043–8.

Statistics Canada (2022), "A fifty-year look at divorces in Canada, 1970 to 2020," https://www150.statcan.gc.ca/n1/daily-quotidien/220309/dq220309a-eng.htm

Tadmor, N. (1996), "The Concept of the Household-Family in Eighteenth-Century England," *Past and Present*, 151, 111–40.

Taylor, D. (2020), "Same-Sex Couples Are More Likely to Adopt or Foster Children," United States Census Bureau, https://www.census.gov/library/stories/2020/09/fifteen-percent-of-same-sex-couples-have-children-in-their-household.html

Turner., Bryan S. (2004), "Religion, Romantic Love, and the Family," in Treas, J., Scott, J., and Richards, M. (eds.), *The Wiley Blackwell Companion to the Sociology of Families* (Oxford: Blackwell)

Wallis, L. (2012), "Servants: A Life Below Stairs," BBC News, 22 September

Weeks, J., Heaphy, B., and Donovan, C. (2004), "The Lesbian and Gay Family," in Treas, J., Scott, J., Richards, M. (eds.), *The Wiley Blackwell Companion to the Sociology of Families* (Oxford: Blackwell), 340–55

Appendix

acesaware.org, "Adverse Childhood Experience Questionnaire for Adults"

Barlow, A., Ewing, J., Janssens, A., and Blake, S. (2018), "The Shackleton Relationships Project Summary Report," University of Exeter

cdc.gov (2020), "Adverse Childhood Experiences (ACEs)"

emdrassociation.org.uk

Felitti, V. J., et al. (1998), "Relationship of Childhood Abuse and Household Dysfunction to Many of the Leading Causes of Death in Adults: The Adverse Childhood Experiences (ACE) Study," *American Journal of Preventive Medicine*, 14(4), 245–58

myrootsfoundation.com, "The 'Do You Know?' Scale"

Acknowledgements

Without my clients' willingness to participate in this project there would not be a book. It takes fortitude and a generous spirit to dare to speak so openly about the most painful private aspects of their lives, then see that experience out in the world for others to read. Their motivation is to help others understand themselves, an aim I hope they can take pride in having achieved. An overriding preoccupation has been disguising their identity—and, to repeat the disclaimer personally, I have made every effort to anonymize people and actual events while remaining true to the spirit of the work.

In order to keep the writing flowing I have not inserted references throughout the text. Instead they can be found in the Bibliography on pages 272–92. Please accept my apologies if there are omissions of acknowledgement or errors, for which I take full responsibility.

The Penguin Life team, have, as ever, been outstanding in their support of me and the book. I'd like to thank my brilliant editor, Venetia Butterfield, who thankfully commissioned it and worked closely with me until she went to a different Penguin imprint. Daniel Crewe has been terrific as my new editor, helping me shape it to be the best it can be. Julia Murday, Kayla Fuller and Alice Gordge have been remarkable in the passion, time and skill they have given to get it out into the world. Hazel Orme is a wonderful copy-editor, editing with precision, intelligence, insight and accuracy while maintaining the essence of my words.

My literary agent Felicity Rubinstein and her colleagues Fran Davies and Hana Grisenthwaite have fiercely fought for and protected my best interests while extending the book's reach as far and wide as possible. I am forever grateful for their warmth, kindness and knowledge.

Professor Tim Bond, who wrote *The Ethical Framework for the*

Counselling Professions was, as ever, very generous as we discussed the important points and potential pitfalls of publishing client work. He is the very human side of ethics, for which I am very thankful.

Geraldine Thomson, my supervisor, has been my much-valued and primary support. Her unwavering empathy, experience and skill are rare gifts. She also helped me at the conception stage of the book as to how I would invite families to be a part of it.

There is a big list of people who have contributed to the accuracy and the content of the book, including Adrian Cayford, Kai Downham, Raffaella Barker, Mary Russell, Sophie Ford, Zoe Blaskey, Professor Eamon McCrory, Dr Renee Singh, Rahul Jacob and Marianne Tatepo. Juliet Nicolson has, as ever, been a stalwart friend and adviser through the project. My thanks to Clara Weatherall and the team at the Maggie Centres, Andrew Anderson and George Bustin for their helpful connections.

Dr Priscilla Short and Dr Lesel Dawson have been phenomenal in the time, knowledge and insight they have contributed to this book, identifying themes, wisdom, theories or ways of thinking that I absolutely missed, always with kindness and a spirit of generosity. I cannot begin to express how much I value the goodwill of these colleagues.

Tilly St Aubyn did the tough legwork of compiling the Bibliography with speed, accuracy and good cheer. Maisy Ash did a masterful job in researching the history of family and distilled it, giving me a coherent narrative to work with.

My children, Natasha, Emily, Sophie and Benjamin, have taught me more about how to be a family than any other source. They have often sparked ideas to include in the text or been kind enough to comment on parts of the book. Seeing them with their partners, Rich, Keenan, Jake and Drusie, is always an inspiration.

Finally, I want to thank my beloved husband Michael, who has been, as ever, loving, wise, patient and endlessly reassuring. He has kept me on the straight and narrow through kindness and humour while I go through my usual turbulence in book writing.

Find me and further information about support organizations for you at www.juliasamuel.co.uk or follow me @juliasamuelmbe

Index

© Justine Stoddart

JULIA SAMUEL, MBE, is a leading British psychotherapist and the author of international bestsellers *Grief Works* and *This Too Shall Pass*. During the last thirty years, she has worked in both public health service and private practice, and she is founder patron of Child Bereavement UK and a vice president of the British Association for Counselling and Psychotherapy. She is frequently cited across the national media, and has presented the podcasts *Grief Works* and *A Living Loss*. She lives in Somerset with her husband, and has four children and nine grandchildren.

GRIEF**WORKS**

**Soothe Your Pain, Build Your Strength
and Heal with the Grief Works App**

Be supported through a step-by-step process to help you live and love again. **Download the Grief Works app today.**
@juliasamuelmbe • https://juliasamuel.co.uk/

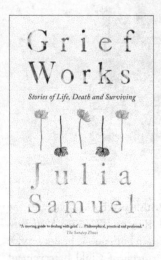
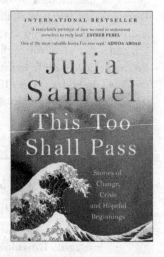